With best
winds in 1996/7 and for
many years thereafter

Adrian Seligman

WAR
IN THE
ISLANDS

UNDERCOVER OPERATIONS IN THE AEGEAN
1942–4

RECALLED BY MEN OF
THE LEVANT SCHOONER FLOTILLA,
THE GREEK SACRED COMPANY AND
AEGEAN RAIDING FORCES

ADRIAN SELIGMAN

ALAN SUTTON PUBLISHING LIMITED

First published in the United Kingdom in 1996
Alan Sutton Publishing Limited
Phoenix Mill · Far Thrupp · Stroud · Gloucestershire

British Library Cataloguing-in-Publication Data

A catalogue record for this book is available from the British Library.

ISBN 0-7509-1180-8

A ship, an isle, a sickle moon
With few but with how splendid stars
The mirrors of the sea are strewn
Between their silver bars.

James Elroy Flecker

Typeset in 10/12pt Plantin Light.
Typesetting and origination by
Alan Sutton Publishing Limited.
Printed in Great Britain by
Hartnolls, Bodmin, Cornwall.

CONTENTS

Author's Note

These stories are based on taped conversations with caique and ML skippers and the soldiers they carried, plus one or two written accounts and a few of my own experiences. All the events occurred as described, but in some instances additional dialogue, thoughts and feelings have been added by the author to bring the stories to life. The names of certain people and places have also had to be changed for personal or security reasons.

Together the tales provide a true picture of the way we lived, the weather we faced and other problems in our encounters with Germans, Italians, Turks and even our own secret services, during an exceptionally fluid and often confusing period of Aegean naval and military operations.

The tapes and transcripts from which the tales were extracted have been retained and the final text has been checked and approved by the tellers, as conforming with the explanations given above.

1 In 1936, when we were fitting out the barquentine *Cap Pilar* for her voyage round the world, we were advised and assisted by Commander Stenhouse RNR, who had sailed as First Officer in Scott's *Discovery*. He told us of old-time sea captains who navigated by courage and common sense alone. 'Lead, log and latitude . . . and then stand boldly on' was their watchword. In 1942 it became ours in the Levant Schooner Flotilla. Skippers had their own personal flags, embroidered by wives or girlfriends, which they carried with them from ship to ship.

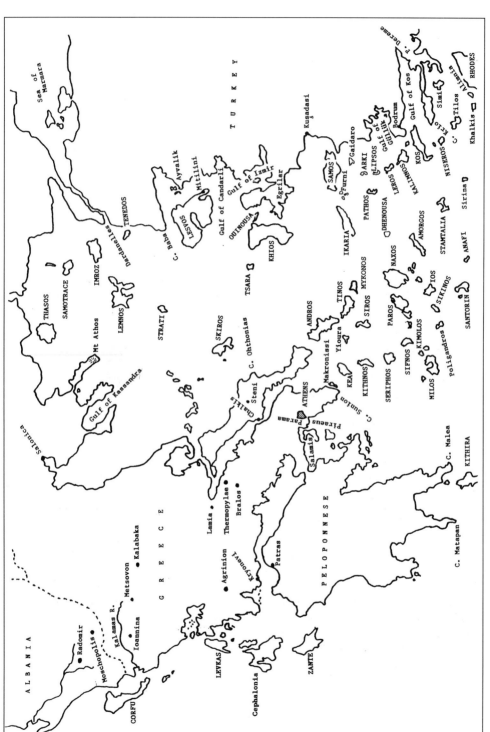

Map 1 Greece and the Aegean.

Introduction:
A Base Too Far

The islands of Antiparos and Despotiko, in the southern Cyclades, have a turbulent history. They lie next to each other in a line of four, which, seen from the air at 35,000 ft, resembles an ancient stone dagger, fallen from the sky and shattered into four pieces – with Paros, the largest, to the east; then Antiparos, less than a quarter its size; then Despotiko, smaller still, and finally the rocky islet of Strongilo at the tip of the dagger, which has a lighthouse on its south-west corner.

Today Despotiko is uninhabited except for occasional shepherds with their flocks, and a solitary monk who takes care of the little church close to the sea on its eastern side. The ruins of a few stone houses show where a small community once lived, back in the eighteenth century when Greece was part of the Ottoman Empire. As that empire began to crumble, pirates of many nationalities moved in and soon infested the whole of the Aegean. One of their favourite haunts was the well-sheltered anchorage between Despotiko and Antiparos, which was protected from northerly gales by the mid-channel islet of Tsimindiri, with shoal water on either side of it through which only seamen with local knowledge and experience could find a way.

One of the most powerful of the pirates was the Frenchman Le Blanc, who commanded a flotilla of three ships, a barquentine and two small schooners. They looked upon the Tsimindiri anchorage as their own and drove away any other vessels who tried to make use of it. They were on good terms, however, with the islanders on both sides, who were generally friendly so long as the pirates behaved themselves; but there were times when, through drink or the desire for women, the pirates became threatening. And instances of sheep stealing for impromptu feasts were not unknown.

On one such occasion, when the pirates had been especially unruly and demanding, the people of Despotiko lost patience and petitioned the Turkish governor of Paros to come to their aid. He reported the matter to his admiral, based on Syros, who despatched a squadron of warships. They approached the island from the south, caught Le Blanc at anchor in the Tsimindiri roadstead and hanged him from his own yardarm. The two schooners, however, escaped through the tortuous channels to the north, where the men-of-war couldn't follow, and everyone hoped they had seen the last of the pirates. There was general rejoicing. And before returning to Syros, the commander of the Turkish squadron rewarded the people of

2 Tsimindiri Island and anchorage today.

Despotiko for their help in ridding the seas of a ruthless and dangerous scourge. Sadly, none of them lived to enjoy their reward. As soon as the Turks were gone, the schooners returned, and the pirates massacred the entire population – men, women and children; five families in all – and burnt their houses to the ground.

For more than a century after that the island remained uninhabited. Many believed it to be haunted by the victims of the massacre. Lights were sometimes seen, and fishermen passing close inshore told of unearthly cries. So Despotiko remained deserted. The anchorage, however, became a favourite meeting place for smugglers from all over the Eastern Mediterranean, who replaced the pirates. They found it a safe and convenient rendezvous for the exchange of contraband cargoes. Safe, in particular, because of those two dangerous channels on either side of Tsimindiri Island: tortuous and rocky to the westward, with a maximum depth of 2.5 metres (if you knew where to find it) and 1.5 metres (in calm weather) over a sandy bottom on the eastern side. No revenue or coastguard cutter, drawing 2 metres or more, as most of them did, would risk either channel; whereas the smugglers' shallow draught caiques could come and go as they pleased.

★ ★ ★

We now move on a hundred and fifty years to the bitter winter of 1941/2, when, after the fall of Greece, Charis Grammatikakis, a brave and enterprising Cretan, hired a 20-ton caique from a friend in Piraeus, and set about evacuating and transporting to Crete Greek soldiers in hiding from the Germans. To do this he first had to obtain a permit to carry a cargo of wine to Paros. But in fact he only loaded a part cargo to make room for olive oil, provisions and water for his 120 passengers, whom he then sailed to Despotiko, where they went into hiding again while he sailed on to Paros. There he discharged his wine and obtained another permit from the Italians who controlled the island to carry a second cargo of wine from Paros to Crete. Then, returning to the Tsimindiri anchorage[1] at dead of night, he re-embarked his passengers and their supplies and sailed them down to Iraklion. The first trip was a success and so on his return to Paros, a week or two later, he recruited three more caiques and schooled their crews in the procedures to be followed.

This was the start of a regular traffic which, over the ensuing four or five months, rescued some 2,500 Greek men and women from the clutches of the Germans – and all in great secrecy, despite the numbers of simple peasant folk who came to know about the Cretan's exploits.

Inevitably, however, the Allied secret services got to hear about it; and this was in some ways more dangerous than anything else, because of the continuing and inescapable rivalry, not only between the different nationalities in the Allied camp, but more especially between different organizations of the same nationalities. For example, where British secret services were concerned, there was always tension between ISLD[2] (Intelligence), MO4[3] (Sabotage) and MI9 (Escape routes), who sometimes found themselves treading on each other's toes; and this, as in the present instance, could lead to disaster.

★   ★   ★

Whether Captain Atkinson was a regular member of one of the secret services, or whether, after an adventurous escape from Greece, he approached one of them spontaneously with his plan for an advanced base on Antiparos, I don't know. He was certainly a man of enterprise and ideas, with more than his fair share of courage, but he was inclined to arrogance – a dangerous fault where secret operations are concerned. However, his idea for a base on Antiparos, through which sabotage teams and their equipment could be introduced into Greece (and as a bonus, escaping soldiers evacuated to the Middle East on the return journey), was accepted. He was allocated W/T operators and a supporting team headed by Sergeant-Major John Redpath, whose primary task was to organize the escape by submarine of 600 officers and men known to be hiding in the Tayeto mountains of Lakonia, while Atkinson himself concentrated on the Athens area.

Meanwhile, according to Antonis Aliprantis[4] who has researched these events in considerable detail, Grammatikakis had been approached by Allied secret agents in Athens; and on 28 September 1941, after embarking sixty Cretan soldiers at Piraeus, he picked up six British officers from a beach further down the coast and transported them all to Crete, arriving at Plaka in Mirabellou Bay on 1 October. Next day he persuaded his brother to join him and they sailed on to Egypt with the six British officers and nine of the Cretans. In Alexandria he was contacted by one of the secret services, who expressed great interest in his activities. He was sent to Cairo where, with secret service backing, he pressed for a submarine to land agents on Despotiko or Antiparos, and embark the escapees that his slower but less conspicuous caiques would bring from the mainland.

Attempts were made to coordinate these two plans – one with the emphasis on sabotage and intelligence, the other with evacuation – into a single, continuous two-way operation. But it wasn't easy. Both Atkinson and Grammatikakis were thrusters, impatient of direction or restraint. Each, moreover, considered himself the originator (and therefore the natural leader) of the enterprise. And over and above all this there was Atkinson's autocratic manner – acceptable, perhaps even admirable, when you were on the right side of it; infuriating, and in this kind of situation frightening, when you weren't.

However, on 14 November men and stores for both projects were landed by submarine on Antiparos. On Grammatikakis' instructions the stores were hidden in an abandoned well, which was then filled with earth and sown with grass and other seeds. Then Grammatikakis sailed on by caique to Paros, to get a permit from the Italian authorities for a voyage to Piraeus and back.

Atkinson and Redpath, both members of the Antiparos party, were welcomed by the little community of Agios Georgios, and were installed in the house of Spyros Tsavellas (later called Casa Rosa by the Italians) which became their headquarters. As soon as they had settled in they went out to the well and dug up all the stores which had been hidden there and transferred them to their new base.

When Grammatikakis returned two or three days later he not only found the stores gone, but the whole party walking about openly in uniform and armed; two of them were even fishing from a boat with hand grenades. He was furious, and the first of a series of rows between him and Atkinson erupted. To his credit, Atkinson kept his temper, but remarks such as 'You and your pals can skulk in the undergrowth if you want to . . . I'm a soldier . . . a fighting man', didn't help. To a Cretan – among the fiercest of the Greeks – it must have sounded like (and was probably meant to sound like) a studied insult. Yet Grammatikakis, with steely self-control, succeeded in ignoring it, and a sort of armed truce was established, which held for several weeks.

★   ★   ★

During this period two attempts were made to start evacuating the lads hiding in the Tayeto mountains. Both failed: the first because the submarine *Trooper* arrived in the Gulf of Lakonia before John Redpath had time to bring any organized parties down to the coast; the second because John and the skipper of the caique which replaced *Trooper* couldn't agree on the pick-up point.

However, two more parties of British and Greeks – more than sixty officers and men in all – arrived at Antiparos from the mainland by other caiques and the problem then was where to hide them. All suitable hide-outs in the vicinity of Agios Georgios, including several of the houses, were occupied, so the new arrivals had to trek across the mountains to Soros, on the eastern side of the island.

The situation was beginning to get out of hand but nobody was really worried. There were plenty of stores, including cigarettes – mostly Craven 'A' – which the boys used for currency and as presents for their girlfriends. Oh yes! Some of them soon found girlfriends. This wouldn't have mattered so much if the girls had all been smokers, but unfortunately most of them weren't, so they passed their gifts on, and before long packets of Craven 'A', became a fairly common sight all over Paros, including Paroikia where the Italian garrison was stationed.

Charis Grammatikakis had two girlfriends – a mature but lively and very beautiful woman from Paroikia, with whom he had been friendly for some time, and a younger girl he met in Antiparos. This led to trouble when Chrysoula, the older woman, in a jealous rage, threatened to betray him to the Italians. She said as much to a senior police officer, who smiled indulgently and patted her shoulder . . . 'But how would that benefit you, my child? Because the moment the Italians came for Charis we'd kill you.'

Chrysoula began to cry. 'But I love him, I . . . I must have him,' she sobbed. The police officer put a friendly arm round her. 'I'll tell him,' he said. 'Give me a letter.' So Chrysoula gave him a letter and in due course a tryst was arranged.

This might well have been the end of the matter, if Chrysoula's father hadn't come storming over to Antiparos, whereupon both he and his daughter were bundled into a back room of one of the houses and locked up. Atkinson and Redpath were on the point of shooting them both. Only Chrysoula's soft beauty and eyes shining with tears saved them. And in the end her father agreed to act as a courier taking food to the soldiers hiding at Soros, while Chrysoula joined up happily enough with the team at Casa Rosa.

★   ★   ★

It seems odd that the Italians had so far appeared oblivious to all these goings on. The truth was that the small garrison on Paros – less than fifty men in all – had been finding life there not only peaceful but pleasant and the last thing they wanted was a fuss which might bring the Germans, whom they hated, and who were openly contemptuous of them, about their ears. So although they had in fact heard about Grammatikakis' 'passengers' on his first voyage to Crete in September, they chose to treat it as just another rumour about smuggling, for which the islands in the west had always been notorious. For form's sake a party of five men – three Italians and two Greek customs officers – had been sent to Antiparos to investigate, but their report was generally dismissive (in fact they'd spent most of their time fishing). And now, two months later, it was possible to discount the sudden influx of British cigarettes as further evidence of persistent smuggling, which was an administrative matter for the local customs officers to deal with, and none of the garrison's business.

The air was cleared a bit on 29 November by the arrival of another submarine which picked up sixty escapees and carried them off to the Middle East. Atkinson went with them and was away for several weeks. When he returned at the end of December it was evident that he had been doing some serious empire-building. He had with him another Army officer, a sergeant, a Greek W/T operator and a prodigious amount of equipment – explosives, weapons and supplies.

Fortunately or unfortunately, depending on which way you look at it, Grammatikakis had left the day before for Piraeus. Fortunately, because Atkinson's great consignment of weapons and stores was landed from the submarine in broad daylight, without any regard for security, and took several hours to disperse to a variety of hiding places – which would undoubtedly have sent Grammatikakis, had he seen it, into a transport of fury; unfortunately, because the Cretan was not there to press personally for the Greek and British soldiers, brought over to Antiparos during Atkinson's absence, to be taken away immediately by the submarine which brought him back. Aliprantis blames Atkinson for not ensuring that this was done, but it was not necessarily his decision. The submarine was due to carry out a further patrol before returning to Alexandria, and it was almost certainly her captain who decided that the passengers must await his return to Antiparos in ten days' time. Atkinson no doubt passed on this ruling with some force; and when he was warned about a possible Italian raid, he replied with characteristic bravado, 'If any bloody Eyeties show their ugly mugs around here, we'll kill 'em . . . all of 'em'.

★   ★   ★

One cannot be sure, at this distance in time, whether or not the agent on Paros (a young Greek born and brought up on Rhodes) had heard about the build-up of four MAS boats, a hydroplane and an assault force of 150 Italian soldiers on Syros, 22 miles north of Paros. If he had, his report would have gone direct to his HQ in Cairo and would eventually have reached Atkinson's HQ, who might or might not have thought it worth passing on to him. On no account would the man on Paros have contacted Atkinson direct, or even through a messenger, for fear of blowing his cover. In any case there might at that time have been no indication of a likely target for such a force. It might have been stationed on Syros – at the centre of the Cyclades group, and more or less equidistant from the principal islands – to be ready in an emergency to reinforce any of their garrisons. And if, by some miracle, Atkinson's crowd on Antiparos had mended their ways (or withdrawn to a remoter island or Turkey) this tale might have had a happier ending.

The posting to Paros in January 1942 of a certain Lieutenant Gali ruled that out. Whether he was in fact seconded from the assault force on Syros, or just a tough soldier, I don't know; but after a brief visit to Antiparos and Despotiko – ostensibly to collect firewood – he certainly stirred up the sleepy Paros garrison. He had brought with him to Antiparos a fatigue party of four or five Italian soldiers and half a dozen local Greeks, who were to collect firewood from both islands. While they were away on the job he suggested to Spyros Tsavellas that they have a chat and an *ouzo* or two in Casa Rosa. Tsavellas, with some embarrassment, regretted that he had lost the key – it must have dropped out of his pocket – which surprised Gali, because he could see smoke issuing from a chimney at the back of the house – thick smoke, as though from a fire just lit. He shrugged his shoulders, but said nothing. When he got back to Paroikia, however, he voiced his suspicions at some length to Lieutenant Rusticelli, the garrison commander. As a result, it was decided to raid the two islands that very night.

A schooner belonging to one Petros Rangoussi was requisitioned and preparations made, with food, water, explosives, weapons and ammunition, for a full expedition. This all took time; time enough for Rangoussi to send a warning message by boat and runner to Atkinson – who ignored it.

★   ★   ★

The encounters which followed were brisk but indecisive. They began with the arrival on Despotiko soon after sunset of a twelve-man Italian patrol. They landed on a beach where they could see a party of men in uniform sitting round a roaring driftwood fire. But before they could get clear of their boat they were recognized, and the men round the fire scattered into the bush. The Italians followed but failed to find them.

The Italians on the schooner reached Agios Georgios about 1 a.m. and went straight to Casa Rosa. The dozen or so British inside, roused by Greek boys who had seen the Italians landing, opened fire. The Italians replied with hand grenades, one of which smashed Atkinson's left foot and damaged his right eye, whereupon Kypriades, the Greek W/T operator, shot and fatally wounded one of the Italians. Then all the British and Greeks hurled themselves through windows at the back of the house and escaped. Atkinson himself was in agony, but succeeded in dragging himself 30 yards through the scrub to a fisherman's hut, where he took shelter. Some Greeks found him there and hid him more securely under a pile of nets and ropes.

The Italians meanwhile had withdrawn to their caique to wait for daylight and to signal for reinforcements from Syros and Naxos. There followed a lull during which two young Greek boys were sent by Atkinson's second-in-command to Casa Rosa to find and recover two suitcases containing secret files, cypher books and money. They failed to find the suitcases but brought away the W/T set and code book.

For all his faults – his arrogance, his impatience, his stupidity – Atkinson had one redeeming quality which dwarfed all the others: courage. This now emerged. Although it was already broad daylight, and in spite of his wounds, he dragged himself from his hiding place to hail a third Greek who happened to be passing, and sent him to Casa Rosa to look for the suitcases. He was also unable to find them – which was not surprising, because they had already been found and removed by the Italians.

It was well on in the forenoon when the Soros party – twenty-one in all – were seen coming down the hill towards Agios Georgios. They had been alerted, as he passed, by the messenger sent to warn Atkinson. About 200 yards from Casa Rosa they stopped, apparently undecided. The silence following the recent gunfire may have suggested that the battle was over and all their friends dead or captured. However it was, they withdrew back into the hills, where they met some Greeks they knew from Soros. The Greeks offered them a boat to get away to Turkey, but they were so confident that a submarine expected before dawn would still arrive and pick them up, that they made instead for the mountains in the south-east of the island and assembled at the head of a cove on their southern side (Map 2), the agreed pick-up point.

They spent the rest of the day, all night and the following forenoon flashing the recognition signal to seaward every ten minutes or so, but in vain. Soon after noon they saw a group of MAS boats and transports rounding Strongilo Island and heading for the anchorage – the reinforcements from Syros. They turned at once to their Greek friends who had offered a boat to take them to Turkey, but it was too late. Nor was there anywhere to hide in the cove or on the barren hillside above it. They were soon spotted by a patrol boat of the approaching flotilla and all were captured without a fight. The submarine never came.

★   ★   ★

The Italians at Agios Georgios meanwhile, whose numbers had been increased by the arrival from Paroikia of Lieutenant Gali with a patrol of twelve men, had made a thorough search of the area, and had soon found Atkinson's hiding place. Before being transferred to Paroikia for interrogation, he had been minutely searched and further secret documents discovered, the most damaging among them being a list of his contacts in Athens. Some of these had, in fact, been warned by the caique first sent to warn Atkinson, and had been able to go to ground. Others were not so lucky.

Grammatikakis, in the meantime, had embarked thirty-five Greek officers and three women in the caique *Thriambos* at Piraeus, and was on his way back to Antiparos. He anchored off Agios Georgios in the early hours of 10 January and was immediately challenged by an Italian patrol boat. He succeeded in escaping in his dinghy to Tsimindiri Island whence, it now being daylight and his boat therefore conspicuous, he swam on to Despotiko, and remained there in hiding for several days. His passengers were taken under guard, in 'their own' caique, to Italian Headquarters on Syros for interrogation. All claimed that they were Cretans returning home (some of them were), and after a few days in custody they were allowed to sail on south to Iraklion.

A signal from the ISLD agent on Paros to Cairo, describing what had happened, including Grammatikakis' escape, resulted in a caique from Turkey being despatched to his aid. But by the time it arrived, Grammatikakis (as impatient and headstrong in his own way as Atkinson) had swum back to Antiparos, and thence to Paros where he went into hiding again in a friend's house. Eventually, after many more adventures, including a 3 mile swim across the open sea with short oars lashed to his arms as floats, he reached Naxos, where he stole an Italian rowing boat and set off for Turkey via Mykonos, Ikaria and Samos. It took him fifteen days of almost continuous rowing, and on arrival at Port St Paul, at the tip of Samsun Dagh headland, he was imprisoned by the Turks. The Greek consul succeeded in freeing him, and sent him by train down to Haifa, where he was immediately arrested as an impostor by the British authorities; they had heard about his setting out to swim from Paros to Naxos, but since he hadn't contacted anyone on arrival there, they had assumed him drowned. He was ordered to be sent to a concentration camp in the Congo, but managed to escape once again and find his way to the Greek government offices in Cairo, where he was enrolled as a chief petty officer in the Greek Navy – a rank he retained until the end of the war.

★   ★   ★

So ended the saga of the base on Antiparos. The captured British were sent to a POW camp in Italy until the Italian surrender in September 1943, except for Atkinson. Antonio Aliprantis tells of his complete collapse under interrogation, but I find this difficult to believe, given Atkinson's great courage. However, his arrogance, coupled with poor judgement when it came to reading a situation, was certainly a defect and one, I believe, that ultimately destroyed him. Under interrogation he was not only uncooperative, but openly contemptuous of his inquisitors, and it may well have been this which led in the end to his downfall: the Italians simply lost patience and handed him over to the Gestapo. Early in February 1942 he was executed by firing squad.

---

[1] This name is used here to avoid confusion. It is usually referred to locally as Despotiko Bay or Harbour.
[2] Inter-Services, Liaison Department, also known as MI6.
[3] Another name for Special Operations Executive or SOE.
[4] *The Secret Allied Base of Antiparos*, published in Athens in 1992.

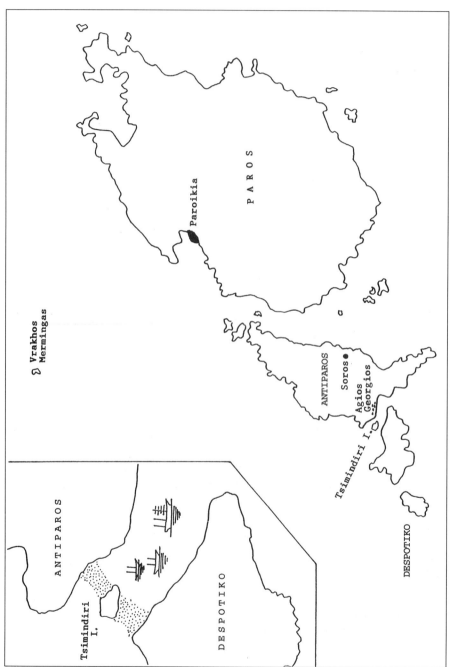

Map 2 The Paros group of islands.

How it All Began

CHAPTER ONE

The Courage of Yanni

Yanni was a fisherman who lived in a small village I'll call Denizi on the west coast of Turkey. He was a timid man, who looked on the sea as his enemy and watched her intently from the dry-stone hovel he used as a boathouse. He never went to sea unless the weather was set fair, and then with a gloomy face because in fair weather you never really knew, did you, when the shift would come? Especially in summer, when Meltemi, the northerly gale, might fall upon you at any moment out of a cloudless sky.

It was difficult to judge Yanni's age. Between fifty and sixty, I guessed. He was an Armenian on his father's side; and as a young man, before the First World War, he had served in British merchant ships out of Liverpool, where he'd picked up a working knowledge of English. Then the war came, and as a Turkish national he would have been interned if he hadn't jumped ship in Port Said.

Yanni wouldn't be drawn on what he did after that, but his intimate knowledge of the Cyclades, and especially the Paros group of islands, made me fairly certain that he'd been in the smuggling business for a good many years. In fact he was just the man we needed, because we were smugglers too, of a kind – smugglers of agents and their supplies in and out of enemy-held territory.

Yanni's only possession, apart from the boathouse and a cottage which he shared with his wife (they had no children), was a 25 ft caique of the shape known in Greece as 'Tricanderi' (photo 3) – that is to say she was a double-ended gaff-rigged cutter with a deep sheer and no freeboard to speak of, and to prevent her from being swept by the sea in heavy weather, she had canvas bulwarks laced to sheer poles on either side for about two-thirds of her length amidships. Yanni kept her in first-class order, working on her whenever it was fine and always with enormous concentration, as though making ready for some prodigious voyage across the Aegean.

'Storm wind in Mykonos channel . . . mountaining sea . . . new canvas bulwarks with strongest rope, isn't it?' I wouldn't answer, because I knew that Yanni didn't really want an answer. He was talking to himself. And if I

3 '. . . the shape known as 'Tricanderi' . . .'

hadn't been young and a stranger to those parts, he wouldn't have included me in his soliloquy at all.

I didn't have a boat of my own just then, in the winter of 1942/3. In fact I wasn't really supposed to be there. But the loss off Benghazi of the Senior Officer of our escort group and his ship had meant that another Commander RN had to be appointed to be senior to the Commanders in Greek-manned escort vessels who had recently joined us, and he would have to take over *my* ship. So I was spare. And to keep me busy I was sent up to Izmir to help Gareth Evans, our consular and undercover representative up there, with sea-borne operations. Gareth had helped me the winter before,[1] when I was struggling to get *Oilshipper*[2] down the Turkish coast. Now it was my turn to help him.

My main task was to keep in touch with one or two of our agents in the islands; I took them stores when they needed them and arranged reliefs. When I had to go anywhere I went in an SOE[3] boat, if there were any about; when there weren't, I had to make do with local boats, whose people, as in most small communities, were apt to be talkative. Except Yanni. He kept himself to himself, so I preferred to sail with him than with any of the others, even though it sometimes took days of coaxing and argument to get him to sea at all. There was always something: a faulty shroud in his boat, a leaky seam, or just the fineness of the weather. Yanni distrusted fine weather almost more than gales and rain. It just couldn't last, you see; and the finer the weather, the deeper his misgivings. 'Moon near to full,' he'd say. 'Soon coming wind . . . blowing like devils . . . Meltemi . . . north wind . . . no hiding from devils blowing.'

Yanni's wife, Zerrin, was a quiet, hard-working woman in her early forties, who kept their cottage tidy, and always made the best of things. Her Irish mother had come out to Turkey in the 1890s as nursemaid to a wealthy Levantine family and, like so many West European girls before and since, she had fallen for a handsome young Turk. As a result, Zerrin was bilingual. But she hated Yanni working for us on operations which '. . . are none of our business. . . . We have no children. He's all I've got,' she insisted. 'So why should I lend him to you for your *games*?' The last word, spoken with force, had a contemptuous ring.

How Zerrin came to team up with a dour old stick like Yanni was a mystery; but she was devoted to him, there could be no doubt about that. She had met him on holiday between the wars; and maybe in his forties he had seemed a romantic figure. Indeed he may have *been* a romantic deep inside; perhaps still was; the expression in his eyes or an oddly poetic turn of phrase sometimes suggested it. He was also shy and gentle by nature, and at heart a man of great courage.

Now, there are many different kinds of courage, some of them overrated. Courage against suffering and boredom. Cold courage. Daring and gallantry, which are less respectable. The ferocious courage of brutes. And we all know the courage of fear: rats have it. Then the courage of hate; Yanni hated Zerrin's cousin, Orhan, though few would have realized it unless they had sat beside him, as I had, and seen him curl right into himself as the fellow came swaggering along.

Orhan had trained in Switzerland for the hotel trade and was serving as a waiter in a good-class Berlin restaurant when the outbreak of war interrupted his career and brought him back to Turkey. He was a loud-mouthed, boastful sort of fellow, always poking fun at Yanni, whom he despised. He also despised Yanni's profession which, he said, any educated man (meaning himself) could learn backwards in six months. He even set out to prove it by getting himself a job in a German-manned schooner which used the anchorage from time to time. She was sort of Q-ship, with guns on retractable mountings that could be hidden away when entering harbour. The Germans had a number of these disguised patrol boats in the Aegean. They were powered by twin Deutz high-speed diesel engines and usually carried a crew of four or five Greeks, with a German NCO in overall charge, and eight or nine soldiers to man the guns and form boarding parties.

Orhan spoke fluent German and English as well as Turkish. He had influential friends ashore, and was probably more of a liaison and intelligence officer than anything else. He may also have convinced his employers that he knew some of the islands intimately, on the strength of yachting holidays before the war. Entirely imaginary yachting holidays; Orhan had never been to sea in his life. Anyway they paid him well, and he was soon strutting around in a reefer jacket and nautical cap. 'Six months!' I

4 An Aegean schooner.

heard him say loudly to his cousin, in English (for my benefit I suspect). 'I know more about sailors' work after six weeks in a ship than your old Yanni has learned in a half a lifetime!'

Yanni, who was also within earshot, said nothing. But he began to spend more and more time away from the cottage, mostly in his boathouse, or down aboard the caique with Memet, his crew – a peaky lad of fourteen and an orphan, who looked on Yanni as a father. Yanni loved him, and went to great pains over his upbringing, teaching him the ways of the sea and ships, especially his own, which Memet was to inherit.

★   ★   ★

They say it never snows in the Aegean south of Izmir. But that year it did. And snow was ideal weather for a job that came up soon after I arrived: it would allow us to cover most of the 90 miles between Khios and Antiparos without being spotted.

Yes, Antiparos. The Atkinson disaster of the winter before had stirred things up to such an extent that our man on Paros had gone to ground, and disappeared into the hills with his W/T set. From time to time we took him stores or fresh batteries, and slowly he'd managed to establish new contacts. But something must have gone wrong; quite suddenly he had moved across to

Antiparos and made an urgent signal for fresh supplies, and also for money –
gold sovereigns, reals or escudos, presumably for bribes. He would be watching
rendezvous No. 3 (map 3) from the hills above it until we arrived.

This was a job for Yanni and no other. As I said earlier, he knew those
islands and the Tsimindiri anchorage better than anyone. But the idea of
asking him to go to sea in a snow blizzard was so absurd that I decided not
even to mention it when I went down to the boathouse that morning. So
how it came into our conversation I don't quite know. All I remember is
referring vaguely to Antiparos and our chap there being in trouble,
whereupon Yanni looked up quickly, with a strange expression in his eyes,
and said, 'When you like going?'

I was astonished. I wondered what on earth had come over the old fellow.
Had Orhan's nagging and bullying got him down so badly that he wanted to
get to sea at all costs? I knew they'd had a row the day before, mainly because
Orhan had been pumping him. The Germans had no doubt guessed that we
would try to make contact with our man and Orhan had probably been told to
keep a close watch on our movements. But because the Paros group of islands
had any number of coves, creeks and offshore islets where a small boat could
hide, I wasn't worried as long as the Germans didn't know our actual route
and rendezvous. What was much more important was that Yanni, who was
not only as close as a clam, but one of the finest seamen I'd ever sailed with,
was ready to take me on a tricky operation in the dirtiest weather they had had
for years. So I wasted no time in stocking up with olives, cheese, hard bread,
sausages, wine and a bottle of local brandy – I wanted to get to sea as soon as
possible before the old man changed his mind.

★   ★   ★

It was barely ten in the forenoon when we left harbour. The German schooner
also put to sea, and soon out-distanced us, disappearing into the wrack on our
starboard bow on a more westerly course than ours. There was a wild sea
running south of Khios, but with a dead fair wind we rode it fairly
comfortably. Yanni had boomed his foresail out to starboard; it was balanced
by a reefed mainsail to port. He also kept his engine in gear and running at half
speed. The sails and engine, together with a strong following wind, gave us
a speed of close on 7 knots. The engine was an old Bolinder semi-diesel, with a
hot bulb on top, which glowed comfortingly, providing us with something
to warm our hands by. That and the gleam from a small boat's compass were
all the light we had when night came on, and it was still snowing.

How Yanni knew where he was I couldn't imagine. He seemed to be
steering by the wind and the run of the seas. Once during the afternoon we
heard the boom of surf coming to us through the snow to port. Yanni
altered course a bit westerly and stood on. Then at dusk a shadow appeared
through the murk to starboard. It might have been a squall cloud, but Yanni
knew better. 'Staphodhia Island,' he said with confidence. 'Antiparos before

midnight.' And sure enough, soon after ten that night we heard more surf rumbling in the darkness, but this time right ahead. 'Vrakhos Mermingas,' said Yanni (map 2), and opened the throttle on the Bolinder, which responded with a healthy bom . . . bom . . . bom noise into the night, increasing our speed to well over 7 knots.

The plan was to round Strongilo Island and land me in a cove sheltered from the north wind on the south-east side of Antiparos. The caique would then stand out to sea again, or hide somewhere, while I trekked off into the hills to find our man and hand over the supplies. Then I would lie up somewhere and come back to the rendezvous after dark on the following night.

It was a simple plan, which had the merit of needing no complicated communications arrangements. It had worked well enough in the past and would probably have gone without a hitch this time if the wind hadn't backed to the north west – the snow clouds lifted, and just as we were closing Cape Kalika, the northern point of Despotiko, a brilliant half-moon hadn't shone out full on to the close-reefed sails of the German schooner – less than a mile away – emerging from the pass between Despotiko and Strongilo Island. There was no mistaking her. But we didn't waste any time wondering how she came to be there, at the very spot we'd chosen for our landfall. She must have heard our engine thumping down-wind towards her; and now her searchlight flashed out, sweeping across the water towards us.

We gybed at once, sheeted the foresail home and headed east up the coast. The schooner followed, but didn't appear to be making any effort to overtake us. The NCO in charge of her must have decided that our position was hopeless; we were on a dead lee shore, and the only shelter within miles was the Tsimindiri anchorage, where the seas were breaking white over the shoals on both sides of the mid-channel island. In calm southerly weather there was enough water over those shoals for a boat of our draught, though the western pass was rocky and the channel tortuous. But now, in a northerly gale, no sensible seaman would have attempted either of them. So we would be forced (the Germans must have thought) to make for Naousa Bay on Paros, where they could easily board us or keep an eye on us until the weather moderated and we tried again to make contact with our agent.

But Yanni had other ideas. I heard him say something to young Memet, who set about getting the foresail in. Then Yanni did an extraordinary thing: he put the helm *up*. The boat's head swung in towards the shore. We gybed again. Then the boy took the foresail halliard to a third sail – a big fair-weather jib, which had been lying there sheeted well aft on the port side. I gave him a hand, and together we got the sail about half-way up – bellying out to port like a half-hoisted spinnaker. It was enough.

★　　★　　★

I would have trusted Yanni with my life anywhere, at sea or ashore. But this time I thought he'd gone mad. It was blowing like fury now, well to the west

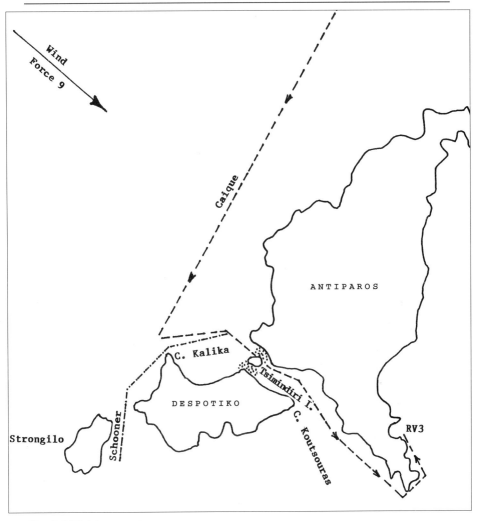

Map 3 Midnight encounter.

of north, out of a clear black sky. The caique, under her press of sail, seemed to lift and charge straight at the surf on the eastern side of Tsimindiri Island, which was now less than 400 yards ahead of us.

We've all known courage – cold courage, raging courage, desperate or dogged courage. But the courage of Yanni that night was a terrible thing. And when I glanced up at his face in the moonlight, I knew that there was nothing I could do, either to halt or to help him.

Memet crawled aft along the deck and crouched beside us. I remember his pinched little face and staring eyes fixed on Yanni at the helm. We were driving diagonally towards the line of surf. The swell was building up under us. Yanni watched for his moment. When it came, he threw all his weight against the tiller and kicked the throttle wide open. For a moment we hung broadside on the face of a comber, heeling far over to starboard. Then the crest of the wave got under us, sweeping us round as it moved forward. Mountains of water poured in over our bulwarks on both sides. The engine raced madly as the screw broke surface for a moment. We slid down into the trough, with another great wave building up astern. I felt her touch and check. Then we were lifting – lifting and flying forward.

★   ★   ★

The wave subsided and dispersed beneath us. Yanni throttled back. Memet went forward to haul down and stow the big jib. Then between us we got the mainsail in, as we motored quietly over smooth dark water towards the other end of the anchorage. For a moment – in the reaction from terror, I suppose, and in the all-pervading peace which followed – I, at least, had forgotten about the schooner. But now we all looked back and to our astonishment saw that she was turning in after us.

'He must be off his head,' I said to Yanni. 'Surely he draws nearly double what we draw?' Yanni didn't answer. Instead he slowed his engine and we sat there watching.

The schooner was sailing wing-and-wing – her mainsail to starboard, foresail to port – and seemed to be aiming at the exact spot where we had crossed the shoal. Soon she had almost reached it. We could see a big wave building up after her. Her stern began to lift. Her bows plunged down. Then her forefoot must have grounded, because all at once she was swung right round to port and broadside to the advancing sea, which rolled her almost on to her beam ends as it poured over her.

She rolled back and seemed to stagger as the next wave picked her up, carried her a little way and dropped her heavily. Down came her mainmast in a tangle of wire and canvas over her starboard bulwarks. The wind filled her foresail, swinging her round to starboard. At the same time another wave struck her awkwardly. Her foremast and sail went overboard to port.

But it was the last disaster. A final comber lifted her into deeper, calmer water, where her diesels were able to take charge and propel her slowly and clumsily, with tangled wreckage hanging out on either side like tattered coat tails, round Cape Koutsouras, at the eastern end of Despotiko. We heard her anchor go down as we chugged quietly on towards our rendezvous in silence – Yanni because that was his natural state, I from shock at seeing a fine ship flung about and smashed like a child's toy. There might have been casualties too; we didn't know. At last I said: 'What made them try it, I wonder, without a local man to pilot them?'

Yanni spoke for the first time: 'They have pilot,' he said.

'Who?'

'Orhan.' And I think for the first time ever, though not the last, I saw Yanni smile.

* * *

When we reached the rendezvous Yanni put me ashore on a shelf of rock in the northern arm of the cove, then stood out to sea again. I shouldered my pack and set off up a track which zigzagged through the scrub and bushes until it came out on to the bare hillside near the top of the ridge. There I waited.

After a while – it felt like ten minutes or so – a figure detached itself from the rocks higher up the hill and came warily down towards me. As he approached in the moonlight, I got the impression of a sensitive youngster with untidy black hair, a straggly beard and piercing black eyes. But there was fear in those eyes, which kept darting glances to right and left, like a bird approaching crumbs on the ground.

And crumbs were all I had brought him – crumbs of food and money and fresh instructions; perhaps also a few crumbs of comfort to know that he had not been abandoned. I passed him the packages one by one, and rested my hand for a moment on his shoulder. He looked at me steadily and, I thought, a bit longingly. Then, all at once he pulled himself together, shook my hand, then turned and strode back into the bush. A boy of twenty, no more – a brave boy of twenty.

* * *

But I never sailed with Yanni again. Though not because I didn't trust him as a seaman. It was what his wife told me later that decided me. And when I confronted Yanni with what she had said, he admitted quite freely – in fact with a grin – that it was true. He was convinced, moreover, that what he had done was to everyone's advantage – even Orhan's, who was most likely in prison now on the island of Syros, where the schooner was based, which would be good for his soul.

Because it was, in fact, Yanni who, while I was away shopping, had told Orhan where we were going that night. And more, he'd actually promised to lead Orhan to a deep-water channel which would allow him to pilot his friends through the Tsimindiri shoals to follow or capture us, as they preferred, on the other side.

That was all that was needed. Orhan's vanity and inexperience, plus the German NCO's arrogance (he must have overruled his Greek skipper) did the rest. Only Yanni – and the Greek skipper, of course – knew that there wasn't any such channel for deeper-draught vessels through those shoals, and there never had been.

---

[1] See *No Stars to Guide*, Hodder & Stoughton, 1947.
[2] *Olinda* in *No Stars to Guide*.
[3] SOE (Special Operations Executive) ran a small fleet of motor boats and a drifter, chiefly on sabotage missions in enemy territory.

CHAPTER TWO

Troubled Waters

Sink without Trace

The colonel was a small man, rather plump, with wispy reddish hair and a short-clipped moustache. I remember especially his eyes – small, greyish-green and watchful – that stared at you unblinking from behind an enormous desk which almost filled one side of the room.

'I sent for you,' he said curtly, 'because there's a special job we want done . . . quickly . . . within the next few weeks.'

I was interested. Although I was only on loan to SOE from the Navy, I found their sea-going team the sort of people I could understand and happily work with. Their CO, 'Skipper' Poole, was a master mariner who had been in charge of Imperial Airways' flying-boat base in Suda Bay, Crete. John Campbell, an old Etonian and an experienced deep-sea yachtsman, was now a Lieutenant (E) RN with a well-earned DSO to his name. Then there was Kenny McKenzie, a fiercely independent schoolmaster from the west coast of Scotland, and young Beckinsale who had joined the Army as a second lieutenant straight from school.

The work they did in their small boats – penetrating deep into enemy-held archipelagos of the Aegean, to land agents or teams of saboteurs and keep them supplied – was a refreshing change from the minesweeping and convoy escort duties which (with one brief interlude piloting Russian tankers down the Turkish coast) had been my normal way of life so far.

'More and more Greek schooners and coasters are working for the Germans,' Colonel K. went on, 'carrying stores and equipment between the islands.'

'I suppose they have to live and eat, sir.'

'We don't think so,' he snapped back at me. 'And you've got to *see* that they don't. We want you to take a caique – one of the dozen or so that have escaped down to Beirut and been left there by their people – and fit her out with a more powerful engine, guns and explosives; then take her up into the Aegean, and whenever you see a Greek ship flying the red and white German Sea Transport flag you'll sink her and machine-gun any survivors in the water.'

'But, sir . . .'

'What d'you mean "but, sir"? This is an order.'

'Not one I can obey, sir. The Geneva Convention is quite clear on . . .'

'To hell with the Geneva Convention!' The little man was on his feet now, glaring at me across the desk. 'The K. Convention's what counts here . . . you'll do as you're told.'

'I'm sorry, sir . . .'

There was a long silence, while Colonel K. continued to stand there glaring at me. Then slowly he subsided and sat staring out of the window to his left. I began to back quietly towards the door. Suddenly he looked round, his face clearing. 'Oh, dear,' he said in a silky tone of voice. 'What a pity . . . now that you know our plans and choose not to obey them, you're a bit of an embarrassment, aren't you?'

'Surely not, sir, if I don't breathe a word to anyone . . .' I had nearly reached the door '. . . about your intentions.'

The colonel smiled a silky smile. 'I'm afraid I can't agree with you,' he said. 'The point is that you know.' He paused, staring at me very hard. 'You may also know that we have a camp in the desert where we send people who know too much and won't cooperate.'

He reached out and pressed a bell on his desk. At the same moment my hand found the door knob. I flung myself out of the room and down the corridor at high speed. Fortunately for me, SOE headquarters in Cairo were made to look like ordinary administrative offices, no doubt for secrecy reasons, so there were no sentries in the corridors or on the landings, and only a commissionaire and a reception clerk at the entrance. My jeep was waiting outside. 'Back to Alex . . . fast,' I told the driver.

★　　★　　★

It was close on midnight when we reached Alexandria. There was a sea mist blowing in across the harbour, as we bumped our way along the rough track skirting its southern shore, lending an almost conspiratorial atmosphere to the ancient sheds and cranes of a deserted fish-dock about a mile out of town near the ruins of the Pharos,[1] where the marine branch of SOE had their base. One end of one of the sheds had been provided with a desk, a chart table, filing cabinets and a few chairs, to serve as an office. The others were filled with stores and equipment or fitted out as workshops. The rusty old coaster *Hedgehog*, which John Campbell used for landings and supply runs to Crete, was alongside the wharf.

I found John alone in the office ashore, lounging in 'Skipper' Poole's chair – tall, dark, athletic (he'd pole-vaulted for England in the Berlin Olympics).

'You've been mixing it with that little swine, K. We've had a signal,' he said as I came in. 'Consider yourself under arrest.'

'Not till I've had a cup of tea and something to eat,' I said. 'What've you got?'

We found a tin of Frankfurters and half a loaf in the Skipper's food locker and put the kettle on the primus. While waiting for it to boil, I told John about my interview.

He didn't appear to be particularly concerned.

'Humphrey'll sort it out for you,' he said. 'We'll go and see him in the morning.'

Fresh Start

Humphrey Quill, a major in the Royal Marines and a Staff Officer (Intelligence), was not only a personal friend but also our official link with C-in-C's office. He was a man of many talents, combining the skills of a highly trained soldier, a real tennis player, a single-handed sailor and a collector of ancient clocks – just the man, in fact, with the breadth of outlook to deal with my immediate problem. He did so very quickly. In less than twenty-four hours I was back in his office.

'C-in-C's furious,' he said. 'I'd already told him about your interview with K. when the fellow came on the telephone to the Chief of Staff demanding your court-martial for gross insolence. He was told where to go in no uncertain terms, and it's been decided to withdraw both of you – John Campbell as well – from SOE. Instead a separate naval flotilla will be formed, to operate with Army raiding forces.'

That was how the Levant Schooner Flotilla was born. We were attached to Coastal Forces Eastern Mediterranean under Commander Ralph Courage DSO, DSC, RN, with John Campbell as his Staff Officer LSF Operations. My job was to fit out all the suitable single-masted caiques I

5 '. . . all the suitable caiques I could find . . .'

could find (photo 5) in Beirut and Famagusta, as well as one or more larger schooner-rigged craft to act as headquarters and supply vessels. When enough of them were ready for sea, I was to take them up to a secluded anchorage in one of the fjords in south-west Turkey, where the schooners would act as advanced bases for the smaller raiding caiques, and also for one or two HDMLs[2] armed with Bofors, Oerlikon and twin Vickers machine-guns, which were sent up to provide additional fire power when required.

Turkey at that time was in a state of what might be called spring-loaded neutrality. She was ready to jump in either direction, depending largely on military developments between her present and former allies.[3] In the meantime Allied ships were permitted to make use of Turkish waters, but not to bring any weapons ashore. Even so, at some points round the coast Turkish Army units acting as coastguards were openly hostile. It was, after all, less than twenty-five years since Germany and Turkey had been allies. However, for the time being our diplomats seemed to have succeeded in pacifying on our behalf useful areas of the Gulfs of Kos and Doris and the Turkish side of the Khios and Mitilini Straits. And in due course units of the Long Range Desert Group and George Jellicoe's[4] Special Boat Service of the SAS came up with their own supply and headquarters schooners to join us, ready to plan and carry out raids against the Italian- and German-held islands of the Aegean.

★   ★   ★

I was sad to leave our cosy little nest on the wilder shores of Alexandria harbour and the adventurous companions I had shared it with. But the new task looked interesting. And because the Mediterranean Fleet, already reduced to four cruisers and a few destroyers, was pinned down by greatly superior enemy sea and air forces, it was the only kind of active operation likely to be contemplated. So we would be able to count on more than ordinary support in stores, equipment and dockyard services.

But one or two fairly tricky problems had still to be solved. The first concerned the boats. We would have to operate mainly during the hours of darkness, so the 15 or 20 hp Bolinder diesels which powered most of the caiques we chose – going 'bom . . . bom . . . bom' for a top speed of 5 or 6 knots, and audible for many miles on a quiet night – would have to be replaced. Fortunately this was not too difficult. A number of spare 90 hp (2,000 rpm) diesel engines intended for Matilda tanks, which the Australians had recently withdrawn from service, were lying in store at Haifa. When our caiques were fitted with these they were able to cruise at 6 or 7 knots – only a knot or so faster than their designed speed, but *at half throttle or less* and therefore in comparative silence.

The crews were another problem. Regular naval officers and ratings, highly trained on modern equipment, couldn't easily be spared for irregular operations such as ours, on which their skills would largely be wasted. So all

6 An LSF caique on trials.

our people, officers as well as ratings, had to be volunteers (photo 7) –
mainly men who had got into a rut somewhere and wanted a more
interesting life. There were also quite a few habitual defaulters who were
allowed to volunteer for the LSF rather than spend long periods in
detention. One or two more difficult characters had, I believe, been virtually
ordered to volunteer under threat from exasperated superiors.

The officers who commanded these men were all young reservists aged
between nineteen and twenty-three, and formal discipline on irregular
operations in enemy waters, frequently 100 miles or more from base, was
not only inappropriate but obviously impossible to enforce; yet no unit I
ever served in – from trawlers to destroyers – was as trouble-free as the
Levant Schooner Flotilla. And I believe the same applied to the Army
patrols we carried.

Navigation was another problem. The only instruments we could use
effectively without giving ourselves away to the enemy were small aircraft
steering compasses with phosphorescent dial-markings, plus hand-bearing
compasses and lead lines. Patent logs streamed astern were useless for our
kind of work – they were always getting foul of something, especially in
emergencies.

We had to make passages of anything up to 80 miles over open water and
arrive at an exact spot – usually a deserted beach or cove – on an unlit coast,
in complete darkness. We couldn't risk even a lighted binnacle. But the

7 'All our people . . . had to be volunteers . . .'. Brian Coleman of LS8 and his coxswain ashore in Alinda Bay, Leros.

8 Stoker Osborne and Leading Seaman Hallybone on duty.

aircraft compasses were, in fact, very easy to use. You simply set the two parallel lines on the cursor to the course you wanted to steer. The helmsman then kept the compass needle (also phosphorescent) between the two course lines.

Only once did the system let us down. On a dark and overcast night, with no landmarks or stars to guide him, the helmsman of one of our boats managed to get the needle between the cursor lines the wrong way round. He must have dozed off and, waking with a start, found the needle across the lines instead of between them. He then, by bad luck, put the helm the wrong way, and when the needle had finally been brought back between the lines on the cursor, he was actually steering 180° off course – i.e., back the way he'd come.

Finding the entrance to a secluded creek or cove at night was the most difficult of all. Recognizable silhouettes – of hills or headlands, rocks and islands – could help, but the final approach often had to be made in stages. First, maybe, a known rock in line with a cliff or gap between hills. You steered towards this until another recognizable silhouette appeared in a different direction, and the course must be altered again until a third feature was established. And so, at last, to the sheltered landing point agreed on.

If the landing point was a beach rather than rocks, the stern anchor was dropped on a long scope of 2 in line when the boat was still half a cable or so (100 yards) off. The boat could then be eased on to the beach and held there with the engine going dead slow ahead, while two soldiers jumped ashore on a recce. If the coast was clear, the others would follow. Then the boat was hauled off, taking the bight of the stern line forward, to swing her round and away. The record for a beach landing, from approach to clear away, was two-and-a-half minutes, and it seldom took more than four.

Ships in Disguise

All this we practised repeatedly in Yeronisis Cove, on a completely deserted stretch of the west coast of Cyprus, until it became second nature. But now the knottiest problem of all began to worry me: when piloting those Russian tankers down the Turkish coast the year before, we had been made acutely aware of the close watch being kept on coastal shipping by enemy aircraft. Every morning a German Ju88 would fly down the coast and every afternoon an old Italian CANT would pass by, always at the same time, so as to reach Cape Khelidonia at the end of its run at precisely 4.30 p.m. I remember it with sadness. We had grown to look on that old CANT as a friend, noting the times at which it passed our successive lie-up anchorages, and working out from these that it had an air speed of around 235 knots.

I remember also an evening in the bar of HMS *Martial*, the naval base at Beirut, telling some friends, including John Reid, CO of a nearby Beaufighter squadron, about all this and feeling rather proud of our ingenious calculations. I also recall the feeling of utter desolation when two days later John showed me a photograph taken from his Beaufighter of our CANT lying flat, still and broken on the surface of the sea, with no sign of life around her.

I still feel sad about my part in that incident. But in the early summer of 1943, with half a dozen LSF caiques fitting out and nearly ready for sea, it was the close enemy watch on coastal shipping that concerned me most. It meant that any craft, seen either from the air or from the islands, steering out into the Aegean or returning to Turkey would be suspect, since no ordinary Greek trading or fishing caiques would have any business in such directions. Nor were there any harbours, creeks or coves out in the islands where we could spend the day safe from prying eyes and wagging tongues, or indeed from enemy patrols. So we would always have to come and go during the dark hours of a single night, which in turn restricted the Army raiding parties we carried to targets in the Dodecanese and, at a pinch, the islands of Amorgos, Stampalia and Scarpanto.

★   ★   ★

I have always looked upon Maurice Green as a co-founder of the Levant Schooner Flotilla, because but for him we would never have been able to carry out the Aegean-wide raiding and reconnaissance operations which became a factor in Middle East planning for nearly two years. I remember him best as a quiet and unassuming soldier with the rank of major, sitting all on his own at the wardroom bar of HMS *Martial* one weekday forenoon. I said 'Hullo' or 'Good morning', as one does, but found it difficult to get any further. He really was an extremely reticent person. However, since we were alone in the bar, I persevered.

I don't know how it came into the conversation; maybe it was some reference of mine to schoolday memories which led to the discovery that we had both been at the same school, though at different times. This, at least, established a common interest and gave us a topic of conversation, and I soon found myself telling him about the problem that was uppermost in my mind just then. 'If only we could hide somewhere during the day and continue the next night,' I said, 'we'd be able to operate all over the Aegean . . . and on the mainland coast as well, come to that . . .'

'Why can't you?' he asked, smiling.

It was then that I discovered not only that Maurice had specialized in art at school but that he was now commanding a 9th Army camouflage unit! For the next two or three weeks we experimented with nets of various shades and patterns, and different kinds of spreaders (long bamboo poles with wire and hessian discs on their ends to break up the lines of a boat's hull when seen from above). The mast of our experimental caique was stepped in a tabernacle, so that it could be lowered to lie fore-and-aft, with

9 '. . . till she looked like part of the rocky headland . . .'

its head resting in a crotch on the cabin top. Additional spreaders could then be erected to break up the boat's profile as well.

Maurice and I got to know each other and became fast friends during those weeks, like kids with a new and fascinating toy. I remember it as an exciting time, full of successes and reverses, and in the end a trip one evening up the coast to Juneh, which was then no more than a village at the head of a bay, with a rocky point jutting out southwards on its western side.

Six of us sailed up there one evening – Maurice and three LSF skippers plus a wife and a girlfriend. We moored the caique against rocks just inside the point and rigged camouflage nets on spreaders till she looked like part of the rocky headland itself (photo 9). Then we took blankets, sleeping bags and baskets of food up a shingle beach into the mouth of a great cave, where we soon had a driftwood fire blazing and the *ouzo* bottle going round while we roasted sausages on sticks.

It was a wonderful night, warm and starry, and we'd almost forgotten why we were there when we were woken next morning by John Reid's Beaufighter roaring overhead to look for us and take photographs. When these were developed and printed later that day, all you could see was a beach, a cave and a rocky headland; but which of the rocks was our caique none but those who knew where we'd moored her, could have told.

From that moment the whole scope and nature of LSF operations changed fundamentally. We became a force to be reckoned with all over the Aegean. Nor was it long before special service craft in the Adriatic, and eventually in the Far East as well, adopted a similar system. That was Maurice Green's contribution to our war effort and the reason why I have always looked on him as a co-founder of the LSF.

[1]   An ancient marble pillar on top of which a fire used to be lighted. By lining up this fire with another down by the shore, ships were guided safely through the outer reefs into the harbour.

[2]   Harbour Defence Motor Launches.

[3]   In the First World War Turkey and Germany were allies.

[4]   Major the Earl Jellicoe DSO, MC.

The City Accountant's Tale

CHAPTER THREE

Champagne Galore

It was early in February 1944. The wind was north-easterly, light to moderate, and it was cold, very cold, and dark, as the caique approached the Arki Islands, whose misty outline was just visible on the port bow. I took hand-compass bearings of both ends of the land, which put us about 3 miles off, so I steered for the northern tip of the main island.

My sailing orders told me to land our SBS patrol – five men and an officer – in Melissa Creek, about a third of the way down the eastern coast. My only guide to it would be a small islet tucked into one corner of a wide bay just north of the creek. On the chart, this islet was distinct enough, but from seaward all we could see was a flat black wall with a gently undulating skyline and no other discernible feature.

About a mile off the northern point, I throttled back to 'dead slow' and turned inshore. We were towing a 16 ft motor dory in which the patrol were to make some of their landings; it surged up alongside, then fell back. The hills inland stood up blank and black against the overcast sky. I steered for the highest point on the ridge, which the chart showed to be opposite the islet we were looking for. Coxswain Hallybone came aft and stood beside me. Soon we could see breakers, and a little later hear the low rumble of surf above the mutter of our engine and the swish and bubble of our wake. But there was still no sign of any break in the coastline.

We stood on. The hills rose higher. Miles, the radio operator, poked his head out of the after hatch. The SBS men crouching on the foredeck watched in silence. Till all at once it seemed to me that a darker, denser patch was growing out of the murky background towards us. Then a pale tongue of sea water appeared beside it, detaching the darker hummock from the rest. We had found the islet.

'Don't knock it over, Skips . . . they'll sue yer.' Stoker Osborne's languid West Hammersmith drawl was somehow reassuring. Anyway we knew where we were now, so I swung her round to port, and twenty minutes later we entered Melissa Creek, where we secured to rocks on the eastern side.

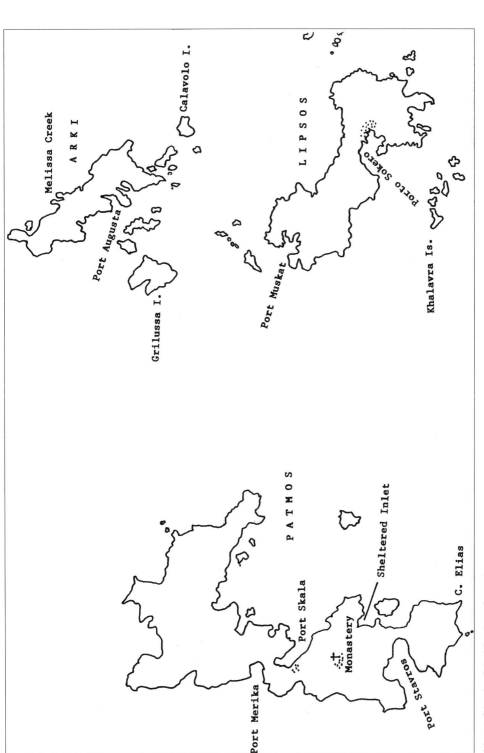

Map 4 Islands of the Northern Sporades.

★   ★   ★

It was beginning to get light as Terry Bruce-Mitford,[1] Corporal Miller and the rest of the SBS patrol scrambled ashore, and set off up the rocky hillside for Port Augusta, the main village, on the other side of the island. We hauled their dory alongside, lowered our mast and spread our camouflage nets over both boats. Then a sentry was posted, and the others lay down wherever they could to catch a few hours' sleep. I sat in the stern sheets for a while to watch the overcast slowly lifting in the east and the sun come staring through. Orange light swept the grey hillside, littered with stones and stunted bushes, then faded again as the sun rose further into the wrack.

The wind had backed and freshened from about north, and a certain amount of swell entering the creek was causing the caique to surge at her moorings. I routed out a couple more fenders from the fore peak, and placed them beside the two already over the side.

This was one of our first operations with an SBS patrol. I wondered how it would go. Were the lads at this very moment sitting over coffee and *ouzo*, with welcoming islanders crowding round them and pretty girls treating them like heroes? Or would we suddenly hear a burst of firing and the crack of hand grenades, men running for their lives, crashing down into the boat? And just how easy would it be to get survivors aboard and the caique to sea with the enemy at their heels?

My thoughts were interrupted by someone calling my name, and Corporal Miller clambered over the rocky foreshore towards us.

'Captain Mitford says will you come and talk to these airmen, skipper?'

I lifted the inshore side of the netting and climbed out on to the rocks. 'Airmen? What airmen?'

'Two Beaufighter blokes what's crashed and wants takin' off. There's no Germans on the island,' he added.

'Then why didn't the airmen come with you?'

'They're bothered about leavin' their hide-out in the village . . . in case a German patrol was to come in.'

I roused Hallybone and told him to single up moorings, ready to cast off fast, and Osborne to stand by with the engine, just in case we came back in a hurry. Then I climbed ashore again. 'All right. Let's go.'

★   ★   ★

We set off up the hill at a steady pace. The going was surprisingly rough, but after about twenty minutes we reached the crest of the ridge and were able to walk downhill in greater comfort. The village of Port Augusta lay scattered round the head of a deep inlet with its only taverna right on the waterfront. Oleander, tamarisk and olive trees spread out before it to the beach itself. The sea was calm, except when sudden gusts swept down the hill behind us to lash its surface and pass on, spray turning to dust up the opposite slope.

We shouldered our way through a small crowd of curious villagers who had collected round the taverna doorway. Inside we found the rest of the patrol talking to two rather bedraggled RAF chaps, who looked and sounded a bit crestfallen. But there was indeed a bottle of *ouzo* on the table, and a motherly woman with a jug in her hand to top up the glasses.

I pulled up a chair and someone poured me a drink. Then we got down to the evacuation question, which wasn't going to be as easy to solve as one might think. Our caique (LS3) and its patrol were committed to a series of reconnaissance landings, on Arki itself, on Lipsos Island, about 6 miles south of Arki, and on Patmos, some 10 or 15 miles further west. We were already overcrowded on board, and would find it difficult to make room for two more.

'There's an Air/Sea Rescue launch on the Turkish coast somewhere,' I said hopefully, to the older of the two airmen.

'Yes. But we've no way of calling them. Our radio's at the bottom of the sea.'

'Where did you crash, then?'

He took me to the window and pointed. 'Over there,' he said, 'near the head of the bay.'

'Oh, so you ditched, did you? Engine failure? Out of fuel or something?'

'No, we were diving on that schooner anchored close inshore, and I didn't pull out in time . . . misjudged the down-draught from the hill here, and pancaked in . . . easy enough to do, you know . . . in the heat of the moment.'

I supposed it was, but I was still puzzled. 'Why on earth were you strafing an unarmed Greek trading schooner?' I wanted to know.

He looked uncomfortable. 'Those were our orders,' he said doggedly. 'Anything with two masts or more in enemy waters.'

'Hmm . . . Doesn't look as though you damaged her much. She's still got her two masts. Anyway, there's no way we can contact Air/Sea Rescue, except through Alex, who'd then have to get on to RAF Cairo to make them a signal.'

'And they might be away on another job . . . it could take days to get them here.' Both airmen looked resigned to the fortunes of war. But in the end, of course, we took them aboard. They were brought down to the caique after dark, so as not to give away our hiding place to possible watchers, at sea or ashore; we might need to use the creek again. In fact, I was rather relieved to have them aboard, safe from enemy patrols.

At dusk we left for Lipsos, and next morning we were blessed by a remarkable stroke of luck. We had entered Port Muskat at the northern end of Lipsos Island during the night, and were safely secured, invisible under camouflage nets and having breakfast, when a large caique flying the white and red pennant worn by vessels carrying stores for the Germans came motoring into the harbour and anchored not 200 yards from where we lay.

Bruce-Mitford finished his breakfast, then ordered two of his men to get the dory ready and her outboard started. They motored over to the caique and were pleased to find that her skipper and crew were only too happy to be 'captured' by the British. Nor was there any problem about a prize crew. Marine Smith of the SBS and the two airmen were just what was wanted.

So that evening, when the SBS patrol came back from its first reconnaissance patrol, both vessels left together – the caique *Eugenia* bound for Türk Bükü, our temporary base on the Turkish coast, and LS3 for Port Stavros, on the west coast of Patmos.

★ ★ ★

As the sun went down, the wind backed to west-north-west, blowing hard. We soon found ourselves punching into a heavy head sea, which cut our speed to 3 knots at most. The fortitude of the SBS lads, crouched on the main hatch with seas boarding green, lashed by spray and only their standard battle dress to protect them, was remarkable.

The caique crew were all aft and fairly dry by comparison. But on rounding Cape Elias, at the southern end of Patmos, we met the full force of the north-westerly wind, kicking the seas up into peaks and pyramids. LS3 staggered and plunged but kept moving. We fought with the helm, and the helm – a stout oak tiller – fought back; there were no steering wheels in those boats.

It was pitch dark and all we could see was the misty loom of high ground to starboard. But after a bit it seemed to me that the caique was riding more steadily and making better way through the seas. We must be over the worst of it, and daylight wasn't far off. I looked aft at our wake to judge our speed. It zigzagged astern, confused but uninterrupted. The dory had gone! Only the frayed end of her painter – a stout 3 in manila – remained aboard. She must have filled and sunk.

★ ★ ★

So now we had to change our plan. The patrol was to have landed by dory in Port Stavros. Instead, we would have to find a sheltered cove where we could get alongside. We found one just inside the southern point of Port Merika, 2 or 3 miles further north, but failed to notice that a look-out post had been established on the point itself. As we approached, an Italian soldier came out of a small wooden hut and sauntered down to the foreshore, obviously intending to have a chat.

By the greatest good fortune, my seaman gunner on that trip was a Dodecanese Greek, all of whom were brought up from their school days to speak Italian. He answered the soldier's hail and a long, involved conversation ensued. Our Greek persuaded the Italian that we were a German armed patrol boat, sent to the Dodecanese to find and destroy the *odiosi* British commandos who were making life so miserable for everyone.

10 Caique LS3 at sea.

Surprisingly, that soldier was the sole defender of the bay and the adjoining coastline. His superiors, with the Latin instinct for what was and was not worth doing, had left him on his own, in favour of a more comfortable life in the lively little town of Scala, just over the hill. So for the next two days, while our patrol was ashore on a prolonged reconnaissance, we moved about Port Merika at will, under the friendly eye of the Italian soldier and almost in comfort.

When the patrol finally returned, we picked them up at the head of the bay and heard that the population of Patmos were virtually starving. So half the patrol took all the food we could spare ashore (we happened to have nearly three months' stores aboard) while LS3 took the other three lads back to Lipsos (where they destroyed the cable station) and then brought them back the following day to Port Merika. That evening, with some relief, we took our final departure from Cape Elias, and stood east-south-east for the Gulf of Güllük.

★   ★   ★

Türk Bükü, on the southern side of the Gulf of Güllük, was a well-sheltered inlet with two small islets close to its western shore. The narrow creek between the islets and the shore, with dense pine forest growing down almost to the water's edge on both sides, made an admirable haven, in which our caiques – and even the large HQ schooners, LS9 and *Tewfik* – were well

11 Supply schooner at anchor in a Turkish fjord.

hidden from the Ju88 reconnaissance aircraft, which every forenoon flew at low altitude along the coast and back, just outside Turkish waters.

We tied up alongside *Tewfik*, the Army HQ schooner, and the SBS patrol clambered aboard her. I followed with difficulty to report to Ian Patterson, the major in charge. We'd been away for seven days and nights and during the whole of that time I hadn't had more than eight hours' sleep. I was staggering with fatigue. The Army doctor on board took a look at me, then fetched the rum jar and poured me half a mugful. 'Knock that back,' he said, and I did. Then I rolled into one of the bunks in *Tewfik's* after cabin (which was messroom, ops room and bunkhouse rolled into one) and went out like a light.

It was eight o'clock in the morning when I went to bed. Every few minutes men must have come clattering down the ladder from the upper deck; others, no doubt, argued over maps and charts on the table; others again were eating and talking, while yet others bandied words from bunk to bunk and bench to bench. The noise in that cabin was unceasing. And it may well have been its very continuity – the steady volume and level of it – that allowed me to sleep on . . . and on . . . and on. I would, no doubt, have slept on until next morning. But around five o'clock in the evening, Corporal Miller gave me a shake.

' 'Ere,' he said, handing me an enormous mug. 'You'd better 'ave a swig of this while it's still goin'.' 'This', to my astonishment, was a mug of the most delicious champagne.

'They has it for breakfast mostly,' said Miller, 'gives 'em a lift to start the day with,' and seeing my amazement, he added, 'That caique we copped in Lipsos 'ad eight dozen bottles on board. They've got through close on three dozen already.'

★   ★   ★

On deck, I found Gordon Hogg, our Pickwickian communications officer, sitting on the main hatch twiddling the knobs of an expensive-looking radio set. 'You're lucky to find us here,' he said, as I came up. 'If Adrian and George[2] hadn't been down the line somewhere, they'd 've had us out of here, quick and lively, for sure.'

'Why? What happened?'

'Plenty . . . and it was all your fault really.' He took a sip from an enamel mug beside him and went on twiddling. 'That caique you sent us was loaded with comforts for the Germans on Leros – radio sets, crates of beer, blankets, boots, bottles of aftershave, two 48-bottle cases of champagne and four enormous packing cases filled with loo paper.' He took another swig at his mug and called over his shoulder 'Bring us another bottle, please, Jacko!' The cook appeared with a bottle of Lanson '38. The words *Nur Für Wehrmacht Offizieren* were overprinted in red on its label. Gordon opened it with practised hands and filled my mug. 'You can imagine what happened,' he went on.

'No, I can't. Tell me.'

'Well, there was a party, of course. And about midnight some of the lads started slinging rolls of loo paper like streamers up into the pine trees and over them. Two whole crates of the stuff went up there . . . you should have seen it next morning – like an outsize eagle's nest made of spaghetti, with more spaghetti dangling and fluttering around it.'

'Quite a picture for an enemy recce plane, what? . . . just when there's all this fuss about compromising Turkish neutrality!'

Gordon nodded. 'But we were more worried about getting raided. So the boats got the hell out of it at daybreak, leaving a dozen or so of the worst offenders ashore – I was one – to clear up as best we could.' Gordon sighed, but he was smiling a plump Pickwickian smile. 'I'm not really the build for climbing trees, but I tried to keep the chaps amused. Anyway, we managed to get most of it down with oars and boathooks before the old Ju88 came by . . . and the rest afterwards. So that evening the boats came in again and everything got back to normal.'

★ ★ ★

Next day LS3 moved on. Those who remained in Türk Bükü enjoyed champagne for breakfast (the ratings preferred the beer) every day for nearly a week. They must have got through another couple of dozen bottles before a prize crew could be assembled to take the caique down to Beirut.

The Ju88 came past every forenoon at about eleven o'clock, but it wasn't until three or four weeks later that he got the pictures he really wanted. Three of our boats, including one unmistakably British HDML, were proceeding peacefully up the southern side of the Gulf of Kos towards our rear base at Port Deremen (now English Harbour) when the Ju88, coming up astern, with engines throttled back and therefore unheard, passed close by us, masthead high. We could see the observer's old-fashioned plate camera levelled at us continuously as he passed, and wondered what would happen next.

Nothing did happen for nearly a fortnight, when we heard that Herr von Papen, the German Ambassador to Turkey, had presented the Turkish Foreign Secretary with 'indisputable photographic evidence of the baseness and cowardice of the British, who take advantage of Turkish generosity to escape their just deserts at the hands of the German defenders of the Aegean Sea'.

The Foreign Secretary's answer, we were told – no doubt apocryphally – was, 'My dear Herr von Papen . . . have another drink.'

---

[1]   Captain Terrence Bruce-Mitford.
[2]   George Jellicoe.

The Parson's Tale

CHAPTER FOUR

Dressed Overall[1]

The moon had already set behind the mountain, but we could see the figures now as darker shapes against the hillside to port, coming down from three different directions.

Friend or foe? The age-old question. I raised my blue-shaded signalling torch and made the recognition challenge . . . MR – MR – MR . . . at the centre group. And waited. I made the signal again, and waited again. There was no reply. Keep calm, I told myself. Anything might have happened . . . lamp burnt out . . . flat batteries . . . they might have lost their torch . . . I might have been flashing the wrong group. I signalled again, this time at the left-hand group – and waited . . . and waited . . . keep calm . . . keep absolutely calm.

We were lying stopped in the mouth of a small cove on the island of Patmos, ready to come alongside, or head out to sea if the correct recognition reply was not received. I looked round the deck of my ML. They were all at their stations: the lad with a boathook up forward; others ready with mooring lines forward and aft; two more with tommy-guns amidships; our main armament (a 40 mm Bofors, a 20 mm Oerlikon and two twin Vickers .303s) all manned and ready; coxswain at the wheel; Number One on the bridge beside me.

I turned to look ashore again. The three groups of figures were closer now, and closer to each other, converging as they came. There seemed to be a great many of them. Three days earlier we had landed a ten-man patrol, but now, lumbering downhill towards us, and already approaching the rocky gully at the head of our cove, there were at least twenty.

Some of them might be prisoners. But we still had to be watchful, until we knew for certain which were the captors and which the captives. I heard the scrape and clunk of the Oerlikon amidships being cocked. The barrel of the Bofors forward was swinging round to port and elevating. I raised my torch and signalled again, at the right-hand group this time . . . once . . . twice . . . three times . . . and there it was at last – QP – QP – QP . . . the correct reply. I hadn't realized that I had been holding my breath, but it came out now with a whoosh, and I expect there were quite a few other whooshes round the ship.

We dropped alongside and waited. Soon the men ashore were scrambling down the rocks close by, large and muscular, small and wiry SBS boys, with ten prisoners – seven dejected-looking Germans and . . . Good Heavens! . . . three women!

The women were shoved aboard first, and straight down to the mess deck, with a few girlish shrieks and giggles on the way. Then came the prisoners with their guards; and finally the patrol, led by a great raw-boned giant of a fellow . . . who immediately collapsed over the engine-room skylight, was violently sick and then burst into tears. None of us knew what to do, except for a slightly built young soldier, who grabbed at his comrade and bundled him off the skylight on to the deck, where he lay face down, still sobbing. The rest of the patrol climbed aboard and found themselves corners round the deck, taking no notice. We bore off from the rocks, and stood out to sea.

The big fellow lay where he'd fallen, face down and still sobbing but more quietly. No one paid any attention to him. 'What on earth's the matter?' I asked the SBS officer, who had come aboard last. 'Is he wounded?'

'Oh, no,' he said. 'He's always like that. You see, we go in with the knife on night attacks. Guns are too noisy. But it seems to affect some of them, especially the big tough ones. Reaction, I suppose . . . or remorse . . . or a bit of both. The smaller guys seem to take it more in their stride. Funny, isn't it?' He was interrupted by a flurry of shrieks and laughter from below. 'I'm afraid we've brought you some pretty odd passengers this trip. I hope they won't make trouble.'

'We'll manage. The lads are fairly sensible.'

'They're a cabaret act from Athens,' he explained, 'comforts for the troops, and all that . . . so we had to bring them away; the Greeks would have cut their throats as collaborators if we'd left them.'

★　　★　　★

Our twin Gardner diesels (we were one of the original HDMLs) (photo 12) gave us a cruising speed of 9 knots. From Patmos eastwards through the Lipsos Channel and well into the Gulf of Güllük, on the Turkish coast, was a distance of some 45 miles. But we had barely covered half of this before the strong westerly wind, with a high sea lifting us along, had veered into the north-west and freshened rapidly. By the time we reached Türk Bükü, on the southern side of the gulf, it was blowing a Force 9 gale. We passed the two islands on the western side of the bay and anchored thankfully under the lee of the second.

A wild day had dawned, and soon the regular Ju88 reconnaissance aircraft would be over, checking on Allied activities all the way down the Turkish coast to Castelorizo. We fought like fury with our flimsy camouflage nets, which kept taking charge and flying into the air like a ballerina's veils. The

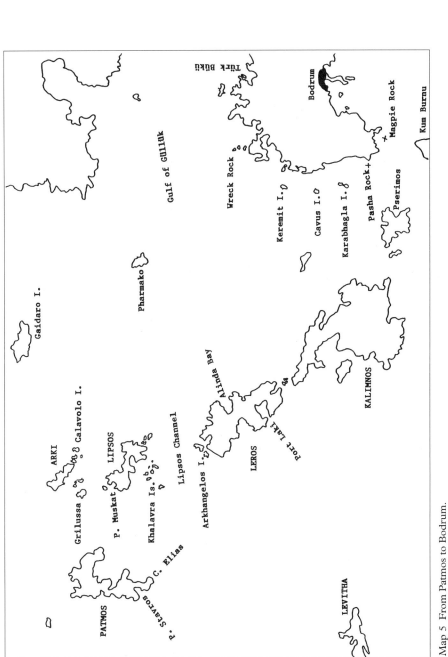

Map 5 From Patmos to Bodrum.

12 '... we were one of the original HDMLs ...'

German prisoners struggled to help us. They were a cheerful bunch, overjoyed that for them the war was over.

At last we succeeded in making the ship look reasonably rock-like, with spreaders here and there to break up her line, and weights secured to the lower edges of the nets to sink them. We had just finished when, to our surprise and pleasure, mugs of hot coffee, followed by great hunks of bread smothered in meat paste, came round – crawled out to us under the nets by two of the prisoners and all three girls, who had taken over the galley. It became their personal domain for the rest of the voyage.

Things were looking up. And as soon as the wind fined down a bit, we could look forward to a pleasant, maybe even luxurious, Mediterranean cruise. But the wind didn't fine down. Not for a day or two anyway. It freshened to close on hurricane force, sweeping across the pine forest covering the land to windward, flattening the crests of the trees and raging out across the water, kicking up clouds of spray. Our anchor dragged. We gave it more cable. It dragged again. We gave it all we had, 'right out to a clinch'. We had to start the engine and go slow ahead before the dragging stopped. And on that first day at anchor we had to keep the engine turning, off and on, almost until sunset, when at last the wind abated a little, and half the ship's company could get some sleep.

There wasn't room below – on bunks, benches, tables and the deck – for more than half of them, including the prisoners, to lie down, so they took it in turns. They had, of course, offered three of the bunks furthest forward to the girls, who accepted two, one above the other, which they shared between them. The heads (lavatory) was a trickier problem, but they solved it somehow together.

For me meantime there were different puzzles to worry about. How long would our food last out? Or our fuel, for that matter, if we had to motor to our anchor much longer?

★   ★   ★

On that first evening, as it grew dark, I left Number One and the SBS officer to make the most of our tiny wardroom, and went up alone on to the bridge, where I parted the nets and hooked them back so that I could look about me. The wind seemed to have freshened again. The coxswain, whose anchor watch it was, had started the engine and was watching lights along the distant shoreline and in the hills above, to check that we weren't still dragging. The sky was clear, jet black and blazing with stars. In the west a wisp of moon low down was close to setting.

It was on just such a night, three years before, that from the farm in Buckinghamshire where I was working we saw an orange glare growing and building up in the south-eastern sky. London was burning. The great blitz of 16 April 1941, had begun. I have always remembered that moment as a turning point in my life, because the year before, at the age of twenty-two, I had registered as a conscientious objector. And now, seeing those flames enveloping Dockland and a large part of east and south-east London, where my family and most of my friends lived, I realized all at once that my place was there too.

Within a few days I was back in Catford as an air raid warden. And when, eight months later, the bombing of London had largely ceased, I looked for some other useful wartime occupation. I still couldn't face either of the killing services (the Army or the RAF), so I joined the Navy, hoping perhaps that my being a martyr to sea-sickness and terrified of the sea would in some way add to the quality of my contribution.

My hope was fulfilled in a manner which seemed to me miraculous. After a year as a rating and six months training for a commission, I was appointed to command an HDML which, with two others, formed the escort for the monitor HMS *Aphis*, bound up the coast from Durban. We had not gone far before we found ourselves punching into a northerly gale of such ferocity that both the other escorting vessels were forced to turn back. We kept going, even though all on board, except the motor mechanic and – surprisingly – myself, were prostrated with sea-sickness. I wondered afterwards whether it had been my terror at the violence of the storm and my desperate efforts to keep station in spite of it, which had driven any thoughts of illness or discomfort from my mind. However that may be, it is certainly a miracle that never again, from that day to this, have I suffered from sea-sickness.

These thoughts and others like them were passing through my mind (I may even have been talking to myself, I sometimes do) when I noticed that I was no longer alone. A bulky figure had come quietly up the ladder and settled in the opposite corner of the bridge, hunched forward over the dodger[2] and staring into the wind in silence. It was Baynes, the big soldier, whom I'd seen sprawled in tears on the deck at my feet the night before.

For a long time neither of us spoke. When the ship was under nets, moored or at anchor, it was normal for soldiers to come up on to the bridge after dark for a look around and a breath of air. There was nowhere else they could go. But I sensed that Baynes had something to say to me; and after a while, haltingly at first, it came out.

'I'm no coward, sorr.' He spoke in a rough Irish accent, half growl, half mutter. 'But I'm no killer, neither . . .'

'So what's troubling you?'

'I joined up to fight killers, sorr, . . . and then . . .', he paused awkwardly, '. . . I found that some of 'em wasn't killers.' Baynes faced round and burst out suddenly 'He was a lad, sorr, and . . . I'll never forget his face lookin' up at me as . . . as I . . . Oh God, sorr!'

There was agony in his voice. But after a bit he calmed down and said more quietly, 'What are we all doing here, sorr, . . . killing a few Germans, bein' killed ourselves, and gettin' hundreds of Greek people shot for helpin' us? What's it all for, sorr? What are we doin' here?'

Baynes looked at me searchingly, as though he thought I might have an answer – a satisfying answer. But I hadn't. I knew that more defenceless Greek hostages were executed every month than all the Allied and Axis casualties put together. And yet, there were strategies – even 'grand strategies' – to be considered, yes, and political balances. But even so I remembered some of the loyal and generous Greek people who had welcomed us to their islands, made feasts for us when they were starving, given us presents, helped and served us – until the Germans heard of it; and then . . . what happened to *them*?

I remembered especially the laughing face of a young Greek girl who came down to the ship and collected all the clothes she could find, to wash them for us. We paid her in soap, some for the clothes and some for herself. She came down again next day with all our laundry beautifully folded and ironed, my pyjamas decorated with a sprig of sweet-scented myrtle in the breast pocket. But when we called at the island again, some weeks later, the people were cowed and distant, and the girl wasn't there. Where was she? What had happened to her, we asked? But no one would say.

We talked on for a while, Baynes and I, about the war; about home; about God, of course, and the meaning of life. Talk during the night always seemed to follow that kind of pattern. And when Baynes eventually went below, I thought for a long time about my own position and the responsibilities it carried with it. I hadn't at that time considered entering the Church. That came much later. But I suppose that my whole life in those days was trending towards it.

★   ★   ★

Two days later the wind dropped at last. By evening it had fallen to a gentle offshore breeze. The sea subsided with it, and at dusk we stowed our nets and got under way. The distance to Port Deremen, in the Gulf of Kos, where we could transfer our SBS patrol to their Headquarters ship and hopefully stock up with a few essentials (we were out of almost everything edible, except salt, pepper, mustard, dried peas and a little rice) was 65 miles – nine hours, running at 7 knots to reduce fuel consumption.

The moon was higher in the sky and brighter than the evening before. Passing inside Büyüktavsan Island (map 6) we could pick out individual pine trees on the thickly wooded mainland opposite. Then on past Wreck Rock, standing up bold and black in the moonpath; and beyond it the open sea spreading dark and mysterious westwards to the mountains of Kalimnos, with the jagged outline of Leros dimly seen on the horizon. We turned south-west past the Sandama Peninsula and Palamüt Bay, and were almost abreast of Keremit Island, with its flashing light, when the lookout on the port side of the bridge said, quietly but distinctly, 'Shipping on the port bow, sir, coming this way'.

It was misty out in the fairway and at first I couldn't see them. Then a patrol vessel, zigzagging ahead of the others, turned at the end of her sweep, exposing a pale flank to the moon. Beyond her I could just make out two lines of dim grey shapes, with two more escorts, one on either side, advancing towards us. It looked like a convoy of lighters or landing craft; and we could see now that they had a total of three escorting patrol craft, one ahead and one on either beam – German R-Boats, specially equipped with 40 mm and 75 mm guns for Aegean patrol duties, any one of which was more than a match for an HDML.

It was a moment for prompt decisions to meet a situation which could at any time become desperate. We altered course to port, making for the inshore channel between Karabhagla Island and the coast. The enemy might not have seen us or, if they had, were perhaps unwilling to leave their charges and go chasing after a solitary HDML. In any case we would be more difficult to pick out against the sombre background of Turkish cliffs and hills.

I reduced speed so as to moderate our wake, shining silver and visible from a long way off in the moonlight. There was little else we could do but wait and hope. Number One came quietly up the ladder and stood beside me. I was grateful for his sturdy and good humoured support. We stood in silence watching the shore, the approaching islands and the convoy, which was coming up to Karabhagla Island from the south on its seaward side, as

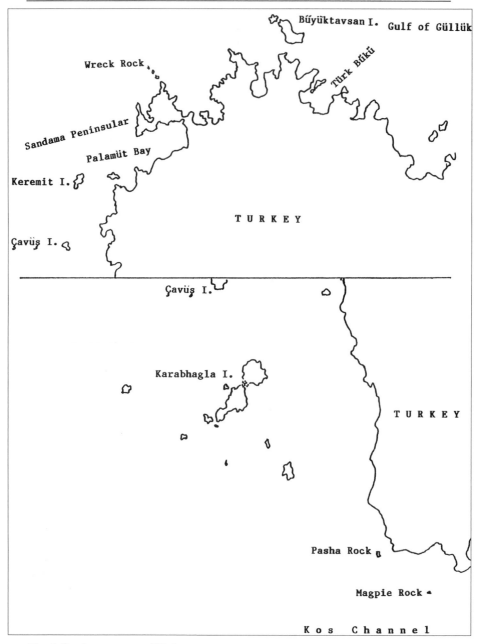

Map 6 South-west corner of Turkey.

we approached it from the north on its inshore side. It looked as though we would both reach it at about the same time.

And that was the moment when a cheerful little voice behind me said, 'You like, kyrios?' And there was one of the girls, the one with the peroxided hair whom we took to be the leader of the troupe. She smiled winningly, head on one side, as she held out before her a steaming mug – half an offering, half a protective shield against the outburst which she knew must come. And it did. But not from me – I have never quite mastered the procedure for shouting at women. Number One was made of sterner stuff. 'What the hell are you doing up here?' he blazed at her in a raucous whisper. 'Get below at once.'

She smiled disarmingly, and with an almost motherly patience in her voice, said, 'Not understanding, please'.

'Get below!'

'You like?' She held her mug out invitingly. And now, behind her on the ladder, I could see her friend – the little brunette with the ample bosom – passing up another mug as she pressed forward behind her pal. The third girl – the quiet one – was waiting her turn on the deck below, carrying a small tray with more mugs on it.

Then two things happened almost simultaneously, completely overshadowing the pantomime on the bridge ladder: the nearest R-boat started flashing, a challenge presumably; and seconds later, before we'd had time to think of a reply, the friendly mountain mass forming the northern end of Karabhagla Island slid between us.

What a relief! What a wonderful feeling of reprieve! But it didn't last long. The northern and central mountains of Karabhagla Island – 500 ft and 370 ft high respectively – are separated by a low isthmus, little more than a sandbank some 300 yards long, over which the upperworks of the R-boat suddenly appeared, less than a mile away, as we drove by in opposite directions. We saw her guns training round towards us, and expected a hail of 75 mm and 40 mm shells to fall upon us at any moment. But her skipper must have realized that there was no time for serious hostilities. And perhaps as a child he'd had an English nanny. Because her bridge signalling lamp blazed at us again, and P–E–E–P B–O' was what he flashed, then disappeared behind the northern mountain and we behind the central one.

The quiet girl came timidly up the ladder with her tray to join her friends on the bridge. The soup which they now handed round was out of this world and made one doubly thankful still to be in it.

$$\star \quad \star \quad \star$$

So there were indeed Germans with a sense of humour, and no doubt some, perhaps many, who wouldn't murder hostages. The General captured on Mykonos by one of our patrols was an extremely civilized and well bred gentleman, who spoke excellent English; but what I remember best about him were his boots. They were beautiful boots, immaculately boned and polished; but when he sat down and stretched out his legs, one saw that the soles were worn right through, leaving great cavities under the balls of his feet. He smiled at our obvious astonishment, and said with a twinkle, 'I allow my servant to polish them till they glow; it's good for his soul and pleases my superiors. But I won't have them repaired. That would be an admission that the war might continue for years.'

He showed us photographs of his family (he had seven children) and of his estates, his horses, scenes from the hunting field and the rollicking, roistering celebrations which followed. There were also grand parades and artillery salutes, with further celebrations. Yet behind it all one sensed the joy, the overwhelming relief he felt now that the war for him was nearly over. He would soon be able to get his boots repaired and made ready for the peacetime pursuits he longed for in his beloved Upper Bavarian estates.

★   ★   ★

Soon after sunrise we passed through the outer islands into Port Deremen and a happy family scene – caiques berthed, one on another, on both sides of the two HQ-and-supply schooners; naked bodies plunging and splashing around them; one or two soldiers or seamen (it was hard to tell which from the odd bits of clothing they wore) industriously fishing from rafts and dinghies; others lolling over rails and lounging or sitting on the hatches with mugs in their hands. In general it was a relaxed and friendly setting. But John Campbell, who was COMARO I[3] at the time, would only let us stay long enough to transfer our SBS patrol to their HQ ship, *Tewfik*, and the seven prisoners to a landing craft in which they and some fifty others were to be sent under guard to Egypt.

In the meantime we took on enough fuel from the Advanced Base's slender stocks to get us to Cyprus, and topped up with basic provisions – tins of sausages, 'herrings in', bully, peaches, apricots, sardines, milk, tea, hard biscuits, sugar, rum . . . But no soap; too much had been 'paid' out by caique and ML crews in the islands, in return for laundry and other less orthodox services. So we'd have to wait till we got back to base.

The girls were bitterly disappointed. They'd been making do with a rub and a wring in sea water and a final rinse in fresh for nearly four days. However, from the Gulf of Kos down the Turkish coast to Castelorizo and on to Cyprus, we were able to make a day-and-night passage; so we sailed at 10.00 p.m., reaching Limassol the following afternoon. The girls were off ashore the moment we arrived, wearing their stage outfits – white silk tunics with crimson hearts here and there and golden miniskirts, which they'd kept carefully folded under their mattresses since coming aboard. The crew were given leave in two watches, with orders to the second watch to be back by 11.00 p.m. At 9 knots our passage time to Beirut would be about fifteen hours, so we'd sail at midnight. When the coxswain came back aboard and had taken over the watch,

Number One, the SBS officer and I went ashore with the sub-lieutenant (I forget his name) who had been sent by the fabled 'Snow White', the Naval Officer in Charge of Cypriot Ports,[4] to berth and look after us.

For a while we were pleasantly occupied, after six weeks away from civilization, in a little homely window shopping and gift collecting, then a relaxed hour or two in a waterfront café. And finally, of course, supper in the local nightclub. There was only one in Limassol, and to our surprise the first act, which came on at 8.00 p.m. was announced as follows: 'And now, Gentlemen, straight from the romantic Isles of Greece by luxury cruiser . . . for your personal enjoyment and entertainment, the wondrous . . . the fabulous . . . the miraculous . . . Patmos girls!' . . . and on they danced, high kicking and yodelling at the tops of their voices.

It was a splendid act, and it brought everyone to their feet cheering. And when it ended, the girls came straight to our table, brimming over with pleasure and excitement. They had had a wonderful afternoon shopping (with dollars saved up in Athens) at the one or two dress shops which were still open in spite of wartime constraints. It appeared, moreover, that those dollars had been saved and the Patmos engagement taken up, expressly in the hope of finding a way of escape through Turkey to the Middle East. They were full of plans and promises for the future. The nightclub here in Limassol had offered them a contract, which they might consider later. But first they were going to Beirut – for them, after Cairo itself, the most glamorous city in the Eastern Mediterranean. And in the spirit of euphoria that now possessed them, they had bought a great box, bigger than a hat box, which they opened on the mess deck later to reveal an enormous cake, covered with creamy icing – a leaving present for their messmates.

But their greatest triumph, which they now displayed – sweeping away glasses, bottles and plates to give it pride of place on the table – was a package containing several large bars of Lifebuoy soap. They lifted them out one by one, turning them this way and that for us to admire, before hugging them ecstatically to their bosoms.

*   *   *

The forenoon was well advanced when we noticed a darkening of the mist ahead and knew that the mountains of Lebanon could not be far off. During the afternoon watch, as we ploughed steadily eastwards with satisfying bow and stern waves streaking out on either side, the decks amidships and aft became scenes of furious activity. Buckets of water for washing, rinsing and double-rinsing were secured along the guard rails on both sides of the ship, while others, turned upside down against the casing, supported shapely little bottoms in jeans and bulkier ones in khaki shorts. Bare arms were plunging and scrubbing and thumping and wringing, as every conceivable garment – mostly female with a few male pants and vests among them – received the treatment they had long deserved.

The bright lights and relaxing comforts of Beirut – the cafés and 'Dancings', restaurants and promenades, bars and hot spots, even one or two welcoming apartments or cottages in the hills with quiet gardens – were in different people's minds, according to their tastes and fortunes. Already the wall of mist ahead was thinning. The first dark stencilling of pine trees and rocky gorges was showing through. And high above them now – although it was already late in May – the snow-covered ridge of Mount Saneen, 10,000 ft above sea level, brooding like a great white bird on a nest of cloud and forest. In two hours or less we would enter harbour.

'Call me when we're coming up to the outer mole', I told Number One, and went below to attend to some of the endless paperwork which seems to make base staffs happy. I could hear the clanking of buckets and the 'spl–o–o–osh' of water pouring into the sea as they were emptied over the side. Most of the laundry would be drying somewhere by now, I thought idly, as I plodded on with my report. When it was finished, I lay down on my bunk and must have nodded off, because the next thing I remember is our leading seamen's voice calling down the hatch.

'We're closing the harbour entrance, sir,' he reported, 'and they're calling us up.'

When I joined him on the bridge, Number One had the Aldis lamp to his eye and was acknowledging the shore station's message word by word. I read it too. It ran: 'IT IS NOT CUSTOMARY TO ENTER HARBOUR DRESSED OVERALL IN LADIES' UNDERWEAR'.

I looked about me, and sure enough, our guard rails were festooned with garments of all kinds, while our forestay was decorated with panties, pyjamas, vests and bras in various interesting shades and styles.

They all had to come down, of course, and at once. But not in anger. Commander Rex Arnot RN, NOIC at Beirut, was a cheerful old fellow, also back from retirement, who loved making memorable signals. Who doesn't? He must already be having a great time in the wardroom bar of HMS *Martial*, the shore establishment, telling them all about it. Besides, we were going to miss our young ladies . . . all of us. They'd been great shipmates and good company through difficult times, and we were grateful.

---

[1]   Flags from stem to stern over the mastheads to celebrate important occasions.
[2]   The wind screen along the fore side of the bridge.
[3]   Commander Aegean Raiding Operations – Southern Area.
[4]   Snow White (so-called because of his gleaming silvery hair and the laughing cabaret girls from Famagusta's 'Chanticleer' nightclub – his dwarfs – who usually decorated his 1908 chauffeur-driven Rolls-Royce) was a retired naval captain of irate disposition, brought back to look after the Navy's interests in Cyprus where he had lived for many years. His favourite 'dwarf' was a lively Hungarian dancer called Peter Pan.

The Artist's Tale

CHAPTER FIVE

A Sail through the Cyclades

Far and few. Far and few
Are the lands where the Jumblies live;
Their heads are green and their hands are blue,
And they went to sea in a sieve.

Edward Lear

Bitter Decision

In the afternoon Commander Andreas Londos of the Royal Hellenic Navy – tall and dark, with a bushy black moustache and flashing eyes – came aboard to wish us luck and give us a few hints about weather conditions, useful lay-up berths and the trustworthiness or otherwise of people on different islands. He finished up by saying, 'and while you're at Polykandros, do me a favour: contact Kapitan Elias Triandafilou – it means "thirty petals", our name for a rose'. He held out a bag of gold coins, 'Give him these, and make sure he signs this receipt. Don't forget.'

I thought this insistence a bit odd. What good would a receipt be in the savage and unpredictable conditions of our secret war. He went on, again rather surprisingly, 'He'll take them to my wife and two beautiful daughters.' His eyes flashed as he said this. 'And remember, if you're ever in trouble, Elias is a good man . . . to be trusted completely . . . he'll help you all he can.' So why the receipt, I thought, as I locked it away with the gold coins in my instrument locker and followed the Commander on deck.

Fortunately for me, Bill Turnbull was coming with us as an extra watch-keeper and we also had a Greek-speaking gunner through whom we'd be able to speak to the islanders and to the Greek Sacred Company patrol who were to look after the shore side of our reconnaissance. They joined us next morning – a captain and two men. The officer, whose name was Caralambos, looked as though he would be more at home behind an office desk in Athens, which was where he came from; he was short, not above 5 ft 6 in in height, with a sallow complexion, drooping moustache, beer-bottle

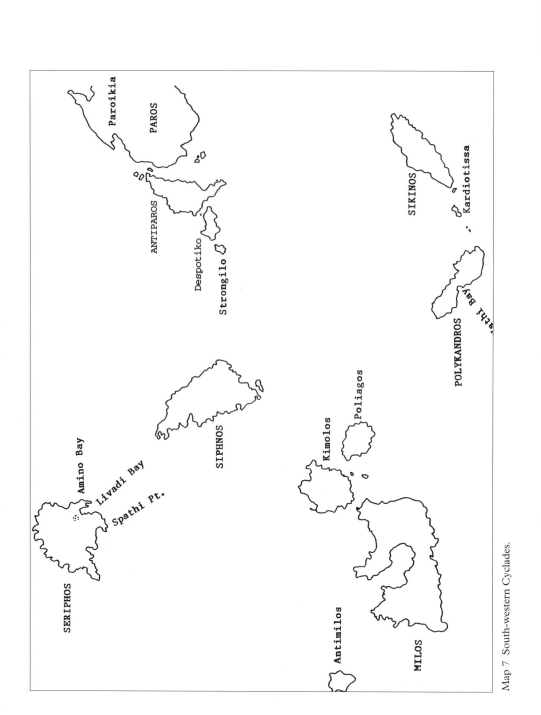

Map 7 South-western Cyclades.

shoulders and a pot belly. He had very small feet and, on leaving Deremen, wore an immaculate bush jacket and drill trousers. I couldn't help admiring the chap, so clearly unsuited to this kind of work, and yet a volunteer for service with the GSC, a famous 'Death or Glory' outfit. The Company had twice before been formed when Greece was in mortal danger, and twice wiped out to a man. There was not one of them today, I believed, who did not expect the performance to be repeated.

Shortly after noon, we headed westward out of the Gulf of Kos, with the Turkish flag at our port yardarm. A light breeze on the starboard bow was kicking up a short sea, making the caique *Maritza* dance and skip. 'This'll slow us down a bit,' I said to Bill, who was standing – tall, fair-haired and grey-eyed – on the stern grating with the tiller lines in his hands. 'Still, at this rate, it'll be dark before we leave Turkish waters.'

I ducked down into the cabin to take a last look at the chart. Down there it smelt of hot diesel oil, and above the swish and gurgle of water passing down our sides, I could hear the 'Da–da–dit . . . di–di–da–dit' from Sparks's earphones, as he crouched on the starboard bunk, signal-pad on his lap, listening to the evening routine.

Back on deck, the coxswain, sitting in the lee of the cabin top, was telling the gunner how he'd painted the town red on his leave in Beirut . . . 'Cor! You should've seen this gorgeous fuckin' piece.' His face was flushed and eyes sparkling as he thought of her. 'Streuth! I'd 've crawled over Dorothy Lamour to get at 'er.' The gunner listened, mouth half open, eyes popping.

The stoker down below was topping up the header fuel tank on the engine. But further along the deck, huddled against a pile of camouflage netting and ammunition boxes, Caralambos and his men, looking green in the face, were far from merry.

'Their heads were green and their hands were blue,' quoted Bill unkindly. And from then on the patrol were always known as the Jumblies.

Night was falling as the light on Cape Krio began to wheel and flash above us. The breeze had gone down with the sun. 'That's the last light we'll see until we get back,' I said to Bill. 'Better have that Turkish flag down and the Greek ensign hoisted.' Then, 'Coxswain, stream the log!' . . . and we headed out into the Aegean.

*   *   *

By dawn we were close under the lee of the rocky island of Sirina. The coxswain lowered the sails and slacked off the tackle on the forestay, which brought the mast creaking down. The crew seized it amongst a tangle of rigging and laid it in its crotch on the cabin top. In the half light, Coxswain Bobby and his lads seemed to struggle like flies in a spider's web of ropes and wires.

As we came into our hide-out the sky was paling in the east. We dropped our stern anchor and ran *Maritza* into a cleft in the rocks. Then, putting grapnels out on either side, we rigged our blotched and brindled camouflage nets, whose mottled shadows on the deck brought back childhood memories of rummaging through raspberry canes in the kitchen garden.

Our two heavy machine-guns were carried up on to the rocks and a lookout was posted. It was less than a year since one of our smaller caiques had been surprised and sunk by two German patrol boats in this very anchorage. By the time the machine-gun posts had been set up the sun was high and the crew were weary. The Jumblies had already set off to search the island for Baba Yannis, a friendly shepherd, and his family, who were the only inhabitants of Sirina. The rest of us had a scratch breakfast and then flopped down where we could under the netting. It was very hot.

★   ★   ★

We hadn't been long asleep when a tug at my elbow brought me back from happy dreams.

'Oi, skipper!' It was the young stoker, who'd been on lookout. 'There's a caique comin' round the point . . . headin' in here, she is.'

'OK. Action stations . . . man the guns ashore.'

Men scurried up the rocks to the heavy machine-guns. Others trained the .303s under the netting towards the south of the cove. We all knew that members of irregular organizations like ours, if taken prisoner, would be shot. And I suppose that thoughts like this were going through the minds of most of us when a long bowsprit and a snow-white jib glided into view, followed by another jib and another and yet another, then a sharp bow and a towering lateen sail. The caique creamed slowly, on the starboard tack, to the other side of the cove, then came about, and passed within 300 yards of where we lay.

'I can see only four men on deck,' I said to Bill, who had picked up the binoculars. 'But there may be more below.'

Bill adjusted his focus. 'They're all dark and wearing odd bits of clothing. They look like Greek seamen to me.'

As he spoke, the caique disappeared round the headland into the next bay and we heard her anchor cable rattle out.

'Now what about it, Bill? They must have seen us lying here. If they tell the Germans in their next port of call, that'll be curtains for us.'

Bill slowly stroked his military moustache. 'We've got to call here on our way back, haven't we?' he said at length. 'I'd say sink her and have done with it.'

I turned to the coxswain, who was gathering up tommy-guns from the cabin top where they'd been laid when the caique disappeared . . . 'Bobby, take Sparks and Guns with you and bring the crew of that caique back here . . . Stokes, you get back up the hill and keep a sharp lookout . . . the most important thing is not to let her get away.'

*   *   *

When Bobby came back with the caique crew, they told us that they *hadn't* spotted *Maritza* under her netting. However, they had now, and the question was what to do with them. Obviously we must immobilize the caique, and I thought we'd better keep her skipper with us as a hostage. If he cooperated, when we came back he could take his caique and clear out.

Bill looked doubtful, but went over with the others to where the caique was anchored and removed her rudder and also her sweeps, which were 18 ft long. Then the Jumblies returned, bringing with them an old man, as rugged and weatherbeaten as the rocks around him. He wore a collarless homespun shirt and *vraka* (Turkish trousers) of faded blue cotton, with a white woollen cummerbund round his waist. His splayed feet were hard as hooves. His face resembled time-eroded marble, with a sprinkling of white bristle on his craggy chin. This was Baba Yannis, our redoubtable ally, who quickly took control of the situation, questioning the crew of the Greek caique, apparently to their growing consternation.

'These men are traitors,' he told me, through Guns, 'working for the Germans on Crete. And this man,' pointing to a greasy-looking individual with shifty eyes and one gold tooth, 'is an Italian black marketeer. He's a 'kataskopos' (meaning 'spy'); he spat the word out with indescribable hatred and loathing in his voice and eyes. 'You must sink the caique or he will escape and betray us all to the Germans.'

I let him run on. But the idea of deliberately destroying a man's boat – or any boat for that matter – made me shudder.

'We've taken their rudder and their sweeps,' I said. 'They can't get off the island.'

Yannis turned to the Jumblies in blank disbelief, rolling his eyes to heaven, then back to me. 'You really believe that?' he cried. 'Of Greeks? Why before you're out of sight they'll have improvised a rudder, and the Germans will be waiting for you when you get back.'

We searched the Italian and found gold ornaments set with glass and precious stones, a gold Napoleon, four sovereigns and an American Eagle. The caique, which had no motor, was loaded with barrels of olive oil and sacks of raisins, which the Italian had been bartering for family jewels (at outrageous rates, Guns told me) with the near-starving islanders.

But I was thinking of the caique as she came round the headland, a vessel of heart-rending beauty, then dropping her sails and anchoring, like a seabird coming to rest. The *kapetanio*'s grandfather and great-uncles had built her. His father had inherited her; together he and his father had gone sponge-diving from her off the coast of North Africa. Now she was his.

Behind me Baba Yannis was vociferous. 'Sink her. Sink her,' he shouted. 'The *kapetanio* must go with you. I, Baba Yannis, will take care of these beauties till you return.' He spoke with a harsh nasal inflection, his voice ringing eerily among the rocks.

Yes, I thought, and you'll soon have the cargo out of her (raisins and barrels of oil won't spoil in sea water for a long time) and the whole of your family are divers, I'm sure.

But he was right, of course. Greeks are born to the sea. The caique crew would quickly rig a jury rudder and be off to another island. There was really nothing for it but to let the old pirate pillage the caique's cargo. He was, after all, our ally.

That evening, at dusk, we unshipped our nets and spreaders, stepped our mast and took the beautiful caique in tow. As soon as we were clear of the entrance and in deeper water I shut off the engine and we hauled the caique alongside.

'Right, Bobby.' It was hard to get the words out. 'You and Guns take axes and knock a hole through her bottom planking.'

'Knock a hole through her, skipper? She's built like a battle ship. Are you sure?'

I gritted my teeth. A great surge of something that felt almost like suffocation was building up inside me.

'Yes, I'm sure.'

And to their surprise, at the fourth or fifth blow they did knock a hole in her. Sea water came gushing in. Bobby and Guns scrambled back aboard, saying 'Cor, skipper! She must've been rotten!'

Maybe she was. But I was watching the *kapetanio*. Tears had come to his eyes as the caique settled, slowly and majestically, in the water. It was more than just his livelihood that was disappearing, but he remained silent as the sea came bubbling up through the hatchway and the stone ballast in her bilges took her gently, inexorably, to the bottom.

I nodded to Stokes to put the engine in gear, and we headed westwards into the deepening dusk.

Time and Tide

All that night we plugged into a short lumpy sea. What wind there was came from north-north-west, which just allowed us to keep the sails drawing. We passed south of Stampalia in the small hours, and at dawn we could see the high, bare rock of Anedro rising above the haze on our starboard bow. The wind rose with the sun, and we were wet and tired by the time we reached our hide-out on the south side of the island. But mooring went without a hitch, the Greek *kapetanio* cheerfully handling warps and jumping barefoot on to the rocks to plant the grapnels. He seemed to bear us no grudge for sinking his caique.

That afternoon I climbed a path which led northward to the highest cliffs. Looking back, I could see the whole sun-bathed island sloping away southwards like a wedge of old cheese, with a giant bite out of the end marking the bay in which we were moored. Meltemi was blowing strongly out of a clear blue sky broken only by an occasional small cloud travelling fast. Northwards the blue Aegean was flecked with row after row of white horses galloping in to dash themselves against the rocks below me. The only life I saw along the way was the odd grasshopper, a few sheep put ashore to graze by some shepherd from another island, a lizard or two basking on the rocks and a solitary snake sliding over the gravelly soil to disappear under a sage bush.

By evening the wind had died away and at dusk we struck out again westwards, to make our first night landing on Polykandros. We were to put our patrol ashore in Vathi Bay on the south side of the island and some distance from the main village. Their task was to discover the size of the German garrison, and make things as hot for them during our short stay as possible. Then they would contact our undercover man, the great Captain 'Thirty Petals'.

We approached the rocky shore wondering what kind of reception awaited us. My anxiety was in no way reduced by the eccentricities of *Maritza*'s exhaust pipe which ran across the deck and over the side, making a considerable din at any time but especially at night. It normally became eccentric when, on closing the shore, we had to idle the engine. It would mutter softly to itself for a few seconds, then suddenly burst into a fearful fit of coughing that could be heard a mile away. To quell the din, some genius had invented a dog-legged pipe which could be fitted to the exhaust and lowered into the sea. This we now did and, gefuffling gently, approached the shore.

We found Vathi Bay without any difficulty and hoisted out our dinghy. Caralambos and his men dropped into it and, loaded down with guns, grenades and other instruments of death, as well as a few tins of bully and boxes of biscuits for the islanders, disappeared into the darkness, pulled by Coxswain Bobby. When he got back we motored slowly to the neighbouring deserted island of Kardiotissa, crept into our hide-out there, rigged our nets and turned in.

★   ★   ★

Coming-to some three hours later in broad daylight, I stretched luxuriously, crawled on to the grating aft and stuck my head over the transom to watch the fishes. To my surprise, a small boat lay tied to our stern in the shade of our netting. Seated in it was an old man, bent over his oars and fast asleep.

So here we were again. To sink or not to sink? That was once again our dilemma. Then, waking with a start, he saw me looking at him, gave a cry of welcome and climbed aboard, embracing everyone in turn. We gave him whatever canned provisions we could spare and after a while he got back into his boat and pulled away. The old fellow had come a great distance with only oars and a spritsail from his home island of Spetsai, fishing for sponges, octopus, or whatever else he could catch. Apparently he thought nothing of sailing and rowing 80 miles between the islands, and had often been three weeks or more away, sleeping in the bottom of his boat or on the foreshore.

We made ourselves some lunch and relaxed again, looking forward to a lazy afternoon. But not for long. We had barely dozed off when the 'put-put-pop-pop' of a semi-diesel engine had us all wide awake again. Two small caiques were approaching close inshore. They were bound to see us, so we brought our grapnels aboard and shoved off into deeper water. Then, mast still down and nets flying, we went full ahead on the engine and shot out to intercept.

The caiques turned out to be full of men and women, dressed in their best clothes and singing loudly. Whether it was a saint's day celebration or they were coming back from a wedding we never discovered because, while we were still puzzling over the matter, the sound of another, more powerful engine was heard, and round the rocks from the direction of Polykandros came another larger caique. And this one was crowded with men.

I snatched up my binoculars and levelled them at the approaching vessel. My fears were in no way dispelled by what I saw, for among the men were soldiers brandishing rifles. Our hearts were in our mouths as we trained our guns on them. I looked again through my binoculars and said, 'Hold your fire . . . I think . . . yes, I'm sure, the chaps with rifles are the Jumblies!'

A tall figure in an open-necked shirt, striped trousers and white woollen cummerbund, with a seaman's cap on his head, stood in the sternsheets steering with one foot on the tiller. His bristly nut-brown face and short-clipped moustache under a hawk-like nose made him look every inch the pirate, as he put his caique alongside us and leaped aboard. Disentangling himself from our camouflage netting, he grabbed my hand, pumping it up and down; then embraced me with a bear-hug and planted garlicky kisses on both my cheeks.

'Captain Triandafilou,' announced Caralambos proudly. 'He refused to wait till dark to come and find you.'

'Greetings from Commander Londos,' I told him through Guns, and brought out the bag of gold from my instrument locker to show him. His eyes lit up. A great chasm of a grin split his face as I went on, 'And here's the receipt for thirty-two coins which the Commander wants you to sign.'

Captain Thirty Petals emptied the bag on to our cabin top and started counting. As he bent over I noticed the butt of an enormous old-fashioned revolver sticking out of his hip pocket. '. . . thirty-one . . . thirty-two . . . thirty-three! . . . Ah!' said the Captain, slowly shaking his head, as he put the last coin into one pocket and the bag with the rest into another, 'I knew that Andreas wouldn't forget me.'

So that was the reason for the insistence on getting the receipt signed. And nothing would now satisfy the captain but that Bill and I should go in his caique to the village of Karavostassi, on Polykandros, for a celebration lunch. The other two caiques followed us, their people still singing. And while we drank *ouzo* after *ouzo*, the captain's wife, a handsome, kindly woman, chased a chicken round the courtyard, killed it, plucked it and set it cooking.

In twos and threes the whole village came crowding into the Triandafilou living room where we sat, to stare and giggle and shake our hands. And when, in the late afternoon, the captain finally took us back to Kardiotissa, half the population came with us in the three caiques – still dressed in their Sunday best, and singing all the way.

★ ★ ★

We sailed again at dusk and headed north to the island of Siphnos. Here at midnight we landed the Jumblies, promising to be back the following night. Then we hurried away to a new hide-out on Seriphos. The principal town, also named Seriphos, stood closely packed round a Crusader fortress on a mountain top overlooking Livadi Bay in the south-west corner of the island. It had originally been fortified against the infidel pirates who used to plague these waters, but more recently fishermen had built a small stone jetty and a few cottages down by the shore. This was the village of Livadi.

Amino Bay, to which we were bound, lay immediately to the eastward, where the chart showed a gantry for loading iron ore. Close beside it on the chart, some well-meaning schooner skipper in Deremen had placed a cross and the words 'Good hide-out'. Arriving off the bay at five o'clock in the morning, we entered slowly just as the eastern sky showed signs of brightening. Ahead I could clearly see the jagged outline of the mountains, and once inside the bay, hills ringed us round: dark shadows against the sky reflected in the calm surface of the water.

I went forward and stood in the bow, searching in the half light for the rocks which were to give us cover. The gantry was visible, but I could see no rocks capable of forming a hide-out. Half a mile away, at the head of the bay, was what I took to be a beach. But all at once the caique gave a sickening lurch, which nearly tumbled me over the bow, and came to an abrupt standstill. I sprang aft and put the engine full astern. There was a roar and a rush of water down our sides, but *Maritza* wouldn't budge. When I stopped the engine there was a ghastly silence, into which Bobby's harsh voice fell like a hacksaw on to emery paper . . . 'The skipper's fuckin' done it this time.'

It was a tense moment – tenser than any in the whole ten days of that operation. As I said earlier, we all knew the consequences of being captured. 'All right! Overboard, the lot of you!' I kicked off my sandals and jumped from the bow. The water came up to our waists. We laid our backs to the hull and shoved for all we were worth . . . for twenty minutes. But nothing would shift her.

I could see now that there were no rocks in the bay against which we could have hidden. And what I had taken for a beach was the far side of a shallow lagoon, contained within the bank of shingle which was now firmly wedged under our keel.

'There's only one thing for it,' said Bobby. 'We'll have to find a fishing boat to tow us off.'

'Try Livadi village,' I told him, 'and take Guns with you to interpret.'

It was going to be a risky business. We knew that there were Germans on the island, and it would soon be broad daylight. But we could think of nothing else, so they put on their oldest clothes, to look as much like islanders as they could, and set off.

While all this was going on, I wasn't taking much notice of anything else, so it came as a surprise, on turning round, to see the old *kapetanio* – our prisoner – with Stokes to help him, putting an anchor and about twenty fathoms of chain cable into the dinghy, which they'd hauled alongside. They worked in silence. There seemed to be complete understanding between them, which no words – if either could have spoken the other's language – would have improved upon.

When all was ready they pulled away astern of us, the old man rowing while Stokes paid the cable out over the boat's transom. When it was all out and the dinghy could go no further, they hove the anchor overboard; then came back for a second anchor which they laid out about the same distance.

Next, the old man had us shift the fuel cans and all other heavy objects – guns, ammunition boxes, fresh water cans, moorings, everything – over to the starboard side, to give the boat a list that way, reducing her draught. After that we unshackled the ends of the two anchor cables and brought them through the after fairleads and over the deck to the windlass forward.

We pumped away at the windlass until the cables rose bar-taut and dripping out of the sea. We went on heaving, straining every muscle to get another half turn out of the windlass, until little by little, but without any doubt we saw that the anchors were dragging home through the mud.

'*Perimeno.*' Panting but smiling the old *kapetanio* held up his hand. '*Perimenome* [wait for the tide], *kapitan.*'

'But there's no tide in the Aegean . . . *Oichi perimene.*' I gestured at the sea and he seemed to understand.

'Lettle, leetle,' he said, indicating about nine inches, by pretending to cut off his left hand at the wrist with his right.

We all had a bit of breakfast then, and squatted around, hoping that Bobby and Guns had been lucky in finding a fishing boat. If they hadn't we were dished . . . as good as curtains it would be. Suddenly, at nine o'clock, the two cables went slack, sinking back into the sea, and *Maritza*, of her own accord, floated stern first into deeper water.

I looked round for the old man, to thank him, but he'd gone below.

★   ★   ★

It was now broad daylight. Perched on its pinnacle and surrounded by white-washed houses, the Crusader fort, like an ancient citadel, looked down upon us (photo 13).

'Hoist the Greek ensign, Bill. We'll just have to brazen it out . . . try to

13 'Perched on its pinnacle, and surrounded by houses, like an ancient citadel, the Crusader fort, looked down on us.'

look like Greek fishermen and see if we can find ourselves a hide-out under the lighthouse there.'

'What if the Jerries are using it as a lookout post?'

'Then our goose is cooked . . . come on.'

While we were talking, the coxswain and Guns reappeared looking crestfallen, having failed to find a boat with enough power to haul us off. When they saw that we were afloat again, they cheered up at once.

We weighed and set off across the mouth of the bay, heading for the lighthouse on Spathi Point. It stood on a crag, over 100 ft high and split in two as though with an axe, forming a deep cleft. Into this cleft we edged *Maritza* and rigged our camouflage nets across the entrance.

From the head of the creek a goat track led up to the lighthouse; and while we were having an early meal we heard a scuffling high up, then stones began rattling down around us, and finally an old man came stumbling and sliding down the steep pathway. He clambered aboard carrying two large bunches of grapes, which he offered to us with a flourish and gestures of welcome.

'Beware of Greeks bearing gifts,' muttered Bill. But Guns told us the old fellow was overjoyed to see the '*Inglezoi*' again; and Stokes, who was cook of the day, rustled up a plate of fried eggs and beans, which the old man gulped down as though starving. He probably was. But he promised, on his honour, not to tell a soul that he'd seen us; so we weren't unduly worried as we watched him clamber laboriously back up the path to the lighthouse. A sentry was posted, and the rest of us lay down where we could around the deck.

Three and a half hours later we were awakened by noises and the clatter of stones, and were amazed to see Bobby, the sentry on duty, leading a procession down from the lighthouse.

'Couldn't help it, Skipper. This is the mayor and bleedin' corporation come to welcome us.'

They all shook hands and clapped us on the shoulders. Mercifully, this time, we were spared the kisses. But even without understanding a word they said, their message of welcome was unmistakable. News of our presence on Seriphos had clearly been too much for the ragged old man to keep to himself; but by good fortune he had met the mayor before he met any Germans. Nevertheless, as soon as it was dark enough, we stowed our camouflage and put to sea. Too much good will, we felt, could very soon lead to disaster.

A Friend in Need

We had now reached the end of our reconnaissance run, and could return stage by stage to Deremen. We were well on schedule, so I looked forward to the pleasure of a long and unhurried sail back through the islands. That night we picked up the Jumblies on Siphnos, and as the blue-shaded flashes from the shore answered ours, I couldn't help thinking, with some satisfaction, how smoothly and efficiently we and the Jumblies had learned to work together.

I thought too soon. When Bobby took the dinghy inshore to pick them up, he found only two – Caralambos and one soldier – waiting for him on the beach. The other Jumbly had lagged behind, we were told when they came aboard, but he would be along shortly. We waited and waited. Ten . . . fifteen . . . twenty minutes went by and still there was no sign of the third Jumbly. In another five minutes we would have to sail, I decided, when all of a sudden, without any warning, Caralambos filled his lungs and bellowed, 'Kyriaco–o–o–o!' and again, louder still, 'Kyriaco–o–o–o!'

It was terrifying. Like many little men, Caralambos had a tremendous voice, which must have carried for a mile in every direction on a still night like this. At any moment we expected an enemy patrol to come crashing down through the rocks and scrub overlooking the beach.

'Silence, for God's sake,' I yelled above the din. But Caralambos wouldn't be silenced. 'Kyriaco–o–o–o, Kyriaco–o–o–o!' There was nothing we could do, short of physical violence, to stop him. And this was just what I had in mind when mercifully there came an answering bellow from another part of the shore – '*Eh, Kapitan Caralambe! Etho eme, vlako* [Here I am, stupid]!'

We felt that the whole island must now have heard us. But we couldn't just abandon the fellow, so away went Bobby once again to pick him up. Then we high-tailed it out of there and, an hour later landed the Jumblies on Kimolos. Leaving them there, we returned to our old hide-out on Kardiotissa, where we were thankful for a quiet day under nets.

★   ★   ★

In the evening we returned to Kimolos and found the Jumblies in a state of great excitement. Our secret service man on Kimolos had just returned from Milos with the news that the evacuation of the German garrison – some eighteen hundred men – had begun. He even knew the quay from which they were embarking and their route through the minefields surrounding the island.

This was vital information for our aircraft and submarines, so I didn't hesitate to break radio silence and pass it on to Deremen and Cairo. Then we made for Polykandros, where the Jumblies insisted they had some unfinished business.

It was not until four in the morning that we crept silently into a cove on the eastern side of the island, and tied up to a small stone jetty. It was very quiet. Not a sound, nor a light from any of the houses ashore. The Jumblies landed silently, crossed the quay, and knocked on the door of a small white-washed dwelling opposite the end of the jetty.

After a few moments the door opened and the figure of a young woman stood outlined against the glow from within. She beckoned, and one of the Jumblies – we couldn't see which – followed her inside, closing the door behind him. The other two leant their guns against the wall and made themselves comfortable on the doorstep. A match flared for an instant as cigarettes were lighted. Bill focused his night glasses on the door, then the windows of the little house. They were heavily blacked out. 'Not taking any risks of the enemy interrupting their council of war,' he suggested.

After about twenty minutes the door opened again, and this time only a man's figure was silhouetted. He paused on the doorstep to hitch up his trousers and attend to his flies. Another man pushed past him. The door closed, and a match flared again as another cigarette was lighted. After a further twenty minutes or so the procedure was repeated, and within an hour all three Jumblies had been processed. Their 'business' now finished, they shouldered their rifles and shuffled back aboard.

★   ★   ★

The next day was spent on Anedro, and in the evening we shortened in our anchor cable, ready to sail at dusk. But when dusk came we found it quite impossible, even with all hands pumping at the windlass, to break out the anchor. We hove away until the hawsepipe had been hauled down almost level with the water. We tried to drag the anchor clear with the engine going at full speed, but *Maritza* only bobbed and curtsied, then began to pirouette round her cable.

The *kapetanio*, who had been watching our antics with interest, now came forward and motioned me to stop the engine. Then stripping off his clothes he lowered himself over the bow into the water. Holding on to the bob-stay he took great deep breaths for a minute or two. Then grasping the anchor cable, he hauled himself down, hand over hand to the bottom. Although the light was fading fast, we could see him clearly, with his feet planted on two boulders, wrenching with great determination at the anchor, one of whose flukes had become wedged under a great slab of rock.

At length, he surfaced, puffing and blowing. '*Andaxi Kapitanye. Molis tofiaxa* [All right, Captain. I've nearly done it].' he called up to me, then dived down again. After nearly half an hour of this he had still 'nearly done it'. It was getting dark when I made him stop and told Bobby to take a hacksaw to the cable. A full length report had later to be forwarded to the Admiralty, stating weight, size, length of cable, weather conditions and circumstances under which the anchor was lost – an ancient regulation presumably to discourage impecunious officers from flogging their ground tackle.

We sailed through the night (photo 14), carried along in comfort by a moderate westerly breeze. The next day was spent at Sirina, where I was able at last to get a few hours of luxurious sleep. I was wakened by a signal

14 'We sailed through the night . . .'. Greek Sacred Company men on passage.

ordering me to rendezvous with two enticed[1] caiques and escort them to Deremen. In fact there were three, and we took them all in tow, our 90 hp engine coming into its own at last. And next day, with engine popping and all sails set, we made a triumphal entry into Deremen harbour bringing a total of twenty-nine Greeks to safety and freedom, not counting our Sacred Jumblies.

★   ★   ★

The story of our ten-day cruise through the Cyclades ends there. But after a day in Deremen we were ordered to escort our three enticed caiques to Cyprus. We handed them over to the naval authorities at Paphos with the twenty-nine Greeks and also our friend the *kapetanio*. It was sad to see him go. He had been a good friend and a loyal shipmate and had helped us when we were in trouble. When the time came to say goodbye, I took the Gunner along with me. 'Tell him I've learned more from him this last month about winds and weather and small boats in the Aegean, than I could have been taught in a hundred years by our own people.'

'Ah, Kapetan,' he replied with great dignity. 'Ours is a small sea with many islands. For thousands of years we and our forefathers have sailed these waters. We know their weather and their winds. We are sea people.'

'But you helped and looked after us. If Greeks had sunk my caique I don't think I would have helped them as you helped us.'

The *kapetanio* pulled a long face. '*Enai to polemo* [It's the war]. And aren't you risking your lives to save our country? As for me, I lost one ship and joined another. Ships are my home. The Greeks are sea people.'

It was a simple and moving message, in simple and sincere language, that Guns passed on to me. I felt that I had learned much more from this man about the sea than just seamanship.

---

[1]   Persuaded to make the long and dangerous sea passage through enemy-patrolled waters to Turkey and on to Cyprus or Beirut and Egypt.

Tales from a Man of Malta

CHAPTER SIX

Love, Life and Death
on Leros

Prelude to Battle

On Malta we had always thought of the Walrus flying boat as a bit of a clown. But it was certainly a game little clown. Like the day in 1941 when one of them found a lifeboat full of survivors from a bombed convoy 50 miles out at sea and landed beside it – a hazardous feat in all but the calmest weather. Undaunted, however, the young pilot then threw them a line and towed them all the way back to the safety of Grand Harbour. At 5 knots it took him all day – and tied to the boat, he was a sitting target for any German or Italian aircraft that chanced upon them. I thought of this as our own Walrus banked steeply and, with a cheery ''Ere we go' from the young pilot, dived down to thread its way through a scatter of rocks and islets to land in Castelorizo harbour.

It was about the middle of September 1943. We were on our way – a squadron leader and I, now a pilot officer (intelligence) – to take over the seaplane base on Leros following the Italian surrender of a week or two before. We spent three days on Castelorizo, where there were, of course, great celebrations and jollity, into which the Walrus pilot and I, both twenty-year-olds, threw ourselves with zest. We became at once close friends, sharing all sorts of intimate secrets, as one always does when times are difficult and the future uncertain.

Every forenoon, about gin time, we swam out to where the supply schooner *Tewfik* lay at anchor. Aboard her were George Jellicoe – just returned from his parachute drop on Rhodes to parley with the Italian general there – and David Sutherland with a detachment of the SBS. They too were making their way up to the Aegean. We all knew that everything depended on whether or not adequate air cover for our advanced forces could be established in time for them to build up enough strength to beat off the inevitable enemy counter-attack.

On the third day, in the afternoon, we flew on up the line to another hair-raising approach between craggy headlands at the entrance to Port Laki harbour, Leros, landing opposite the seaplane base on the other side of the bay. A fast motor launch swept alongside to take our bow line to the buoy and carry the squadron leader and myself to the quay, where smartly turned out Italian officers – about twenty-five of them in all – were drawn up to receive us. The pilot remained in the Walrus to listen to the afternoon routine from Cairo.

After the initial hand-shaking down the line of officers (I couldn't help thinking that we resembled the Queen and Princess Elizabeth at a charity performance), we all crowded into the officers' mess. It was a lively occasion full of back-slapping, champagne and pretty waitresses who ogled us shamelessly. But they weren't really waitresses, I found out later; they were the inhabitants of three '*Palazzini*', one each for officers, NCOs and men, thoughtfully provided by a discerning government.

In due course our pilot joined us, but he seemed distracted and restless. Fighter aircraft had been reported in the area, and although night was coming on he wanted to get airborne so as to be as far away as possible before the moon rose. After a while he left us and a little later I heard the Walrus revving up. I went to the window in time to see him gaining speed for take-off down the bay. Soon he was a diminishing speck between those two dark headlands, like jaws closing on him at the harbour entrance. I said a small prayer for him as I turned away.

★   ★   ★

My task as interpreter kept me fully occupied from the outset, although to carry it out effectively one obstructing hurdle had to be cleared or kicked aside: the thin blue pilot officer's ring on my sleeve was the same as that worn by warrant officers in the Italian Air Force. Our hosts needed some convincing that I was indeed commissioned, and therefore qualified to hear and pass on their innermost thoughts and opinions. When they were eventually reassured, and especially when they discovered that my Italian was good enough for me to understand and appreciate their most intimate jokes and stories, they took me to their hearts. I was allocated a charming little villa reserved for VIPs, all to myself (the squadron leader was given another). It was a fully equipped two-bedroomed cottage, a little way away from the main buildings and very comfortably furnished. It backed on to a low cliff face formed by excavation of the terrace on which the workshops, offices and hangars stood. A deep cavern had been quarried out of the cliff itself to serve as an air raid shelter.

As soon as I could escape from the proceedings in the mess, which had become increasingly uproarious, I made for my new home-from-home and was soon in bed and asleep.

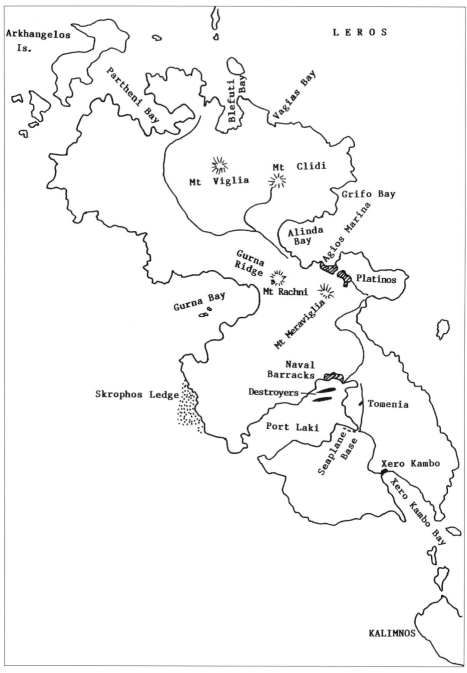

Map 8 Leros.

★   ★   ★

Next morning tea was brought in to me by one of the loveliest girls I had ever seen. She was dark with flowing black hair, brown eyes and a tawny skin glowing with health and vitality. Slender arms emerged from the shoulders of a pale green dress that clung invitingly to full bosoms and a willowy body. Small bare feet, long elegant legs and shapely thighs matched the delicate hands which placed the tea tray gently on the stool beside me.

That was my impression of Maria as I first saw her through the haze of a hard won morning-after-the-night-before. Welcoming but quiet and demure, her very presence was soothing. I wanted to be her friend.

'Thank you, thank you, what is your name?'

'Maria.' She smiled a kindly smile, quite different from the brazen glances flashed at us by the 'waitresses' of the evening before, yet warm and – 'companionable' is the word that best describes the open unselfconscious nature of that smile.

'I have switched on the heater. The water will soon be warm. Is there anything else you would like?'

I was approaching twenty-one and she was perhaps a year or two older; but her calm and self-assured manner forbade any kind of gallantry. I thanked her again and got out of bed. She handed me a bath towel and turned to go.

'If you need anything, please ring the bell,' she said at the door, then left, closing it quietly behind her.

★   ★   ★

The next few days were filled with such a variety of demands for my services that I had little or no time to look about me. It was always late when I got to bed after averagely alcoholic evenings. In the morning, Maria and her tea tray were a welcome sight, but I was too bleary-eyed for more than the ordinary courtesies.

Then the bombing began, though not, at first, against the seaplane base. Two fleet destroyers – *Queen Olga* and *Intrepid* – had entered harbour and anchored half a mile away in the upper arm of the bay. An enemy agent (there were many among the local people) must have informed the German Command by radio, because within a short while formations of Stukas and Ju88s came over. No Italian anti-aircraft batteries opened up on them, fearing no doubt that they would become targets themselves. The Italian naval barracks were flattened and *Queen Olga* was sunk straight away by a direct hit amidships. *Intrepid* was also hit, but was successfully towed into shallower water, and so did not sink immediately. Three more attacks soon followed, resulting in further direct hits and in the end *Intrepid* capsized and was a total loss.

From the seaplane base we watched, fascinated but helpless. Then followed the lugubrious task of recovering bodies from the oil-blanketed water and bringing them ashore for identification and burial. This was my first experience of destruction and death on such a scale. And before it was over I suffered another more personal sadness when they brought me our young Walrus pilot's parachute and parts of his aircraft found by fishermen a little way offshore. He must have been jumped by fighters within minutes of take-off. His body was never found.

This was baptism by fire with a vengeance. I slept very little that night, and morning found me lying on my back staring up at nothing, trying desperately to come to terms with life as it would have to be faced from now on. Maria came in quietly. I could feel her eyes upon me as she placed her tray gently on the stool, then sat down on the edge of the bed, and next moment a warm little hand . . . comforting . . . caressing . . . was laid over mine. A thrill of gratitude ran through me as I turned and saw the human sympathy in her eyes.

We talked then quietly about many things, but chiefly about ourselves. We wanted to know each other better. And as we talked I grew calmer, more hopeful and more at ease.

'Why do you look after me so kindly?' I wanted to know.

'You remind me of someone who was also kind.'

'A man?'

'A fine man. I have his child.'

This, spoken so easily and naturally, came as a surprise, though perhaps it shouldn't have; there was a hint of motherliness in everything she said and did.

'You're married then?'

'No. We were never married. He had to go. He was in the Army.' The quiet sincerity in her voice was deeply convincing, and after a pause she went on. 'I used to bring him coffee in the morning . . . here in this room. I was very young and he was kind to me.' She paused again, looking away, and for quite a while there was silence between us. When she turned back she said, 'You must have Mediterranean blood . . . maybe Italian?'

'I'm Maltese.'

'Ah. I felt . . . I knew there was something about you.' Then smiling again, 'Maybe I should have brought you coffee. Anyway it's comforting to have someone to look after. I miss my little boy . . . he'll be six next week.'

We talked on of more homely things: of her village on the south coast; of her little boy, looked after by her mother; of her father who owned a caique and used to sail to North Africa for the sponge-diving. Now he fished in local waters mostly for octopus and conger, but sometimes also for deep sea bass and tuna. And finally about herself. 'They call me catering manager, but truly I'm their liaison, their only firm link with the Greek people of the island. Many still don't speak Italian.' She laughed. 'They need someone like me more than they know.'

Next day the raids began again. But this time the base itself was the target. Ju88s and 87s came over singly or in groups, attacking methodically – first the hangars and workshops down by the quay, then inland among the offices and living quarters. I was pleased that my little house was set further back on its own. Hardly a worthwhile target, I thought. But when Maria joined me in the afternoon, we decided to move a bed, my suitcase, a jug and bowl for washing water, and other necessities including a primus stove and oven and a can of paraffin into the cave, just in case.

The bombing continued all the while, but more randomly now, as though the pilots were searching for targets, mostly down by the quayside and among the workshops. All at once there was a massive explosion, far louder than all the others and much closer. We rushed to the cave mouth and looked out. The little villa had vanished, leaving only a tangle of timber, tiles, bricks and plaster in its place. Maria stood gazing at the remains for several minutes, then shook herself with a sigh and came back into the cave. She sat down on the bed, motioning me to a place beside her. 'The end of a chapter,' she said laconically. Then we kissed and for a long time forgot about everything except each other.

⋆   ⋆   ⋆

The bombing ceased a little before sunset. I went down to the mess, which surprisingly, was still intact. They were all there, including the squadron leader, who seemed pleased to see me. 'Ah, Grech – just the fellow I wanted. We have seven aircraft still serviceable, and I've decided to get them back to Alex while they're still in one piece. You'll be left in charge here. OK?'

'Who'll turn over to me, sir? One of the Italians?'

'There isn't anything much to turn over, except a bunch of keys. Maybe some of the stores haven't been hit; but I daresay Jerry will be over again tomorrow and the next day.'

'What about the people?'

'Most of them seem to have scarpered, and I don't suppose the rest will hang about; they've all got friends in the villages. . . . Anyway, we'll be off before daylight, so you'd better have a good look round.'

I spent an hour or two at this with one of their supply officers, mostly to check where the various keys fitted, and labelling them accordingly. Apart from this, everything was in such a mess that it wasn't worth worrying about.

The Italian officers were in holiday mood, singing and laughing as they filled their Cant Z501 and 506 aircraft with clothes and personal belongings of all kinds. They were obviously thrilled at the prospect of escaping entirely from a war which no longer interested them. A little before dawn I went aboard the leading Italian aircraft to say goodbye. The cabin was filled with personal effects and clothing: a dress uniform, civvy suits, shirts, pyjamas, a gaudy dressing gown, all hanging from the roof and reeking of perfume; handsome suitcases, jackboots, shoes and slippers on the floor, with more of

15 Telegraphist Miles receiving a routine transmission from Alexandria.

everything neatly piled here and there. A little before sunrise the formation took off, one by one, across the bay, circled the base once as they formed up, then headed south-east and disappeared behind the mountain.

The W/T office was still manned and in touch with the flight. One of the warrant officers and two of the boat's crew were also hanging about. I gathered that they planned a few days' peaceful fishing as soon as the bombing let up. The sick bay staff had stayed with their patients, but were arranging to move them out to one of the villages where there was a doctor. In due course I strolled back to our cave where I found Maria with coffee and breakfast things laid out on a small table she'd found amongst the wreckage. The bombing soon began again, but sporadically now, and all the bombs fell down by the waterfront.

During the next two or three days there was clearly nothing useful to be done at the base, so we kept away from it, going for walks along the southern shore line and up into the hills where the scent of myrtle still lingered in the gullies and autumn crocuses flowered among the rocks. It was now late on in September and the weather was perfect – sunshine from morning till night and warmer than it had been earlier in the month.

There was a line of bathing huts down by the beach and a boom of light logs running out to a buoy a little way offshore. This was obviously intended to provide a clear pool for swimming, free from surface contamination. It came into its own now in holding back the oil slick from the sunken destroyers, which covered most of the rest of the harbour. Every afternoon when we came back from our walk we threw off all our clothes and plunged into the water. Maria in her birthday suit looked stunning, and I suppose that in those days I must have been a well built lad. I think that we genuinely delighted in each other and were truly happy for a while.

In the evenings, when the bombing was over for the day, we foraged among the wrecked buildings for anything which could be useful 'at home' – blankets, cushions, chairs, an oil lamp, two hurricane lanterns and one or two small items of furniture. People from the nearby villages also came down to see what they could find. They took no notice of us, nor we of them. There was indeed a strange 'honeymoon' atmosphere about everything we did and said. We spoke kindly, sometimes lovingly, to each other and always with studied courtesy. It was almost as though we were in training, together but separately, for a return to civilized living when the crudities of war were over.

I think we both had these feelings, though we didn't voice them. And in the back of our minds other influences were beginning to take shape. The bombing had now moved inland to the town of Leros, whose inhabitants (we found out later) left at dawn every morning to spend the daylight hours in caves on the slopes of Mount Clidi. The Navy, I knew, had established their headquarters in a villa, portentously known as Navy House, on the western shores of Alinda Bay. The SBS had their command post on the high ground between Alinda and Gurna Bays.

*   *   *

Early in October the weather broke at last, and a gale of wind with rain confined us to the cave for two whole days. The morning of the third day was clear but cold, so I busied myself with one thing and another around the base. I had some weatherproof clothing of sorts – an anorak and a scarf. But Maria had next to nothing, so she stayed in the cave with a blanket to keep her warm.

Small parties of SBS and other Army units visited us from time to time in search of stores and equipment that might be useful. I invited them to help themselves from any sheds or workshops which had been bombed and could no longer be protected, in any case, from pilfering by local people. By good fortune the food store had escaped, but I kept quiet about that. Maria always made tea or coffee for our visitors and sometimes offered round a bottle of Bardolino from the case we kept for ourselves at the back of the cave. Their surprised looks when they saw her, and the way their eyes followed her around, were amusing; but since she could speak no English, and they no Greek or Italian, no embarrassing situation ever developed.

Two Navy chaps I knew – Frank Ramseyer and Martin Solomon – also turned up one day. We filled the back of their jeep, mostly with hardware and cordage. I deflected their enquiries about food and especially certain Italian luxuries, including costly wines and liqueurs which I sensed were the main objective of their visit. Martin, a cheerful pink-faced youth, exuberant and full of fun, had earned a DSC when in command of an MTB at Tobruk the year before. Under point blank fire from German tanks surrounding the harbour, he had laid a smokescreen down both sides of the bay which allowed other ships to escape, he and Geoffrey Searle (ML 355) being the last to leave. Martin and I became great friends in spite of his enthusiastic passes at Maria, which she evaded with grace and good humour.

By now there was hardly anyone left at the base except ourselves and the two boatmen, who were making a reasonable living from their fishing. Fortunately their ready-use fuel store in a small hut a little way up the hill had not been hit. For the rest, an uncomfortable silence had descended upon the base, which we found disturbing. A stray dog or two could sometimes be seen roaming around, but there was no other animal life; even the seabirds with their lively music had abandoned the place in the absence of cookhouse scraps or any other titbits.

We gathered firewood, mainly from the wrecked buildings and kept a cheerful blaze going in the mouth of our cave. Maria had found a few books and magazines in the mess, which helped to pass the time. But mostly in the evenings we would sit quietly in the cave mouth watching the sun go down between the headlands at the harbour entrance, listening as darkness came on to the sound of migrant birds high up – storks and cranes talking among themselves as they passed overhead bound for Egypt and the lakes of Africa.

It was a comfortable pause in both our lives. Perhaps too comfortable. There were night as well as daytime raids on the north of Leros now. And one evening as we watched the flashes and the necklaces of tracer weaving upwards into the northern sky, there came a moment which we both knew could not be long delayed.

'They're having a bad time up there. A counter-attack may be coming. I ought to be with them.'

We looked at each other in silence for a while. Then Maria said, 'I miss my boy.'

That night we made love for a long time, again and again; then slept, Maria in my arms. In the morning we felt at peace and chatted happily over coffee. After that we tidied up together, then each collected a few belongings into the Army packs we'd found ourselves. When everything was cleared up or put away, we had a last look round then set off towards the head of the little inlet where our ways would part.

'I'll come back from time to time,' said Maria when we got there, looking at me with a shy smile.

'So will I. There'll be supplies and reinforcements coming in.'

But it was only a way, for both of us, of saying 'It's been a wonderful time, but who knows if we shall ever meet again'. Then Maria took the road south to Xero Kambo and I turned north for Temania and Alinda Bay. I looked back once. She was standing at the roadside watching. She waved and I waved back. Then I shouldered my pack and tramped on up the hill.

Invitation to the Dance

'Gotcher!' David Sutherland leapt out of his jeep and grabbed my pack which I'd set down beside me where I squatted at the roadside. It had been a longer march to Alinda Bay than I'd imagined. And harder – especially where I'd had to climb a rocky hillside and fight my way through dense scrub and boulders, between the suburbs of Platinos and Agios Marina, to avoid the centre of Leros town, which was being systematically ploughed up by enemy bombers. I climbed into the back of the jeep, and off we rattled up a track, which David's driver seemed to know by heart, to the SBS command post on Gurna Ridge.

'You've got a new job,' David said when we got there. 'You're now *my* interpreter . . . you don't speak Greek as well as Italian, do you?'

'I'm learning.'

'Never mind. Italian'll do for now.'

I was given a commando carbine and some ammunition. For self defence, they told me, 'in case the buggers decide to drop in on us'. Stewart Macbeth and Dick Harden joined us and we all strolled down to Navy House, which seemed to have become the unofficial wardroom and officers' mess for all units in the area. I found myself in the welcome company of people I knew: Charlie Clynes, who had been in the Malta garrison; Max Bally, the Davis Cup tennis player, now an intelligence officer; Hugh Stowell, Staff Officer Operations to Captain Baker, the Senior British Naval Officer (SBNO) Aegean; and, of course, Martin Solomon and Frank Ramseyer. Meeting them all again in such a friendly and comparatively relaxed atmosphere did a great deal to ease the pain of parting from Maria. Some said there'd be no counter-attack. We were too well dug in, and the Navy would deal with any invasion fleet that Jerry could put together. We'd be in Athens by Christmas.

But the bombing continued. We had to sleep on bed rolls wherever we could find a corner, though Navy House was not at first a prime target, and the kindly Admiral Mascherpa, Governor of the island, had lent us his personal chef, so the fifteen or twenty officers in the wardroom lived in luxury for a time. We were nevertheless surprised one day when we were served roast beef as the main course at dinner. Next morning Hugh Stowell was asked by the Admiral's secretary if he had any idea what had happened to the Admiral's horse which had gone missing. He couldn't say that we'd eaten it, or part of it; but he was pretty sure that that was what had happened. Poor generous Admiral Mascherpa was upset. He loved his horse. But maybe they were not separated for very long; when the Germans finally captured Leros, the Admiral was shot as a traitor.

And the bombing, though sporadic, continued. All day, every day. Navy

House, though sometimes the target, was never hit. The bombers may not have known exactly which villa it was. The continuous racket and moments of nervous tension began to tell on some of us, however. Martin Solomon and I both became 'bomb happy', and one morning Captain Baker sent for us. He told us to stand at ease, then produced from a drawer a well worn Bible, in which he'd flagged a dozen or so chapters.

'Make yourselves comfortable in the anteroom,' he said, 'and read these aloud, taking it in turns.'

It was an extraordinary situation. A Roman Catholic and an orthodox Jew ordered by a devout Protestant to read chapters from both the Old and New Testaments. A chapter from St Paul's Epistle to the Ephesians was one of them, I remember, and there was another from Judges. And it worked. We read slowly and carefully, and as time went on it was, I think, the sonorous and compelling phraseology more than its content which soothed us completely. We paused occasionally to re-read a passage and became in the end not only calmer but imbued with fresh hope. I'm sure the revised version of the English Bible, in which so much of the magic of the original phrasing has been lost, could not have had the same effect.

I grabbed my carbine and made my way up to the command post on Gurna Ridge, where I found David Sutherland poring over signals which had come in that morning.

'They're on their way,' he said, looking serious. 'If only we had more air cover.'

*   *   *

About the middle of October several submarines – one of them the *Severn* – began to bring in consignments of jeeps and Bofors guns, smothered in non-floating grease and lashed on top of the boats' casings with steel wire rope. David and officers from the Buffs and the Royal Irish Fusiliers took delivery of some of the jeeps, and one was allotted to me. Hugh Stowell got another.

I was now kept busy ferrying men and stores around the northern area, where the Buffs were deployed on the slopes of Mount Viglia to cover Partheni, Blefuti and Vagias Bays, with another company to defend the Italian battery on Mount Clidi. On one occasion, Frank Ramseyer, a Lieutenant Commander in the RNVR, sent me to act as conducting officer in an Italian F-lighter armed with a 75 mm gun, to Blefuti Bay, where it was thought most likely that the enemy would try to land. They did, as a matter of fact, a few days later, but by then the F-lighter had been withdrawn.

And still the bombing continued, more intensely now. It really looked and sounded as though the Germans were building up for something. However, two attempts to bring substantial invading forces across the Aegean to Cos and Kalimnos were frustrated by the Royal Navy, who in the process suffered severe losses from mines; they were now also being targeted by glider bombs, forerunners of the 'Doodlebugs' which were soon to be launched in strength on London.

One forenoon, when David had offered me a day off, I drove down to the seaplane base, where I knew there would be no bombing – there was nothing left to bomb. But there, at the door of the officers' mess stood Maria! I could hardly believe it; I had been down two or three times before, on jobs which would anyway have kept me too involved to do more than wave to her if she'd been there; and now, here she was, laughing and excited, with her arms round me, and her cheek against mine.

'I thought you'd never come,' she said, as we kissed affectionately. 'But I couldn't hang about in the village for ever. And Pietro is so happy with my mother. So this morning I thought I'd come and have a look at the old place.'

'I did the same . . . Oh, it's so good to see you.'

After a while we felt hungry. 'If you can find me a little money to buy eggs and oil for a mayonnaise we can have a banquet,' Maria said.

I gave her what I had in my pocket, and off she went to the houses at the head of the creek. I had brought with me the storeroom keys, so I busied myself for an hour loading up the back of the jeep with tinned foods, biscuits, cases of wine and anything else which might make life a little easier at Navy House. When there was no room for any more I went up to the cave, where Maria had everything on the go – a great lobster, which her father had caught the day before, was boiling away on the stove, while she whipped her mayonnaise to setting with a fork.

It was a meal to dream about – and sometimes I dream of it still. The weather, which had been stormy for days, was bright again, so we took everything down to the benches in front of the bathing huts, where we could luxuriate in the brilliant sunshine and gorge ourselves in comfort. Maria had shelled all the joints and claws as well as the great body of the lobster and adorned the meat with blobs of the most delicious mayonnaise. She'd also found a lettuce whose crisp inner leaves filled a large bowl to overflowing. We picked from the bowl each separate leaf, dipped it in a vinaigrette dressing and crunched it happily, along with great gobbets of lobster and draughts of cool Soave brought up from the food store. All we lacked was bread, but the salad made up for that. And during occasional pauses to savour and masticate, we sat back holding hands and gazing out over still blue waters to hillsides clothed in many shades of green, with here and there a splash of autumn colouring.

When we had eaten we threw off all our clothes and plunged in as we used to do. The water was still warm; and when we came out we lay dozing side by side in the sunshine, listening absently to the thump and rumble of war far away to the northward.

*   *   *

October was a disastrous month for the Navy. Four cruisers, five more destroyers, an MTB, three MLs and numerous smaller craft were lost or put out of action. The sowing of mines in the Kos and Kalimnos channels, and the arrival in the Aegean of the glider bomb, had completely altered the balance of power in the war at sea. The glider bomb in particular, launched and radio-controlled from an aircraft, and power-driven to its target with a warhead carrying well over 500 lb of explosive, was a weapon against which there was no immediate defence.

The loss of life from the powerful explosions caused by these weapons was horrifying. Of those who were not picked up immediately by rescuing craft, few survived. On one occasion, a bedraggled figure in underpants only and in the last stages of exhaustion struggled ashore in Xero Kambo Bay, claiming to be an officer from HMS *Hurworth*, mined several days before in the Kalimnos Channel; the Army patrol which found him was highly suspicious, fearing a plant. Hugh Stowell, himself a former destroyer officer, was sent for and was able to identify the poor fellow as Lieutenant Middleton RN.

And the bombing continued. The Levant Schooner Flotilla boys, who carried LRDG and SBS patrols across the Aegean to islands in the Western Cyclades, to report on enemy shipping movements, used to anchor their caiques close inshore on the northern side of Alinda Bay, opposite Agios Marina where all their supplies and spare equipment were stored in a cellar. We saw them from Navy House rowing across the bay, then waiting on the quay to watch the Ju88s coming down in orderly procession one after the other on their parallel bombing runs through the town. As each one passed, the LSF party would make a dash for their cellar, and bring out whatever they needed before the next stick of bombs came whistling down.

From Navy House we had a clear view down the bay and out to sea. One night, early in November, we saw a glider bomb, easily recognizable by its red tail-light, pounce on a Brooklyn Yard Mine Sweeper (BYMS) passing the entrance to the bay. 'Pounce' is an exact description of the way the bomb came cruising along then suddenly tipped up and fell upon its wretched victim. The funnel and deck clutter aft took the full force of the explosion, thus saving the lives of the people in the great palace of a wheelhouse further forward. They now called us up to report the damage and request instructions. We signalled back telling the captain to make for Port Laki round the northern end of the island. He would be met at the harbour entrance and piloted in.

I drove at top speed in my jeep down to the seaplane base to find our motor boat and, if possible, her crew. It was a moonlit night with a clear sky and bombers overhead, which seemed to be concentrating on gun positions in the mountains and round the coast. I found our two boatmen turned fishermen landing their evening's catch on the quay. We motored out to the harbour mouth and a mile or so beyond. In the bright moonlight, I remember, the sea looked black and bottomless. Then slowly round the northern cliffs and down past the Skrophes shoals came the BYMS which, we could see as she approached, had been badly damaged. And she was low in the water aft, where bomb splinters must have holed her. There was an air of silence about her above the slow, laboured beat of her screw turning at half speed.

I called her up with the recognition signal of the day, and when the correct reply came back I signalled 'Follow me' and turned back towards the harbour mouth. Slowly she swung round after me, and we had almost reached the entrance, when all at once a loud voice speaking urgently in English rang out. I thought at first it must be the skipper of the BYMS calling us on his loud-hailer, but couldn't quite catch what he was saying. It sounded like a warning – certainly the word 'trap' came into it. Then to my horror, the BYMS began to alter course away down the coast towards German-held Kalimnos. I flashed and flashed, but there was no reply, and I realized that the voice on the loud-hailer was coming from somewhere to seaward.

There was nothing we could do but watch appalled. The BYMS had increased to full speed, and it wasn't long before she rounded the southern headland of the bay and disappeared.

⋆   ⋆   ⋆

By a remarkable coincidence, I heard the rest of the story in 1953, several years after the end of the war, from the captain of a 'Hansa' cargo vessel on her maiden voyage out east. She was celebrating her first call at Chittagong with a party on board, and I, as manager of a firm of jute exporters, and therefore a major shipper, was received by the master personally. It wasn't long before we discovered that we had both been involved in the battle for Leros. And after we'd well-I-nevered and slapped each other on the back for a bit, Captain Loetzmann said, 'I remember one night in particular, because it gave me my first chance of a decoration . . . I was just twenty, in command of an E-boat patrolling to the east of the island – and pretty pleased with myself, I've no doubt – when we saw what must have been one of the first glider bomb attacks on a ship in the Mediterranean area. Poor creature, I felt sorry for her. She was a small and most unwarlike-looking craft with a tall and strangely palatial design of wheelhouse.

'Sure, she was a BYMS,' I couldn't help butting in. 'We were watching her from Navy House at the head of the bay.'

The captain looked astonished. 'Then it was you we saw signalling?'

'Not me personally, but never mind.'

'Anyhow, that was when my four years at an English public school came in handy. I was able to read your signal.'

'So you knew that she was bound for Port Laki north-about?'

'Indeed . . . and that gave me a better idea than wasting a torpedo on such an unimportant target. Instead I turned away to round the southern end of the island and be ready to meet and board her at my convenience.' Loetzmann chuckled. 'One gets a bit carried away when one's young. On the way round I called up Kalimnos, where we had two batteries of eighty-eights covering Leros strait, asking them . . . no, I expect I told them . . . on no account to fire on a small vessel which I proposed to board and capture. After that it was easy. When she was about to enter harbour I called her up from seaward by loud-hailer. I was down moon, so she couldn't see me properly. There was a small boat in the harbour entrance signalling her.'

'That was *me*,' I had to tell him, 'and we could hear you shouting, but with your loud-hailer aimed at him, we could only make out odd words.'

'I'm glad of that.'

'Why?'

'Well, I hope you will forgive me, but what I said was "Take no notice of that fool flashing . . . it's an Italian trap . . . follow me".'

'And he did, poor fellow . . . kind of wolf and Red Riding Hood stuff.'

We had a drink on that. Then he said, 'I suppose it was, but if you'd seen the relief on the poor chap's face when we boarded him and he knew it was all over, you'd have felt, as I did, that it had all been worth while'.

I met Captain Loetzmann again on several occasions, when we happened to be in Chittagong at the same time. But I never did remember to ask him which public school he'd been to.

Pigeon Shoot

Back at Navy House intelligence reports were coming in of a fresh German invasion force building up for an attack on Leros. Two earlier attempts had been driven off or destroyed by the Navy and the RAF. This third one had already reached the Eastern Cyclades and was expected to make for Cos or Kalimnos to refuel before the final assault. From now on we stood-to at nights, my position on the first night being with Andy Lassen and his SBS patrol on the lower slopes of Mount Clidi. We covered the shallow valley running down to Navy House, looking white and peaceful in the moonlight. I remember a flight of geese honking to each other in a companionable way as they passed overhead flying south. Otherwise the expectant silence continued until dawn and after.

The next day Frank Ramseyer sent me in our F-lighter with its 75 mm gun round to Blefuti Bay on the north coast to cover the entrance. We remained there for two days, then heard that the enemy invasion force had been held up by bad weather. The F-lighter was brought back to Alinda Bay and we all looked forward to a night's sleep. Hugh Stowell even insisted on going to bed in his pyjamas. We admired this defiant gesture, but had failed to allow for the time it takes for a field reconnaissance report to be coded up, transmitted, decoded, considered by staff, recoded, promulgated, again decoded and finally distributed. At midnight we were shaken awake with 'Stand-to! . . . Stand-to! . . . Enemy approaching' and dispersed again to our battle stations.

16 Stoker Wildgoose calling 'Hands to breakfast!'

I rushed up on to the isthmus between Alinda and Gurna Bays, where the SBS and a mortar company of the Buffs were deployed. I was put in charge of a motley little gang consisting of two naval ratings, a REME technician, two infantrymen (one a corporal) and two Italians. One of the Italians threw down his rifle in tears, crying 'I am cook, Signor, not fighting and dying'.

'You'll die without fighting if you don't pick that up,' roared Corporal Banks, poking his Sten gun into the fellow's stomach. The cook picked it up, still weeping, and the incident passed.

We were to cover the road leading up to the Buffs' main position overlooking Partheni and Blefuti Bays. The Germans had succeeded in getting ashore at three points along the north-east coast, including Grifo and Vagias Bays, and had fought their way up the precipitous slopes of Mount Clidi to capture the Italian battery at the top. A landing craft which entered Blefuti Bay would have been shot to pieces by our F-lighter if it had still been there. However, the Buffs were able to rake it with heavy machine-gun fire, killing half its occupants; the rest surrendered.

The Buffs also drove back an enemy company near Grifo Bay, taking more prisoners. But a second enemy thrust along the north shore of Alinda Bay met with little or no resistance. Looking down from our position on the isthmus we saw a party of four or five German soldiers enter Navy House, which now stood empty, Captain Baker having joined the Army commander in the HQ tunnel on Mount Meraviglia. We kept a watch on the intruders and it looked after a while as though they had decided to settle in; we imagined them guzzling our precious whisky and beer. After about an hour, we saw two of them come into the garden. One, a very fat and dumpy soldier, was struggling to get into what looked like a naval officer's jacket. Whether it was Captain Baker's or Hugh Stowell's we couldn't see, but the fellow's antics made us all laugh and we were still watching them, fascinated, when a voice behind me – I think it was David's – called out, 'My God, look at that!' and pointed.

We all turned and looked. Low down over the sea to the westward came three formations of twelve or fifteen aircraft each, in line astern, heading straight towards us. As they reached the Gurna isthmus they rose to pass over it and began to disgorge strings of white and grey parachutes. For several seconds there was no reaction. Then all at once the sky was criss-crossed by machine-gun tracer from every direction, with rifle and bren-gun fire from a company of Royal Irish Fusiliers occupying the centre of the isthmus. We all joined in, I with my carbine, the others with rifles and automatics. Some of the enemy were killed in the air, some wounded. I have a nightmarish picture in my mind of their wriggling, jerking bodies, like grubs on fish hooks; others hanging limp; parachutes here and there torn by bullets or failing to open, their occupants hitting the ground with sickening thumps, and bouncing, like birds at a pigeon shoot. Many landed on boulders or in rocky gullies and suffered broken limbs. Bodies lay around everywhere – on power lines, in trees and bushes and on the ground.

The paratroopers who landed unhurt began to consolidate their positions on Mount Rachni and the eastern side of the isthmus. We moved back to where a company of the Buffs was holding the southern slopes of Mount Viglia. As evening came on the weather closed in on us, the wind freshening to gale force from the south-west with rain. It was a wild night and cold, even for November. Reinforcements expected from Samos failed to reach Partheni Bay. During the night the cook left us, and we never saw him again.

The next day, with my chaps crowded into and on to my jeep (which had been left at the roadside near company headquarters), I was sent up to help with the prisoners taken by the Buffs at Blefuti Bay. On the way up I heard for the first time the strange tumbling and whirring sound made by spent bullets as they fell here and there around us.

At Blefuti we took over a party of thirty wet and frightened German prisoners and marched them round to Partheni Bay, where we locked them in a torpedo store at the base of the jetty there. Immediately there were forceful complaints in loud German accents from the powerful-looking Hauptmann Schmidt, who was in no way cowed like the others.

'Do you not know, young officer,' he rasped, 'that it is against the rules of the Geneva Convention to hold prisoners in a place which may become a target of war?'

We moved them to a rope store not far away, but the Hauptmann was soon at it again. 'Here we have no washing or toilet facilities,' he complained.

'Nor have we.'

'Do barbarians wash?' he asked with a sneer.

'They do after cuttin' a pig's fuckin' throat.' Corporal Banks, who had drawn his sheath knife, had to be physically restrained. The German grunted, sweeping us all with a look of utter disdain.

I told Frank Ramseyer, when he came along, about the trouble we were having with the Hauptmann. 'Take him out and shoot him,' he said without a moment's hesitation. I didn't take him seriously, although I believe he meant it; but I thought it wouldn't do any harm to teach the brute a lesson. So we put him in a jeep under guard, with his hands tied behind him, then we drove him slowly out to the end of the jetty where we hauled him out and stood him with his back to the sea.

'There's great washin' and toilet facilities right behind yer, if you'd care to step back, sir,' said the incorrigible Banks, pointing his Sten gun at the fellow's midriff. To do him credit, the German just glared at us in silence; but his face had gone deathly white. We let him stand there for several minutes, then we hustled him back into the jeep, and untied his hands (I think he was grateful for that) before driving him back to the rope store. We had no more trouble from Hauptmann Schmidt, then or later.

⋆　⋆　⋆

On the third day of the battle an urgent appeal was made for reinforcements from Samos, and although a 380-strong detachment of the Greek Sacred Company was ready to embark, no suitable craft could be found to transport them. In the end it was decided that our F-lighter must attempt to reach Samos with the 250 prisoners so far captured, and hand them over to the garrison there, returning with the Greeks.

We sailed soon after midnight, with Hugh Stowell in command, myself as interpreter and a Petty Officer diver (who'd been sent up to salvage the two sunken destroyers' confidential books) as coxswain. My REME technician kept an eye on the Italian engine-room staff, while half a dozen soldiers guarded the prisoners in the hold. We also carried (to my surprise and I think Hugh's as well) a consignment of mortar bombs and other ammunition for the Samos garrison.

It was a still, clear night with stars, but no moon. The boom was lowered to let us pass and we stood out into the channel between the northern end of Leros and the Arkhangelos Islands. There were no other vessels in sight, but out beyond the islands we could see dark shapes, which might have been E-boats or our own MLs on patrol. There was no way of telling, because we had no W/T aboard; in any case communications with the naval staff on the island had ceased when Navy House was evacuated. However, none of the patrolling craft seemed interested in us. If they were enemy vessels they probably thought we were a landing craft on the way back from putting German reinforcements ashore.

When we reached open water we steered to pass west of Gaidaro Island, 15 miles away to the north-east. As we approached it, the moon rose over Turkey and silhouetted two destroyers heading south at speed. They may have been the escorts for the original German assault force to the eastern side of Leros, and also for the reinforcements which had just arrived. In any event, they probably didn't see us down moon and a few minutes later we had put Gaidaro Island between us. We slowed down after that so as to reach Port Tigani[1], the southern port of Samos, at dawn.

★   ★   ★

As soon as we were moored Hugh went ashore to report to the Naval Officer in Charge. He was away a long time and when he returned he was in a sombre mood. Conflicting reports were coming in from Leros, and there were doubts about the wisdom of committing the 380-strong Greek Sacred Squadron unit to the battle.

Tension was high among the local inhabitants as well as the military. Orders had been received from Cairo to evacuate the garrison and as many civilians as possible by whatever means could be found. A few Army caiques and the LSF HQ schooner LS9 were on their way; and HDML 1004, bound for Mykonos to pick up an LRDG reconnaissance patrol, had been commandeered by NOIC Samos.

Then the bombing began, concentrating first of all on Port Vathi, the principal harbour on the north coast of the island. We landed our POWs, but the Army wanted nothing to do with our mortar bombs, so we dumped them in the sea and withdrew to an anchorage on the Turkish coast. When we returned in the evening, we found the 220 men of the Samos garrison busy trying to work out ways of escape. One joker, I think he was a captain, wanted to connect up all the moorings and other ropes in the harbour to make an escape line three quarters of a mile long, which would be secured between the Samos shore and the Turkish island of Bayrak Adasi, for the troops to pull themselves across to safety. What he hadn't worked out, it seemed, was how they would keep themselves afloat on the way over. Andy Lassen, who was there with his patrol, decided to make for the hills, to be ready to harass the Germans when they arrived.

Before leaving the island in ML 1004 that night, NOIC ordered us to re-embark our POWs and proceed to the Turkish port of Bodrum, at the entrance to the Gulf of Kos. From there, next morning, Hugh Stowell took the F-lighter on down the coast. But I was not aboard her. 'We've got a job we'd like you to "volunteer" for,' Vem Whittall, the British consular representative in Bodrum, had announced. '. . . I think you'll find it amusing.'

---

[1]   Its Greek name is Pythagorion.

CHAPTER SEVEN

Mountain Rescue

It was a wild night, blowing hard from the north-west with rain and sleet. The RAF high speed launch (HSL), capable of 43 knots in moderate weather, had to throttle back to 25 or so, thumping and plunging into a heavy head sea as she fought her way up the Turkish coast towards the northern end of Leros. The island had fallen to the Germans, but one or two Raiding Forces patrols were still trapped in the mountains. Fortunately, however, three pick-up points had been agreed beforehand and we – myself and a Greek guide – were at present on our way to one of them at the foot of Mount Clidi to bring out any of our lads we could find.

A mile offshore we stopped and a small boat was lowered. An SBS corporal dropped into it. We followed. Someone called 'Good luck!' out of the darkness. I felt a little flutter of fear – until then I hadn't really thought about danger, but it was too late now.

The HSL got under way, towing us slowly towards the shore, her engines muttering softly and almost inaudibly above the roar of the gale. About 200 yards from the coast, in the lee of a jutting headland, we cast off. The bulk of Mount Clidi stood over us, black and forbidding, as the corporal shipped his sculls and began to row towards a rocky beach, backed by low cliffs, at the foot of the mountain.

The boat grounded on the rocks, listing over to port. The Greek and I staggered out and set off on a recce of the foreshore and the barren hillsides above. There were one or two small caves in the cliff-face higher up, which we reached with difficulty, but there was no one in them. The going was rough and I was soon exhausted. The sky, though heavily overcast, seemed to be lightening in the east, so I looked round for some thick scrub or a cleft in the rocks where I could lie up during the day, while the Greek, who was a local peasant and therefore had a reasonable alibi, went off to search the other side of the mountain.

We heard the HSL rev up and stand out to sea. What we didn't know was that she had left without her boat. Our somewhat clumsy leap ashore from the boat's gunwale had very nearly capsized it, causing it to take water and become unmanageable. There was no bailer, and after trying for a while to scoop some of the water out with his hands, the corporal had clambered ashore, leaving a swamped boat adrift among the rocks.

Eventually, just as it was beginning to get light, I found a deep fissure and dropped thankfully into it. It was open to the sky, offering little, if any, protection against the weather, but I was too tired to care about that. Nor did I notice, in the dark, that a coastal pathway ran right across it. I was cold, wet and worn out, so I settled down as comfortably as I could among the stones at the bottom of the crevasse, and was soon asleep.

★   ★   ★

I was woken by voices and the tramp of boots, and looking up, found myself staring straight up successive trouser legs of a party of German soldiers, as they stepped across the mouth of my hiding place. They had a donkey with them, which balked at first, but was finally half dragged, half lifted across the gap.

To say that my heart was in my mouth throughout the performance is putting it mildly. I was terrified – I knew they shot people like me. In fact (I heard afterwards) an SOE chap had been landed at the southern end of Leros that very night, on a similar mission, and had been caught and shot on landing.

But the Germans passed on, and for a while there was peace. Then a Feisler Storch came flying along the coast at zero feet, obviously searching, and once again I shrank down into the lowest, darkest corner of my refuge. Though I didn't know it at the time, the swamped rowing boat had been found, so they knew that someone had landed.

For a long time (it seemed like hours) the Feisler Storch went on searching up and down, up and down the beaches – with me pressed hard into what shadow I could find at the bottom of my cleft. And every time the aircraft passed over, I found myself looking straight into the eyes of the observer in the rear cockpit. And still he didn't see me.

Ironically, it may have been the very absurdity of my choice of hiding place that saved me. Neither the soldiers nor the aircraft observer could have imagined that a trained intruder would choose such an open and completely unsheltered lie-up. But that was it, you see – I wasn't a trained intruder. And there was also an astonishing intervention by the Almighty – it could have been nothing less. When I'd recovered my composure a little after the soldiers had moved on, I opened one of those American 'K' ration packs wrapped in wax paper, which had been issued to us, and pulled out some of its biscuits, raisins and chocolate. The food put new heart into me. Then I discovered that the pack also contained five Marlborough cigarettes! This was wonderful – I could have a smoke to calm my tattered nerves. But I was to be disappointed. After searching desperately, opening every tin, box and bundle in the pack and shaking them, I had finally to accept that there were no matches. So I couldn't have a smoke after all, which increased my craving for one about five fold.

And yet it was this that saved me. If I had been smoking when the Feisler Storch came along a few minutes later, that observer would almost certainly have seen either the glow from the cigarette end or the smoke rising. And what convinced me that my life was saved by heavenly intervention was that although we virtually lived on 'K' rations for months after that – and I must have checked several hundred of them – I never found another without matches.

★   ★   ★

When night fell, I climbed out of my cramped hiding place and my Greek guide rejoined me. He had been back to his home village, where he had heard that there were British men hiding somewhere on Mount Clidi. The villagers hadn't looked for them, for fear of German reprisals, but they had been in good shape when last seen. My guide had checked all the caves he could find on the eastern side of the mountain (he'd taken a flock of five or six goats with him, as cover for his movements) but he had failed to find any patrols.

We now set off again, this time without goats since it was dark, and we were able to climb at a good pace. We searched the northern and western slopes as high up as we dared (there was an old gun emplacement on the mountain top, where a German lookout might be posted). We peered and poked into every cave we came to, some of which were only reachable by me standing on the Greek's shoulders.

At last we had to give up. The HSL was due back at 2 a.m., and it was now well after midnight. We started down the eastern slope, the Greek, who was more sure-footed than I, leading the way. I found the scramble downhill more difficult and just as exhausting as climbing. The hillside was covered with rocks, half buried in scrub, and lower down there were larger boulders, singly and in groups. Trying to climb over one of these, I tripped and went flying. My string of picturesque oaths, as I picked myself up, was essentially Anglo-Saxon and in the age-old cadences which alone can bring relief to jangled nerves. What it also brought, which I hadn't bargained for, was a rough grip on my coat collar yanking me to my feet. Then a torch shone in my face and a broad South Pacific voice said, 'Can't mistake a good old Pommy bawl-out . . . no Kraut could match it.'

'It's the tempo that beats 'em,' said another voice out of the darkness.

'Arr, and lucky for him . . . I was just goin' to let 'im 'ave it.'

I saw the glint of a knife in his other hand as I shook myself free, feeling distinctly ruffled. It was good to have found some of our boys – Kiwis of the Long Range Desert Group – but we'd had a hard day, and they might as well know it.

'Where the hell have you been hiding? We've searched every cave on the mountain.'

'Only fools hide in caves,' drawled the New Zealander. 'That's the first place they look for you.'

'Then where *were* you hiding?'

'Under the rocks, here . . . dug in a bit . . . the others are sleepin' there now.'

We woke them all up and made ready to leave. There were eight in all, including the SBS corporal, who had been hiding nearby and now joined us. The wind had veered and freshened from north to bring a short steep sea curling round the headland on to the beach. There was a feel of snow in the air. I started flashing the call-up sign with my blue-shaded pocket lamp, and went on flashing for five, ten, fifteen, twenty minutes, out over a black unanswering sea. I began to wonder whether something had gone wrong – engine trouble? the weather? a change of plan? Were we to be abandoned after all? My fears of the day before came crowding back – ugly, aching, debilitating fears of capture, brutal interrogation, torture even, and then the firing squad. Until at last, after nearly half an hour of agonizing suspense, the hoped-for answering flashes blinked back at us – just discernible against a background of tumbling waves with occasional breakers.

The relief was overwhelming (and almost equally debilitating) as we left the sheltering boulders to make our way down to the foreshore. Out on the open hillside, the full force of the gale hit us. To seaward there was nothing but tumultuous darkness, in which sea and sky seemed to merge into a single turmoil, until all at once a darker shape appeared in the midst of the maelstrom, growing and hardening at last into a boat.

We crowded round her, but there was clearly no room for eleven of us – the boatman, seven LRDG chaps, the SBS corporal, my Greek guide and myself – so one after another we plunged into the sea, some grabbing the boat's gunwale, others the line by which she was still connected to the HSL. But now another problem hit us: the last man turned away; he couldn't swim.

For several minutes we tried to reason with him, then roared at him. To no purpose. He was scared stiff, and would face anything from anyone rather than that black and raging sea. In the end, by tying my inflatable lifebelt on to him, and with one of his mates putting an arm round his waist to hold him up, we persuaded him to come with us. He was a brave lad at heart.

When all was secure, I flashed the letters 'LD' – the agreed signal – to the HSL lying 100 yards offshore. We heard her winch start up, the rope rose out of the water and five minutes later we were alongside, with eager hands helping us inboard up her scrambling nets. Then what joy to hear the four powerful Rolls-Royce/Packard motors open up to full throttle in a crash start. And away at 40 knots towards the dark but welcoming hills of Turkey.

CHAPTER EIGHT

Cretan Reconnaissance

By the autumn of 1944 western Crete and some of the larger Aegean islands were still occupied by the Germans, who had also taken over any Italian garrisons that remained, forcing them to continue under German orders. But most of mainland Greece had been liberated, and Athens was celebrating. The streets were full of fiercely mustachioed characters draped in bandoliers and carrying rifles (many of them German Mannlichers). These were the *andartes* or guerrillas (photo 17) – some right wing, some Communist – who had come down from the mountains and flooded into all the cities in search of food and a bit of riotous living.

There was very little food to be had, and no money; but plenty of liquor, so the fun tended to be fast and furious, with regular troops, British as well as Greek, making the most of the carnival atmosphere. Wandering into Eddy's bar one evening, I found that it had, in effect, become the SBS orderly room. There was Andy Lassen, as dashing and scruffy as ever, and several others that I hadn't seen since the Leros party, so there was much 'do-you-remembering' between drinks. But when I mentioned to Andy that I'd learned Greek, he sobered up instantly and grabbed my arm.

'I need you,' he said in that fierce, tense voice of his, blue eyes suddenly blazing. 'I need you now . . . at once.'

Next morning Andy, who was not a very senior captain, barged into the office of Air Commodore Tuttle, AOC Greece, with me in tow; and in his inimitable manner – disarmingly direct and downright, so that even generals found it difficult to take offence – told the AOC that he wanted me seconded to the SBS *at once*, for an operation on Crete.

The AOC was too taken aback to refuse, and that very night we set off for Iraklion – Andy, his squadron of thirty SBS men and myself – in an alarmingly noisy tank-landing craft. My brief was broad but quite specific. I was to contact local bands of EOK (right wing) *andartes*, gain their confidence, and with them seek out targets for Andy and his men to attack – barracks, fuel stores, vehicle parks, ammunition dumps, airfield installations, road blocks, outposts, regular patrols and so forth. I was also to train my *andarte* comrades in the use of weapons which Middle East Command would air-drop to them.

★   ★   ★

17 'These were the *andartes* . . .'

After a few days in Iraklion, Ian Smith of the SBS and I, plus a corporal with a W/T set, set off by jeep with stores for a month or two in the mountains, and two 2-pounder guns for the *andartes* we would be contacting.

The Germans had blown the bridge across the Mousselas gorge, so we had to abandon our jeep and cross on a 'span and pulley' erected by an SBS advance party. Then we went on into the mountains on foot, with mules found for us by the mayor of Kournas village to carry the guns and W/T equipment. We spent the night in a deserted shepherd's bothy built of stone with an earth roof laid on timber rafters. It rained incessantly. The reek of goat was overpowering. The rafters, infested with a phosphorescent mould, glowed green in the darkness above our sleeping platform.

Next day, at first light, we trudged on across scree-covered hillsides into the German-controlled area of the island. At every village we came to, a dog

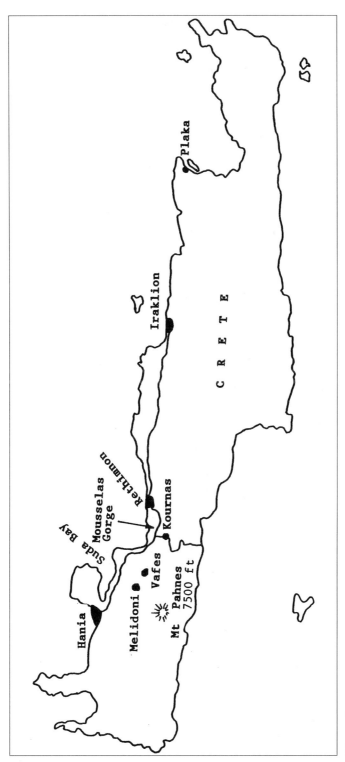

Map 9 Crete.

would start barking and go on barking till we had passed. But no door ever opened and no one was to be seen. They might have been ghost villages. Actually, as we soon discovered, their people were destitute: the Germans had pillaged them, removing almost all their food. And in Crete, the laws of hospitality demand that food must always be offered. So although they knew exactly who we were and where we went, they preferred not to see us.

It was nearly dark when we reached the village of Embrosneros, to be met by one of the local EOK *andartes* who took us to his house for the night. It was small and low-ceilinged. The air was close and very smoky. His wife and three children were grouped round a peat fire in one corner, sipping at bowls of a herbal brew which we were also invited to taste. It was bitter but warming. There was no meat, nor eggs nor even cheese. The Germans had taken everything.

In the morning the woman came with a bowl of water and beckoned us outside. Not a word was spoken until we had rinsed our hands and splashed water in our faces. Then she greeted each of us with a word and a nod and withdrew. Her husband saw us off, the children watching round-eyed from the doorway.

★   ★   ★

We plodded on into the mountains, keeping well away from the main track. It was cold and damp, with morning mists swirling around us. The loose scree was the devil to walk on. My mule was as uncooperative as only a Cretan mule can be, and I was already tired from the previous day's march; so I may perhaps be forgiven for thinking that I was seeing things when out of the mist ahead there appeared a wild figure in red silk pyjamas and no shoes, leaping from rock to rock down the hillside, uttering loud and lurid imprecations.

It was Paddy Leigh-Fermor, captor of General Kreipe and still, to this day, a hero to Cretans everywhere. He had been asleep in a house in Vafes village when the rumble of approaching vehicles was heard, and next moment a German tank and two personnel carriers came crashing into the village. He'd flung himself out of a back window and scarpered up the mountain side in the dark. And here he was, 'bloody freezing'. We managed to find him a sweater to keep out some of the cold. Then we got down behind a boulder and brewed up. The hot tea put new life into us all, and after a short rest, Paddy made off back to his village, while we slogged on across the scree with our mules.

In due course we reached Melidoni village and were welcomed by the mayor, who offered us a house to lie up in. But with Paddy's recent experience in mind, we felt that somewhere more remote would suit us better. Eventually, higher up the mountain but not too far from the village, we found a gully choked with scrub and a few trees. Here we set up an aerial and were soon in contact with Andy, in Iraklion, who ordered Ian Smith and one of the mules back to base.

It was a lonely moment. From now on, the corporal and I were on our own, responsible not only for our own lives and actions, but for the lives of all who helped us. We had been shown a small house, little more than a hut really, where a young woman lived with her two children, aged two and five. When the British had been driven out of Crete, two years before, her husband had hidden an escaping British officer, who was eventually found and taken prisoner. The Cretan was shot. His wife was left with nothing but her hovel and two chickens. When one of them laid an egg, she bartered it for olive oil with which to cook herbs and grass to feed her children. On this alone, they had survived.

★   ★   ★

The villagers of Melidoni and nearby hamlets soon found our hide-out, as did some of the *andartes* belonging to an EOK band based in the mountains behind us. This was worrying at first, but had advantages too, the chief one being that we always got timely warning of enemy patrols in the area. That was how I heard about an Italian outpost, on a low hill not very far from where we were camped. I made my way down there one evening and, guided by men's voices in the darkness, was able to creep close enough to hear what they were saying. It was not very informative, except for the general discontent and war-weariness which seemed to have gripped them, plus hatred of the Germans, who treated them like dirt. I was not surprised, therefore, when next day a Cretan boy came with a verbal message, to say that some Italian officers wanted to make contact.

A meeting was arranged among pine trees just off the main coast road. There I found three very frightened Italians, two trying to keep out of sight in the bushes while the third spoke to me in a hushed voice.

'We and all our companions wish to surrender to the British,' he said. 'Will you accept our surrender and arrange protection for us all?'

I was astonished and also excited, with visions of nothing less than a DSO – perhaps even a 'Well done!' from the king himself – for capturing a whole Italian unit single-handed. So back I went up the mountain and made a signal to Andy in Iraklion, asking for transport and an armed guard for my prisoners. His answer came at once. 'Not bloody likely. We're not going to feed any bloody Eyeties. Let the Krauts do it.'

★   ★   ★

My next attempt to get closer to target was not much more successful, but at least I gained from it in experience. It involved borrowing some clothes from a kindly farmer, and going down with my *andarte* friend into Hania itself, where the Germans had their headquarters. I suffered most from the borrowed clothes. Not only were they filthy and stinking to high heaven, but never in my life had I felt such coarse material – presumably homespun –

against my skin. I looked like one of those medieval peasants you see in films, and the expression 'sackcloth and ashes' took on a whole new meaning for me.

But they did their job. At the first German road block we came to, the sentry took no notice. Nor did another sentry, nor troops we passed on the road. At a village on the coast road we caught a bus, paying the driver with a small bottle of olive oil, and left it in the outskirts of Hania, where we were able to mingle with the crowd. However, this also presented problems, because my Greek, though good and reasonably colloquial, was mainland Greek rather than Cretan, so I pulled my scarf over my mouth and pretended to have lost my voice.

This worked well enough for casual meetings, but when we reached the *andarte*'s house, his wife wasn't deceived for long. 'What's the idea?' she said in Cretan. 'Either you've brought me a British soldier or a deaf mute. Which is it? Anyway he smells.'

But she was a kind-hearted woman and made us a splendid vegetable soup. We also managed, after a day or two, to glean quite a bit of useful intelligence in tavernas and coffee houses round the town. So at last the operation was getting into its stride.

It was also on this visit to Hania that I made contact with one of our secret service people, who was running agents in Hania itself. Angus, a classical scholar from Edinburgh, was one of those fiercely religious Scots for whom Hell Fire is an ever-present reality. Three years on an archaeological dig in the east of the island had nevertheless given him a near faultless Cretan accent and command of dialect, allowing him to move about at will to rendezvous with his 'Joes'.

One of these was Eleni, a girl of sixteen working in a café in the centre of town. She came of a respectable middle-class Athenian family, who had found refuge with Cretan relatives when their profitable grocery business was virtually destroyed by the invasion. She was no beauty, but her lithe, athletic figure and quick smile could be enchanting. And coupled with a burning patriotism and hatred of anything German, these attributes made her one of Angus's most valuable agents. 'Aye,' he would say, 'She's a braw lassie with her hairt afire.'

And so it was. You would see her moving quickly about the tables, occasionally pausing to chat with a customer, then flashing off again with rattling tray. And it would have been hard to guess what moved her, when you saw her laughing and joking with two young Germans, who had obviously fallen for her grace and humour. I believe that broken English was their common language.

Angus was a solid citizen and I liked him. But no one could have claimed that he wasn't a bit of a prig . . . 'I know she don't like 'frattin' with 'em, especially officers; but we must all make sacrifices . . . all of us.'

★   ★   ★

It was now mid-December. Already there was snow on 7,500 ft Mount Pahnes, and all along the southern range. On the mainland there was trouble brewing, which soon erupted into open hostilities. On one side were British and Greek forces under General Scobie, supported by EDES *andartes* loyal to the Greek Government in exile; on the other EAM and ELAS, the Communist-controlled *andarte* bands, backed by Russia, who were determined to take over the whole country and turn it into another Communist state allied to the rest of Eastern Europe.

In Crete, though, the position was not quite so clear-cut. Although there were ELAS bands in the mountains throughout the island, they were Cretan ELAS bands, with an inborn distrust of mainlanders. Nevertheless ELAS everywhere were anti-British at this time, and indeed were actually fighting the British on the mainland, instead of the retreating Germans.

On one occasion the tragic results of this affected me personally. Charlie Clynes, an old friend from Malta days and now an SBS lieutenant, was driving westwards out of Iraklion when an ELAS sniper opened fire on his jeep from a nearby rooftop. The corporal with him was killed outright but Charlie, hit in the stomach, lingered on. If it had been possible to fly him to Athens immediately, he might have been saved. As it was, though, I was only able to reach his bedside just before he died. I was deeply affected. But also forewarned and on my way back into the mountains with my EOK guide and his mule, I kept a bright lookout. Even so, I was unprepared for what actually happened.

We had left the road and were following a track southwards into the mountains. Scree-covered slopes swept up on either side of us to ragged cliffs, whose heads disappeared in cloud 6,000 ft above. As we were passing through a dense patch of scrub and trees at the head of a gully, I chanced to look over my left shoulder and saw that we were no longer alone: a man with a fiercely curled moustache and black beard had emerged from the trees and was walking quietly beside and a little behind me, his Mannlicher rifle in the crook of his left arm. He was wearing the traditional garb of the mountain Cretan, which all ELAS *andartes* wore – knee-length boots, baggy black trousers and dark shirt, crossed bandoliers, black headscarf and a black sash round the waist, with long knives stuck into it. I glanced to the right and was just in time to see two more ELAS men come silently out of the trees to join us.

We walked on. The silence persisted. Our soft-soled desert boots made little sound on the dusty track. The sharp crack of a mule's hoof striking on stone broke the silence now and then, but that was all. I looked at my EOK guide and could see that he was worried. There was no love lost between EOK, who were Cretan nationalists, and the ELAS Communists. There had in fact been open warfare between their mainland equivalents.

At the head of the next gully we entered a glade of trees, and there stood four more ELAS *andartes* blocking the way. Their leader, an older man with a bushier black beard, sat on a rock to the left of the track. We stopped and, leaving my guide with the mule, I strolled over to a rock on the opposite side and laid my carbine beside it. Then I sat down, at the same time unbuckling my belt with its revolver holster and tossing it to the ground at my feet. My guide slumped down nearby. The ELAS men did the same. The mule wandered over to some bushes and began to browse.

For a little while longer the silence continued. Then, 'You wish to speak with us?' said my guide in Cretan.

'We do not speak with traitors.'

'We cut their throats!' One of the band leapt to his feet, drawing a knife with a 12 in blade from his sash.

The old man waved him back. 'Your people are killing our ELAS brothers on the mainland,' he said calmly, looking at me. 'Is there any good reason why we should not kill you?'

'I can think of three,' I said. 'First, because you would receive no more ammunition or supplies from Middle East Command.'

'We took what we wanted from Italians who surrendered.'

I tried again. 'Only if we fight on together can we get the Germans out.'

He shrugged his shoulders. 'To be replaced by whom?'

'The people must choose.'

'If the traitors in Cairo let them.'

'There will be free elections,' said my EOK guide. 'They have been promised.'

'Promised! . . . Promised by whom? By the Cairo gang?' They were all shouting now and advancing towards us. One or two had drawn their knives. 'We'll feed you to the dogs . . .'

But once again the old man checked them. They subsided, muttering, and the silence returned – a menacing silence, broken only by the hoarse croak of a raven, repeated three times, from the cliffs above us; and I remember thinking . . . 'if the birds don't get to us first'.

But I was more hopeful now. They'd had their say and shown their strength, their dominance over us. If we could keep them talking we might yet be allowed to go on our way unharmed. My guide knew this and started by asking about their own plans. Had they seen or heard of enemy patrols in the area? Were there any Italian outposts worth attacking? How about air-drops of supplies? And soon they were hard at it, vying with each other over schemes for hostile operations, giving advice, telling tales, remembering past successes.

The old man listened, but said nothing. Occasionally a smile would struggle to the surface through his great beard and his eyes would twinkle. Suddenly he turned to me:

'And what was your third reason?' he asked.

'Third reason?'

'Why we should not kill you.'

I felt a prickle of alarm. I'd hoped all that was over; but here we were again, back where we'd started. I thought hard for a while, then suddenly

18 Early morning tea. Seaman/Gunner Reg Osborn on the tiller with Able Seaman 'Curly' Critchley.

an idea came to me. There was one man above all others – a Cretan who, though he had died a year or two before the war, would live for ever in Cretan memory. I rummaged in my pack for the litre flask my father had given me for my eighteenth birthday – a truly man-sized accoutrement, which I'd filled with whisky only yesterday in the mess at Iraklion. I unstoppered it and held it up. 'To Venizelos!' I took a swig and passed it to the nearest ELAS man. He drank and passed it on. 'To Venizelos! . . . Venizelos! . . . Venizelos!' It went from hand to hand round the whole band, and my guide as well. I blessed my father's memory for thinking man-sized, as he always did. The ELAS leader drank last and handed me the empty flask, smiling. 'Better go now,' he said, and we went.

★   ★   ★

It snowed in Iraklion at Christmas. In the mountains it was bitterly cold. Andy sent us up some extra rations, but there was no time for a party; we'd got wind of an impending German drive through the island, and all intelligence sources had to be put on special alert.

My first call was on Angus, who was based in Rethimnon. One of his 'Joes' had been the original source of the rumour, and Rethimnon was the nearest main town to the German-controlled area, which began at Georgioupolis, 16 km westward along the coast.

I found him in a room on the outskirts of the town. He looked worried and on edge. 'Yes,' he said, 'one of Eleni's friends, an officer, said he'd have to be away for a few days . . . they were going to field-test some new equipment. He was in full battle order when he left.'

'Left where? Is she sleeping with him?' I had to know. The value of the report was affected by her closeness to the fellow.

Angus looked away again. 'I don't know . . .', and with sudden ferocity, 'I tell ye I don't know!' He looked very stern and seemed to be suffering. 'She's friendly with him . . . very friendly.' He sat down, elbows on the table, head in hands, staring straight before him. 'We must all make sacrifices,' he said at length. 'All of us; the Lord's work must be done.'

It was clear that I would get nothing concrete out of him in his present mood, so I left and made my way through the mountains to a village overlooking Suda Bay, which I reached next morning at daybreak. I had a contact of my own there, who told me about two large vessels, probably troop carriers, which had come in the night before and left again before daylight. Several Arado seaplanes had also been in and out, and at least one tank-landing craft.

I sent my *andarte* friend – the one whose house was in Hania – to find Eleni herself, if he could. When he came back two days later he told me that she now worked in a German officers' mess. He hadn't seen her himself, but a friend had told him that she was very busy; many new officers had joined the mess and had to be looked after. This sounded ominous. I sent a long report by radio to Andy in Iraklion, repeated to Middle East HQ in Cairo. After that we just had to watch and wait.

For several months the state of tension continued. Alarms flared up and subsided. There were occasional ambushes and one or two brief skirmishes between patrols. In one of these a young EOK fighter was wounded and captured; and a few days later Eleni reported that he was to be executed.

For reasons of *andarte* morale it was essential to rescue him; so a meeting was arranged, through the Bishop of Hania, with a senior German officer. He was told that the Allies had started collecting the names of potential war criminals; anyone found guilty, for example, of complicity in the murder of prisoners, would certainly be hanged.

Jim Henshaw of the SBS was the British envoy to the meeting. He was a cheerful young officer. 'And of course,' he said, 'if you want to come out and fight, the fresh Aussie Division just landed in Iraklion will give you full satisfaction, I'm sure.'

The German consulted his general, who ordered the immediate hand-over of the *andarte* boy. 'And now how about a game of football – your lads vee ours?' suggested the incorrigible Henshaw. The German, surprisingly perhaps, was not amused. And not long afterwards – in May 1945, I think – the enemy withdrew from the island altogether.

★   ★   ★

I never heard to what extent Eleni's 'sacrifices' contributed to the outcome. Nor did I see Angus again before the German withdrawal. But a year or two later, in London, I ran into another secret service chap who had worked with Angus. I asked what had become of him.

'In South Africa, I believe,' he said . . . 'and did you know Eleni too?'

'I knew about her from Angus. She was game for anything apparently.'

'She certainly was – brave as a lion – and I dare say a little harmless vanity came into it as well . . . a sort of latter day Mata Hari by all accounts.' He paused, reflecting. 'The trouble is that you can become addicted to almost anything, if you go on too long.'

'Go on?' I was puzzled. 'Too long at what?'

'Well,' he said, 'it's a strange tale really, because at first her only motive was to get the Germans she hated out of Crete. For that she was prepared to make any sacrifice . . . even sleeping with one of their officers. And when he was posted, with another . . . in fact, two others; one in a Panzer unit and one in sea transport. And after that, well, one thing led to another.'

'And Angus? How did he take it?' I wondered.

'Ah! . . . You knew the old devil pretty well, didn't you – "The Lord's work must be done" and all that?' But which of the Lord's works? That was the battle old Angus had to fight out with himself. Was it the battle to defeat a brutal invader who was tormenting and murdering God's Cretan people? Or was it the fight to save a devoted young woman's soul? Which was the more important to God?

Poor Angus. He brooded and wrestled with himself for weeks. In the end he decided that there was only one way to settle the matter. So he married her. I believe they're very happy.

The Civil Engineer's Tales

CHAPTER NINE

Beach Party with Fireworks

The bombing began at dawn. After landing some 400 men and twenty Bofors guns, as well as a quantity of high octane fuel in drums for the Spitfires, our three LCTs (3, 114 and 139) lay beached a little way south of Kos harbour, with bow-flaps down and stern anchors out. I was First Lieutenant of LCT 139. As soon as the sirens ashore began sounding I 'cleared lower deck' and sent all hands to action stations. Then I started searching the north-western sky through night-glasses, and it wasn't long before I picked up a line of four black dots over Kalimnos which soon became aircraft – Ju88s – coming towards us in a shallow dive. As they approached, another line appeared some distance astern of them, and then another. This was my first experience of a low-level bombing attack, and it promised to be a testing one.

At first the enemy's main target was the harbour itself, but one or two overs fell close to where we lay. Our two 20 mm pom-poms opened up with a will, forcing the bombers to climb steeply at the end of their run. And each successive wave came in higher and higher, till they were almost out of range of our guns.

Now we ourselves became a main target, bombs falling all round us; but still we suffered no direct hits – probably because these Ju88s were essentially shallow-dive bombers, and were not fitted with the right sights for level bombing at 2,000 ft and more. At all costs, therefore, we had to continue firing so as to keep them at that height.

I trained my glasses on each aircraft in turn, until I saw the bombs leave its belly; then I sang out 'Bombs away!' and shifted to the next in line. The pom-poms should have done the same; but our gunners, who had been through the whole North African campaign, seemed to have other ideas. To my horror, on the first cry of 'Bombs away!' all firing ceased. And when I looked round I saw both crews crawling under their guns, with their arms crossed protectively above their heads. I rushed over and booted each of them up the backside, shouting, 'Carry on firing, damn you!' which, to do them justice, they did.

The bombing continued with five or six minutes between waves. There were more near misses, some of them very near; but the policy of keeping up a steady pom-pom barrage seemed to be paying off. And twice during the next hour and a half we were cheered by the arrival of a flight of Beaufighters from Cyprus. However, they were at the limit of their range for fuel. And though each of them succeeded in driving off a wave of attacking bombers, they were unable to follow up and shoot down any of the attackers before being forced to return to base.

An elderly able seaman (he must have been at least thirty-five) was standing near me as we watched the last Beau depart. When they had all gone, he reached for the nozzle of his inflatable lifebelt and blew it full and tight. 'This is the only fuckin' air support we'll be getting from now on, sir,' he said resignedly, 'so we'd best make the most of it.'

During the next lull I told the cook-of-the-day to make tea for all hands. We had a complement of sixteen. He went down to the galley, which was ventilated by an overhead grille in the casing close to where I was standing. He soon had sixteen steaming mugs ready on a tray, and was just about to bring them up on deck when we received the near miss of the century, which lifted us almost out of the water and let us fall back again. Immediately there burst up through the galley grille a stream, a rushing torrent of the most lurid and picturesque invective, which went on and on without pause or repetition. I listened spellbound to the swing, the balance, the variety and the magical phrasing of the outburst. And looking down through the grille I saw the cook standing in front of his tray, which was smothered in a thick coating of oily soot from the galley chimney. Every mug and the tray itself had to be washed and rinsed several times, and the whole job started again from the beginning.

But this was the last calamity – for us anyway. During the afternoon a young officer come along the beach with a message from Army Headquarters. 'We're giving up,' he said shortly. 'Evacuate as many as you can.' Then he handed his message to the CO and left. He looked utterly downcast, and I was sorry for him. But now there were more urgent matters to attend to. A company of the Durham Light Infantry had halted on the beach abreast of where we lay. 'My own regiment,' I thought (I was born and brought up in Sunderland), and set about getting them all aboard.

Some two-thirds of them – about a hundred men – were safely embarked when, to my amazement, we began to drag away from the beach; men were hauling on the stern anchor line aft, but on whose orders I had no idea. ''Vast hauling aft!' I yelled, ''Vast hauling!' But no one took any notice, and soon we had left the beach altogether. There was nothing to do but raise the bow-flap, as the ship was turned to go alongside LCT3, whose engine wouldn't start, and embark her crew. When they were all aboard we headed north-east for Bodrum in Turkey, leaving about thirty of our lads bawling insults after us from the beach.

I felt shattered, and did not trust myself to join the others on the bridge.

Instead I found things to do amidships and forward. Several plates had been badly strained by near misses, and we were leaking quite heavily. The Chief – an engine room artificer – got the bilge pumps going, which more or less controlled things for the time being. So I went below, and had just reached my cabin when a voice over the Tannoy reported 'E-boat approaching Red 095'. With what I felt was commendable presence of mind, I went straight to the confidential book safe and whipped out the envelope containing our NAAFI money. Then I carried the safe up on deck and flung it over the side.

The E-boat never materialized. Whether it was a figment of someone's bomb-happy imagination, or perhaps the conning tower of a submarine which then dived, I don't know. But I had our NAAFI money safe in an inside pocket; and in due course I was able to claim a refund on 'lost in action' grounds, which added greatly to the comfort of all on board (double of everything for everyone) over the next few weeks.

That was the only time in my life that I have ever knowingly committed a dishonest act. It was in a good cause, I felt then, and still believe. But there you are.

* * *

My first ship in the Levant Schooner Flotilla was the 15-ton caique LS10, commanded by Frank Banner, an experienced and exceptionally God-fearing Essex yachtsman. And although I too had sailed small boats since boyhood, I was unversed in the ways and habits of the LSF, which were something of a mystery to most people in those days. So I was considered a 'makey-learn' for a week or two.

At sunset on 20 January 1943, five ships of the Flotilla, together with two 70 ft HDMLs and two Fairmiles,[1] sailed into the teeth of a north-westerly gale bound for Cyprus. Adrian, in LS9, our HQ schooner and supply ship, assured us that the wind would soon moderate. But he was wrong. It freshened, and later backed to the south-west. The ships were scattered – north and south and back towards the Lebanese coast. One small caique sank under tow, fortunately after her crew had been taken off her into LS9. Yet all except two of the Flotilla and escorts eventually reached Famagusta.

LS10 herself was soon in difficulties. But her problems were not due to the weather, more to the practice of putting dockyard work in Beirut out to private tender without proper supervision by Admiralty staff. This was our first passage – in effect our sea trials – after being fitted with a new 90 hp Leyland high-speed diesel tank engine and additional long-range fuel tanks. Unfortunately though, the fitters (or possibly an enemy agent) had left quantities of cotton waste inside the tanks, which quickly blinded our fuel filters. After only twenty minutes or so at cruising speed our engine stopped.

19 Under tow in heavy weather.

The whole fuel line had to be disconnected, cleaned out and reconnected, a task which took about half an hour. But twenty minutes later the same process had to be repeated. And so it went on throughout a wild mid-winter night: twenty minutes on course north-west, making good 3 or 4 knots into the gale and heavy head seas, then half an hour driving back south-east (and later north-east) at 2 or 3 knots towards a lee shore in the region of Tripoli.

None of us got any sleep that night, nor the next, nor the one after. It was the longest stretch of my life that I'd ever been without sleep. And when we finally regained the shelter of Beirut harbour, and I managed to stagger ashore, I remember the whole quayside seemed to be rising and falling under my feet as I stumbled along it.

Frank wouldn't leave the ship. And since there was only room for one in the cabin aft, which we shared 'watch-and-watch' at sea, I went over to HMS *Martial*, the naval base, where I had a bath and a shave and put on my uniform before going along to the bar. There I found an Army doctor who insisted on taking me to a party in town.

'God, no!' I told him. 'As soon as I've had something to eat I'm going to get my head down . . . I've got to.'

'Nonsense!' he said firmly, and feeling in his jacket pocket pulled out a couple of benzedrine tablets, which he apparently carried around in quantity loose.

'Take these,' he ordered. I swallowed them and, to my astonishment, in a few moments felt as fresh as a daisy. And after the party, which went on into the small hours, I went back to my cabin at the base, where I lay reading for the rest of the night. I was quite unable to sleep.

After her fuel tanks had been emptied and cleaned out, LS10 was fitted with twin filters, so that if one became clogged you could switch to the other and keep the engine running while you cleared the first. In due course all the other caiques were also given twin filters. But now another problem faced us. On passage from Cyprus to Castelorizo, a week or two later, bound ultimately for the LSF advanced base at Port Deremen in the Gulf of Kos, our stern gland began to leak alarmingly; a leak which grew progressively worse. Frank stopped the engine and, the wind being southerly, fresh to strong, we made sail and continued happily on our way at 5 or 6 knots. She made less water with the engine stopped, but there was no way of plugging the leak while the shaft was in place, so we had to keep the bilge pump going.

In Castelorizo we hauled her out and immediately saw what was wrong: a clockwise-turning shaft had been provided with a clockwise-unscrewing stern gland, which soon allowed sea water to seep, and later pour, into the hull. We withdrew the shaft altogether, and nailed a copper tingle (patch) over the open stern tube. Then we were towed back to Beirut, where the defect was put right. And two weeks later we finally reached Deremen, fit and ready for operations.

★　★　★

While we were in Beirut, with the ship in dockyard hands, I lived at HMS *Martial* and seldom went down aboard, until one day a signal came in from Alexandria appointing Frank Banner to a staff job, and at the same time giving me my first command. It was a moment in my life at sea that I shall always remember. I walked along the quay to where LS10 was lying. Frank was ashore somewhere, but I was interested to see, as I approached, that there had been some changes in our crew as well. Recruitment to the LSF was from volunteers only, from every branch of all three services. For a while we even had an American field ambulance lad in the Flotilla – I forget which ship carried him – and there were always Army and RAF officers and men among us.

As I came alongside LS10 a rather scruffy-looking youth in khaki looked up from his work and greeted me with a grin.

'You the new skipper?' he called out.

'Yes.'

'Would you like a cup of tea?'

'Yes, I would.'

'Then you're just the bugger to 'op down 'ere and make it – ain't yer, eh?'

I hesitated for a split second, then hopped down and made it. I had seen the scandalized face of our coxswain – P/O Ware RN – emerging from the forecastle hatch, and felt that I could safely leave it to him to explain to Gunner Bye of the Royal Artillery, recently of detention barracks in the Canal Zone, precisely where he got off.

Discipline in the LSF was pretty basic, but on the whole comparatively easy to maintain.

---

[1]   110 ft Motor Launches – both faster and more heavily armed than HDMLs.

CHAPTER TEN

Of Monks, Marines and Tinkerbell

After landing an SBS patrol from LS10 on a reconnaissance of Lipsos in the Northern Dodecanese, we decided to lie up for the day on Patmos, just over 6 miles west of Lipsos, where there was not only an interesting monastery to visit, but a number of inviting coves and creeks near the southern end of the island. We found a well sheltered inlet close south of Port Scala on the eastern side, and soon had the mast unstepped and our camouflage nets hauled over. I climbed ashore, leaving P/O Ware in charge and noticed at once that we had spread the wrong nets. They were predominantly grey in colour, and the rocks here were a reddish brown. We should have rigged our orange and brown nets. However, it was too late now to change them, in the growing daylight, when a passing shepherd, or even an enemy patrol might catch us in the act. So leaving strict instructions that no one was to go ashore till I got back, except in an absolute emergency, I set off up the hill to the village and monastery at the top.

The going was pretty rough in places, especially where the goat track I was following zigzagged up a dry watercourse, choked by large boulders with stunted trees and bushes amongst them. I clambered on for maybe half an hour, when all at once I found myself crossing a smooth surface which looked and felt like concrete. Indeed it was concrete; it was the roof of a pill-box, built into the rock with a gun-slit in front.

The concrete looked comparatively new: there was no moss, nor any sand or bird droppings on its surface. For all I knew it might be occupied and, with the sun just risen, the guard asleep inside. I slipped away as quietly as I could, and made off back to the ship for hand grenades and a tommy-gun.

I was shocked to find that the coxswain himself, whom I'd left in charge, was not aboard. When he turned up at length, however, he had a disturbing report to make. A party of Italian soldiers (who had, of course, been disarmed by the Germans when Italy surrendered) had come strolling along a path which crossed the hillside higher up. Opposite the rocks where the caique was lying under her grey nets with darker grey patches, they had suddenly stopped, staring down at her and talking excitedly among themselves. P/O Ware had decided on the spot that he must go ashore and speak to them. He had found them extremely friendly, and one of them, speaking passable English, had even asked, as they walked along, whether we could take them with us.

I was unconvinced. They might well have wished to be taken away from the war zone, even as prisoners. But if we refused them, as we must for lack of space (the patrol on Lipsos, who were to be picked up again that night, might have taken prisoners themselves), their next best plan would be to earn themselves Brownie points with the Germans by reporting our presence to the first patrol they chanced to meet. And this may well have been what they did, as we soon found out.

The coxswain was sent off to find his Italian friends and tell them that we had no room for them, while I made my way back to the pill-box. After searching around for a bit, I found a small door behind some bushes on one side. I entered in the approved commando style, tommy-gun leading; but there was no one there, so I set off up the hill again, and eventually reached the famous monastery. I was warmly welcomed by the monks, offered coffee and goat's cheese with olives and shown round. I was even able to buy a few postcards with a little Greek money I had with me. But in the middle of all this jollity and mutual congratulations, a Greek lad came in and whispered urgently to the Father who was showing me round.

'The Germans know you are here,' he told me. 'They're coming to take you and your boat.'

I hurtled back down that goat track – literally hurtled, leaping from boulder to boulder. How I avoided breaking my neck on the way will remain a mystery for ever. And at one point on the way down I saw in the distance, across a steep-sided gully, what looked like a party of marines or sailors, with ribbons at the backs of their caps, marching stolidly up the hill to the head of the valley. They might then have made for the monastery to interrogate the monks or, if the Italians' directions had been specific enough, straight down to where we lay.

I didn't wait to find out. The moment I got aboard we stowed our nets and spreaders, and singled up moorings, ready to leave. We were on the point of starting up the engine, when our W/T operator told us to hold on and listen. We all held our breath, and sure enough, in the sudden silence which followed we could just hear a light tapping, as of someone operating a morse key. It sounded fairly close. In fact it seemed to be coming from the other side of the low, rocky point to which we were moored.

I crept up the rocks a little way. The tapping grew louder the higher I climbed until all at once, to my relief, I saw that I need go no further: the masthead and signal yard of a naval patrol craft – probably an E-boat – had appeared above the ridge separating us from the next cove. She must have been sent to search the coves, probably for us. And why she moored where she did was anybody's guess.

I slipped back aboard, and we shoved off at once, but without starting our engine. Fortunately the wind was northerly, light but steady, and the mouth of the creek open to the south-east. So we set the jib and let her gently gather way, moving silently out into open water, where we hoisted the mainsail and gybed, bringing the wind over on to the starboard quarter to round the southern end of the island.

As soon as I felt that we had enough solid rock and jutting headland between ourselves and the E-boat, I got the engine running, dead slow at first, then a bit faster. But now, in broad daylight, we must do everything possible to look like an ordinary fishing or trading caique, which meant that our speed must be kept down to less than 5 knots until we were well clear of the land. Our four machine-guns had to be dismounted and sent below; and all except two of the crew must keep out of sight, leaving only the helmsman and one other on deck. We steered for Kinaros, a small uninhabited island some 22 miles away to the south-west.

From now on it would be a question of luck and little else. The wind began to freshen as the sun rose higher. A moderate sea with occasional white caps helped to mask our bow wave and wake. So I was soon able to open up to full throttle without any risk of our engine being heard up-wind in Patmos. After a while we began to take heart. There was no sign of any pursuit, so the Germans ashore couldn't have alerted that E-boat to our presence on the island – if indeed they really knew about it. A formation of Ju52s, escorted by ME109 fighters, passed overhead high up, bound no doubt for Rhodes or Kos. They took no notice of us. Nor did a small T-class destroyer close to the southern horizon, also eastward-bound. They were all far too busy with their weightier and much more immediate military objectives to take any notice of a happy little caique bounding along through a short steep sea across the open Aegean.

It was a sparkling day – a day to remember – with flights of shearwater rising ahead of us, sweeping low across the sea and settling astern – a day on which we were able at last to sail our caique and still keep to the strictest schedules of course and speed which our operations demanded. The wind increased from fresh to strong. Our speed rose to nearly 8 knots, and now that we were out in the open sea, well away from prying eyes, the rest of the ship's company could come on deck again (photo 20). Soon we were all singing and laughing like schoolboys as the little ship creamed along. And it was barely noon when we gybed and then rounded-to into the mouth of a secluded creek on the south-west corner of Kinaros.

We moored and camouflaged alongside some rocks near the head of the creek, and I took the first lookout duty myself, from a point on shore screened by a large boulder, a little way up the hill from where the caique was moored. After a while, looking around, I noticed a small hut – probably a fisherman's shelter – on the hilltop above me. So when I was relieved by the coxswain at the end of my watch, I took a tommy-gun and stuck a couple of hand grenades into the top of my trousers and set off to investigate.

The tommy-gun was a mistake. Its great round ammunition tray dug into my ribs unmercifully as I climbed up through the rocks and scree; so I was pleased to be distracted after a bit by what sounded like a goat bell coming

20 'Our speed rose to nearly 8 knots . . . the rest of the ship's company could come on deck.'

from not far away round the slope of the hill to my left. One or two hearty roasts over driftwood fires for the next few evenings would make a welcome change, I thought, from our usual supper of 'herrings in', or bully or beans and bacon. And I could hardly miss the animal with a burst of tommy-gun fire as soon as I sighted him. So I set off round the hill in the general direction from which the occasional tinkle seemed to be coming.

The going was a good deal easier in this direction, and I was soon making good progress; but the goat seemed to be finding it easier too, because his intermittent tinkles continued to keep well ahead of me. I persevered, however, until a glance at my watch and a look at the sun, now low in the western sky, told me that it would soon be time to stow our camouflage nets and get the caique ready for sea. We had a midnight rendezvous with the patrol we had landed on Lipsos.

Ten minutes later I decided reluctantly that my dream of a hearty roast or two would have to be abandoned: it was time to turn back. I straightened up and set off again in the opposite direction. And after a few minutes, damn me if that insolent goat wasn't following me. His tinkles were just as loud and rather more frequent than before, in spite of the fact that I was now lolloping quite rapidly from rock to rock, going down as well as across the hillside towards the sea.

And another thing. He was not only keeping pace with me, but sort of in step as well. Every time I jumped down there came a tinkle. And yes, when I looked at my belt I saw that the ring on one of my hand grenades was striking against its stem, with a pretty little tinkle at every step. The only goat on Kinaros that evening was Sub-Lieutenant Alexander Thwaites RNVR.

★ ★ ★

One further incident before we finally left the island made us think very hard about how we should conduct ourselves in the future. Having at last found a goat track along which I could actually walk in reasonable comfort, I was strolling down towards the head of our cove when all at once a light aircraft came sweeping very low round the side of the hill behind me. I flung myself down and lay flat as he came roaring over, to disappear again behind the slope ahead. It was a Feisler Storch, and he was so low that I was on the point of having a go at him with my Webley .45, but thought better of it.

I felt sure that he must have seen me; but when he didn't come back for a closer look I began to wonder. Perhaps he had been searching the coastline to his right. When I got back aboard I discovered the answer: our W/T operator had been trying all afternoon to contact Cairo; but because we were moored close up to the base of a high cliff, which curved round to the south of us as well, Cairo had been unable to hear his signals. However, the Germans on islands or in ships to the west had heard them plainly, and after pinpointing our position with direction-finding aerials, had despatched the Feisler Storch to look for us.

Fortunately, though, the rocks here were grey and black, rather than red and brown, so our light and dark grey nets had proved fully effective. And as soon as the sun was well down, the wind having dropped and the sea subsided, we got under way and stood north-east for Lipsos at a good 7 knots.

The Surgeon's Tale

CHAPTER ELEVEN

The Other Side of the Coin

'The Eyeties say we're being attacked, sir.'

I woke with a start, wondering for a moment where I was. Then a bugle call from the Italian gun position on the hill behind us brought me to my senses. The orderly put down a mug of tea beside my bed. I got up and looked out of the window. It was a fine clear morning on the island of Kos early in October 1943. The sun had just risen. In the channel between Kos and the misty outline of Kalimnos to the north, where the night before there had been nothing but empty sea, lay a fleet of transports, landing craft, patrol boats and two destroyers, with planes circling overhead. Across the low-lying fields, intersected by drainage ditches, that lay between us and the coast, lines of field-grey figures were advancing in open order, apparently unopposed. Memories of OTC field days at school, and the fun of firing blank ammunition, came back to me. But on this occasion they weren't firing blanks, and it was all too clear that we were on the wrong end of a combined operation, for real.

Since this was the first time I'd been in the front line – in fact in any line at all – it came as a bit of a shock. I was living in the padre's house close to the Italian settlement of Marmari, which consisted of a church, a school, a few houses and a general store. There were no Allied troops between us and the sea, except those guarding a landing strip for Spitfires, who had been surprised and overrun already. I put on some clothes and a Red Cross armband which I'd never bothered with before but thought that now was perhaps the moment. Then making use of dead ground (which I must also have learned at school), I worked my way up to the buildings where our patients were housed. Some of them – the lucky ones – had been flown out the night before. They were the last to get out for several months, though we could not have guessed this at the time.

I was now temporarily out of the line of fire. A few stray bullets came through the windows high up, but that was all. In fact, though, everything had happened so quickly that I was reduced almost to a state of disbelief while waiting for the Jerries to arrive, which they shortly did. I walked down

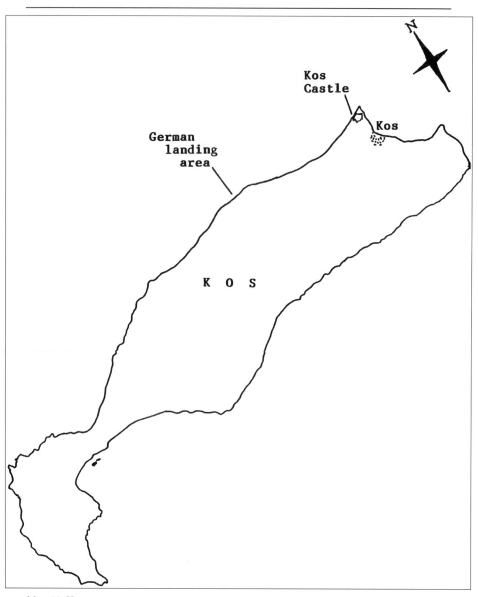

Map 10 Kos.

to meet them, and saluted the officer in charge, who looked relaxed and confident as he studied a map in a large plastic case with a lanyard clipped to his belt; he even apologized for their intrusion into our peaceful lives. We walked together up to the settlement, where he became at once deeply involved in deploying his troops.

I was turned over to a *Feldwebel* who was a very different kettle of fish. With the muzzle of his revolver rammed into my back, he demanded harshly, 'Show me your buildings and all who is in them.' It was hardly the happiest situation to find oneself in at breakfast time, dressed only in tropical kit of shirt, shorts and desert boots. He coveted my good wool stockings, and made no bones about it – 'Ein paar strumpfe bekomme ich' – and I had perforce to find him another pair. However, we were soon fully engaged in dealing with the wounded (ours and theirs) as they came in, on stretchers or limping and staggering. We had set up our light portable operating table in a classroom close to the school hall where casualties were assembled on stretchers. The hall had windows too high to see out of, or to be seen in through, and one wash-hand basin but no water. Our orderlies ran tirelessly to and fro to bring water from a conduit in the road outside.

British, German and Italian wounded on their stretchers were lined up in the hall and corridor, and were seen to in order of severity of wounds. Many had suffered rough and exhausting journeys to reach us and were in shock due to pain or loss of blood and dehydration. These we treated by the time-honoured method of a cigarette, hot sweet tea and occasionally morphine supplied to us in ampoules (and when these ran out, tablets dissolved in a teaspoon of water over a methylated spirit flame and drawn up into a syringe).

The invading force had brought with them no surgical team or equipment of any kind; it looked almost as though they had expected the assault to be such a pushover that no serious casualties would be suffered. They had, therefore, to rely on whatever we could provide from our resources, which the sudden onset of battle had already strained to the limit.

The conditions under which we had to work were in any case somewhat primitive and far removed from the modern concept of bright lights, sterile stainless steel, gowned surgeons and nurses, and tiled floors. Sometimes we didn't even wear masks or change rubber gloves between cases, because these, like most other stores and equipment, were in short supply. Nevertheless you can do a good deal of effective surgery with very few instruments, provided that you are fully equipped for anaesthesia – in which we were fortunate.

All the instruments and drugs we possessed had been brought in on our backs; there was also a small generator for our operating light, which soon packed up and ceased to function. After that I had to operate with a battery-powered headlight, whose headband cut into my forehead and was a pain. So was the German medical officer breathing down my neck to make sure that I wasn't deliberately knocking off German wounded – an ill-mannered and domineering fellow, extremely difficult to get on with. His junior, on the other hand, was a friendly and unassuming little Austrian, who told us with considerable emphasis that his only military training had consisted of leading a mule up and down a mountain in Greece.

Our own team consisted of a surgeon (myself), an anaesthetist and five orderlies, two of whom were Quakers from the Friends' Ambulance Unit and therefore conscientious objectors. But their work and behaviour were exemplary. No task was too hard, too exhausting or too dangerous. There was nothing they wouldn't tackle except cleaning a gun; but since a single service revolver was the only weapon we had, this didn't really matter. The original British occupying force, which took over from the Italians, had also brought with them a dentist and, bizarrely, two malariologists, whose only function was to examine the bambinos' tummies for enlarged spleens. What became of them I have no idea.

$$\star \quad \star \quad \star$$

We soon ran out of sterile towels, but the work had to go on, as fast as possible and for as long as we could see to operate. I found that I could manage well enough by laying my sterile instruments on a boiled macintosh sheet. It was sometimes possible to assess injuries with the patient lying on a stretcher; but all too often clothing and equipment which couldn't be removed without causing acute pain made this impracticable until an anaesthetic had been administered. Only then could mud- and blood-stained uniforms be taken off – or more often cut off and dumped on the floor. After a while the operating room grew steamy and the floor was cluttered with piles of foul and bloody clothing, while the wash basin became clogged with a sludge of plaster of Paris.

It was important always to find not only where a missile had entered but also where it had come out, thus indicating its probable track through the body and the organs likely to have been damaged. However, a great many lives were saved at this time by prompt first aid; but in some cases timing was also of vital importance. When a German soldier had his arm blown off above the elbow, someone very sensibly applied a tournique; unhappily it was left on too long – more than twenty-four hours. By the time he was brought to us, the stump below the tourniquet, starved of blood, had turned black; a gas-gangrene infection, which spreads through bloodless muscle, had extended to his shoulder and into his body. The poor fellow reeked of its sickly sweet smell, which is the smell of death.

$$\star \quad \star \quad \star$$

For some time we had no idea how the invasion was going. The Germans had landed half-way along the north coast of the island, right opposite the Marmari settlement, cutting the only road between Kos town and

Antimachia airfield. They then spread out to right and left, still encountering little or no resistance, until one force reached the airfield, where the RAF regiment defending it was soon overwhelmed. The other force approached Kos town, where the Durham Light Infantry were dug in together with some Italian units, who were now our reluctant allies but looked on by the Germans as traitors.

The DLI fought bravely and well but they were heavily outnumbered, and without effective air support they were unable to check the German advance for very long. By the morning of 4 October the fighting appeared to be over. Nevertheless, occasional German aircraft continued to fly up and down the coast, frequently passing directly over Marmari; so, in order to establish our medical identity, we made a large cross out of piled-up corn cobs laid out on a nearby threshing floor. The cobs being yellow in colour, the German pilots may well have taken this as a symbol of abject surrender. At all events they left us alone.

And alone we remained. There are no prizes for becoming a POW and little scope for heroics. Being a medical officer is in some ways quite difficult, despite the advantages and privileges accorded to you under the Geneva Convention. In the interests of the wounded (from both sides) you have to be reasonably cooperative at all times and in all situations. Even so, I sometimes wondered, during the weeks that followed, whether I ought to try to escape. Some did. But being the only surgeon on the island I could not, in all conscience, abandon my patients to get away – even if I'd known how. After a while, however, a steady stream of Allied prisoners did manage to escape to the mountain villages or, in some cases, to caves along the south coast of the island, where they were met by British intruder patrols and eventually picked up by British-manned caiques.

Some brave enthusiasts tried to swim across the 3 mile wide Kos Channel to Turkey. A South African medical officer from our unit nearly made it; but when he had almost reached the opposite shore he spotted a boat flying a red and white flag which he thought must be Turkish; so he waved and shouted to attract the crew's attention, only to find that she was a German-controlled Greek vessel with a German armed guard on board, flying the red and white German Sea Transport pennant. However, his attempt was recognized as a sporting effort, and he was returned to us in good order.

★   ★   ★

Food on Kos was by no means easy to come by. When there was a lot of work (and we were operating on virtually all the Jerry wounded as well as our own) they did send us in some rations. Our staple diet nevertheless was tomatoes picked in the fields and cooked in olive oil, plus whatever our ingenious orderlies were able to steal. However, the island commander did, on one occasion, send us a flagon of wine which went down very well.

Then there was the time early on in the battle, when several officers and men of the DLI were wounded by a mortar bomb which exploded among them. Most of their wounds were such as we could deal with fairly well; but there were one or two that I still remember in detail after so many years with regret that I didn't do better. One, a private, had suffered a perforation wound through the right side of the abdomen which I explored and closed in the usual way. He was nursed and fed in our room and seemed to be doing well until unfortunately he developed an infection which led to his death. We dug a grave near the other British graves, and the *Feldwebel* insisted that we bury him with military honours, including a firing party; the Germans had an innate determination to do the right thing on such occasions. I suggested that we could manage without too much ceremony, but the *Feldwebel* was adamant. Since there had been so many killed, however, they had run out of blank ammunition and would have to '*scharf schiessen*'. At the appropriate moment, therefore, a firing party goose-stepped up to the graveside, fired three crashing volleys of live ammunition and departed, leaving us to fill in the grave. It has always saddened me that I didn't do better for this inoffensive nice man, and I hope that his soul will forgive me.

Some of the others I need not regret so much. One German, shot in the head, had an open wound on the left side, with the brain tissue bulging out. I cleaned it up as well as I could, but he was unconscious, with stertorous breathing, and nothing could prevent his death. The German commander had awarded him an Iron Cross, and a deputation of senior officers arrived in the ward to decorate him. I stood to attention in my white operating gown; and as the medal was pinned on the man's chest a cloud of black flies rose from bandages round his head and danced over him, as though a part of the ceremony.

Not all my efforts in brain surgery ended like that. Another German had been hit in the forehead, exposing the brain. Although we had no diathermy[1] to arrest bleeding (you cannot tie off the small vessels in the brain substance) I managed to stop what bleeding there was and remove the piece of metal which had done the damage. I closed the scalp round a small rubber drainage tube, gave the wound a dusting of sulphonamide powder and to my great surprise all was well. In due course the patient was evacuated to Athens by plane, and as far as I know he survived.

* * *

When the initial surprise and upset of the invasion had subsided, we concentrated on dealing with as many of the wounded as possible – British, Germans, Italians and Greeks – and settled down to being POWs. The buildings we occupied were guarded by a few Wehrmacht soldiers, but Greeks from the villages managed to slip past them from time to time, bringing us grapes and little skinny chickens which were very welcome. They couldn't have been more friendly and brave. It seemed as though the

Dodecanese had been invaded so many times over the centuries that one more invasion had made little impact. Yet the assault had taken a distressing toll of Greek civilians as well as soldiers. A young man had picked up a hand grenade which then exploded, blowing off both his hands and blinding him in both eyes. Mercifully he died under sedation with morphine.

A problem which affected all of us, both prisoners and guards, was dysentery due to the flies and the lack of sanitation. I suggested to our captors that with so many bored prisoners around it might be a good idea for some of them to dig latrines. And in a curious way, although I was also their prisoner, the Germans were quite happy to take such instructions from me. Some also preferred to seek medical advice from me rather than from their own MO, whom they disliked as much as I did.

The fact that I was able to converse easily and accurately in German may have had something to do with this, and I was reminded again and again of six happy months in the early 1930s, before Hitler came to power, when I stayed with the friendly and talented family of Freiherr von Kunsberg in Heidelberg, where I rowed on the River Neckar with athletic young Germans of the Heidelberger Ruderklub.

Memories like these, as well, of course, as the Hippocratic oath, which seemed to assume a new and important meaning on the island of Kos where it was first enunciated, did much to colour my whole attitude towards the German people, and made it easier for me than perhaps for others to

21 Coxswain Simmonds at the helm of LS3.

develop that relationship between doctor and patient which is such an important factor in the healing process. I just could not look upon the whole German race as some sort of devils, and frequently had long discussions with those in my care on many subjects, both deep and trivial, that affected us all.

I remember also that although Hitler's conquests now extended from the Atlantic to the Urals, the rank and file of German troops on Kos were worried and unhappy at being separated from continental Europe. They also found it difficult to understand why we weren't both fighting the Russian Communists – 'With our Army and your Navy we could rule the world' was the attitude of many. In the meantime, however, they felt isolated – cut off by the Royal Navy for whom they had such a healthy respect that they had begun to wonder how they would ever get home. Or, if they couldn't, how they would continue to receive their rations, their mail and – already beginning to loom invitingly through the tangle of more immediate worries – their Christmas parcels.

★   ★   ★

During this interim period of comparative quiet, we thought we might be evacuated to mainland Greece. The *Gradisca*, a hospital ship taken over by the Germans from the Italians, had arrived in Kos harbour. Her captain came over to Marmari to find out how many German wounded there were and to arrange for their embarkation. I asked whether our unit could be taken off too, but he told me the ship was full. He looked embarrassed, and it was clear to us all that he was simply obeying an order. The Germans must have felt they needed us on the island. We were particularly disappointed when we heard later that on her way back to Piraeus the *Gradisca* had been intercepted by a British destroyer and ordered instead to proceed to Brindisi, where all her British patients were taken off and the same number of wounded Germans embarked in their place.

Meanwhile German forces were building up for an attack on Leros, a much more difficult and hazardous enterprise, since the element of surprise had gone and the island had been heavily reinforced. Everybody knew that a tough fight was in prospect and many were not at all keen on becoming involved. This gave us our only chance to strike a small blow for the Allied cause by giving Apomorphine, which makes you vomit, and medicines which cause diarrhoea, to any who wanted them.

While the Leros assault forces were building up, the Royal Navy bombarded Kalimnos harbour to the north of us. We watched the salvoes containing tracer shells curving across the night sky followed by explosions in the harbour area. The Allies also had a go at Kos town and harbour, where a few branches were knocked off the revered Hippocratic tree beneath which Hippocrates is said to have taught his pupils in ancient times. I seldom saw the unpleasant Prussian MO, who was at this time preoccupied with some Turkish girls he had found, while the Austrian was dealing with the wounded at the nuns' hospital in Kos town.

After several days of heavy fighting, which we could only speculate about, Leros was taken by the Germans. In addition to the infantry assault and exceptionally heavy bombing, there had been a drop of some 500 paratroopers, who had met such ferocious opposition that few survived to tell the tale. A landing craft filled with a hundred or more of the wounded was beached near our salt flats, and the casualties brought from there up to Marmari, where they were laid on straw spread over the church floor.

They lay in rows, dirty and dispirited, with blood-stained uniforms cut away to expose wounds, and some roughly bandaged; there had been no opportunity for more than perfunctory first aid. Some complained. Some, less seriously wounded, talked too much, thankful to have survived. Some were pale and ominously silent – exsanguinated, infected or with bad head wounds. All wanted water. It might have been a scene from the Napoleonic wars, with light through windows of the little church casting pools of sunshine on the dishevelled remains of the victors of Leros. A German NCO and I examined the shattered young bodies, some no more than eighteen years old. We dealt with those that were operable. But for many, unconscious from head wounds and with mangled limbs or multiple injuries caused by falling on rocks, made worse by the time lag since being wounded, there was little we could do.

Eventually, after several days, we had done all we could and had to resort to a frustrating existence of little work and progressively less food. But one evening, shortly before Christmas, our small party was loaded into a lorry and driven up the road to the airfield at Antimachia. Our guards scanned the skies for the Ju52 transport plane which was to take us off, but none came. Crestfallen, we had to return to Marmari. However, a few days later the aircraft finally appeared and we piled into it. We flew to Tatoi airfield in Greece, unchallenged, to our great relief, by the RAF Beaufighters from Cyprus which sometimes flew over the island. We spent the night in the guardroom at Tatoi with the German contingent, a noisy occasion due to the Christmas drink ration that they had just received – more expeditiously than the poor fellows on Kos, but I doubt if that worried them, or anyone else just then.

---

1   A method of sealing blood vessels by means of an electric charge delivered by needle.

From Here and There

CHAPTER TWELVE

The Fall of Samos

'You'll have to make other arrangements. I'm taking over HDML 1004.' The officer at the desk was senior to me. He stood up, moved some papers from the right side to the left, then abruptly sat down again. After a pause he picked up a pencil to sharpen it, laid it down with care in front of him, placed a ruler beside it, then a pen and paused again, darting sharp glances here and there, then up at me standing before him, then back to his papers.

He was clearly in a disturbed state of mind, and one couldn't altogether blame him. Leros had fallen the day before, and the softening up of Samos had begun. The bombers were concentrating on Port Vathy, in the north; but they'd soon be here over Pythagorion as well. Then would come the invasion barges and landing craft. He had no way of defending the port or his people. The 220-strong garrison of the island was to be evacuated, leaving him a sitting duck – a sitting buffoon, he must have felt. I could sympathize, but that didn't help me or Captain Moir Stormonth-Darling and his Long Range Desert Group patrol. One of our caiques had landed them on Mykonos, and they should have been picked up again nearly three weeks ago. But by some mischance – engine failure or stress of weather – two attempts had failed. So now I was on my way in a more powerful craft to make sure that the third attempt succeeded.

I moved to the window feeling embarrassment as well as sympathy. How rarely, I reflected, had we in the LSF been subjected to pressures like this. We felt safe and detached in our little boats, almost separate from the grander and more obvious aspects of war. Only once had I, returning from Naxos in LS8, been an actual target – and then it had been in error. It was on a calm night with a brilliant moon. We were lying throttled back off Alinda Bay, Leros, waiting for sunrise before venturing within range of the nervy Italian gunners. Suddenly a submarine surfaced less than 200 yards away to starboard, and next moment tracer from a heavy machine-gun came streaming across our bows. I rammed the tiller hard over, turning towards it, and dived down into the cabin for my uniform cap and jacket. Then a loud and raucous voice, which I remembered well from lively evenings in the

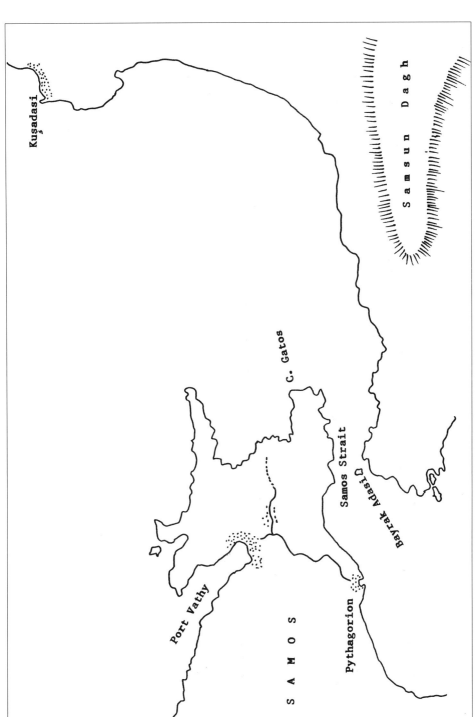

Map 11 Samos Strait.

wardroom of the submarine base on Manoel Island, Malta, boomed out over the loud-hailer 'What ship?' My relief was so overpowering that I let go with the most violent string of expletives I'd ever been sufficiently inspired to put together: 'What the blank, blank, blank and blanking blank are you playing at, Johnny Wraith? This is Levant Schooner LS8.' (Exchanging recognition signals would, I believe, have been less convincing.) Then HMS *Trooper* dived. And that, sadly, was the last I ever saw or heard of Johnny Wraith. *Trooper* struck a mine and was lost with all hands not long afterwards.

But now, standing there gazing out across Pythagorion harbour towards pine-clad hills and mountains, I remembered also how easy it had been for us, when fetching stores from Agios Marina on the south side of Alinda Bay, to note the exact direction in which a shallow-dive bomber was pointing to make his run, and move out of the way until he had passed. Back on the north shore among olive trees on a terraced hillside, where we had made our camp, we dozed and drank tea in peace all day, between night-time forays westwards into the Cyclades. The harsher conditions of war certainly seemed to have passed us by. I turned back to the desk, where the officer was still shuffling papers impatiently, hoping I'd go. I had to have one more try.

'The patrol on Mykonos are at the end of their tether, sir. They're right out of supplies, and German search parties are closing in. If we don't get them away tonight . . .'

'I can't help that,' he snapped, 'I've got my own people to think of . . . I've made a signal telling C-in-C what I'm doing. You'll have to find another boat.'

I wanted to suggest that *he* might find another boat. But I knew it wouldn't do any good, the man was desperate; so I left the office and went back aboard to collect my rucksack. My only hope now was a boat from one of the intelligence services – SOE or ISLD. My immediate need, therefore, was someone within reach who had sufficient authority to persuade one of those services to help me. The obvious answer was Commander Wolfson RNVR, head of naval intelligence at the British Embassy, Istanbul (known all over the Middle East as 'W'), who had played a major part in our Russian tankers[1] operation. Somehow I must get into Turkey and up to Istanbul; but in the general confusion which seemed to have descended on Samos, it was difficult at first to see how this could be done.

⋆   ⋆   ⋆

I set off inland on the road to Port Vathy in the hope of finding a vessel leaving for Kuşadasi, the nearest Turkish port of any importance. It was a lovely autumn day with a clear sky and very little wind. The brownish-green of the hillsides was relieved here and there by drifts of blue and yellow flowers. Clumps and twists of dark green oleander, some of it still bearing one or two late flowers, marked the courses of mountain streams. Spires of cypress stood singly or in groups along the way, with autumn scilla everywhere, and in the background the 3,700 ft Mount Ambelos cloaked in pine forest. My spirits rose as I trudged along the road, which now began to climb, winding its way towards a saddle between the foothills of Mount Ambelos and the mountains further east.

I had been on my way for about half an hour when I heard a truck rumbling up the hill behind me. It came roaring past in second gear and stopped a little way ahead. A grinning face with red cheeks and a black moustache poked out of the driver's window and called cheerily, 'Were you wanting a lift, sah?' It was A.G., an Army captain who had been attached to our Beirut base and was very much one of the gang. But something had gone wrong and here he was now, a private soldier driving a truck in Samos.

Nothing could have been more heartening than this meeting with an old friend, someone who was actually pleased to see me, at a time when I felt rejected, friendless, stripped of my command and driven into the wilderness, with responsibility still weighing heavily upon me for the rescue from enemy territory of men who depended absolutely on the LSF. I climbed aboard and we drove on up the hill, chatting happily about old times and mutual friends, until we reached the pass and stopped. A rough and very rocky road led off to the right here, to a village on the outskirts of Vathy itself, which covered the northern slopes from there to the sea. This road, I thought, might take me to a coastal village with boats that could carry me across the narrows to Turkey.

I said goodbye to A.G. and started up the side road, which became increasingly boulder-strewn as it climbed steeply between peasant houses towards a terraced slope covered with olive trees. Further on still I could see grey cliffs and pine trees. But now I halted. The growing sound of aircraft made me look to the right. Coming towards me in line astern, but with longish gaps between them, were four Ju88 bombers. I watched them carefully and saw that they would pass over the village higher up the hill. I waited nevertheless.

As the first stick of red and yellow bombs left the leading aircraft I could see them very plainly, falling among houses further up, and on down the northern slope into Vathy town and port. The next stick crossed the village closer to where I was standing, and the next stick closer still. I walked on quickly. The wind from the exploding bombs caused the dust to rise and blow about in the street, and my most vivid memory is of a woman dressed in black coming out of a house on my left, blonde hair blowing wild across her face as she screamed at the top of her voice for her little boy, a lad of seven or eight, who now came running up the street, laughing with pleasure and excitement, to be gathered up and carried into the house. The next stick of bombs fell behind us as I trudged on up the hill.

Soon I reached the olive groves, where the road petered out into a rough track leading towards a tree-filled gap in the grey cliffs. When I came to it and passed through, I found myself in one of the prettiest little mountain valleys imaginable – running from south-east to north-west, not more than 100 yards wide, with cliffs on either side and full of flowers. A fast-running stream, gabbling between bushes and boulders and patches of soft green grass, zigzagged over the valley floor.

I sat down with my back to the base of the near-side cliff. As I did so, a Ju88 appeared quite suddenly at the valley mouth to my right. He came through at eye level, not more than 30 ft above the ground. He passed me so close that his rear gunner saw me sitting there and waved. I can't imagine to this day why I waved back, but I did. It was an instinctive reaction, I suppose, but a shameful one, as he dived down low over Vathy to deal death and destruction among the people there.

I got up and walked to the valley mouth on my right, where the path ended abruptly at the top of a high cliff. About a thousand feet below me was the sea, glittering in the morning sun, and beyond it, across the Samos Strait, the imposing bulk of Samsun Dagh in Turkey. But nowhere was there any fishing village with boats which might lift me across that mile of sun-bathed sea. It was nevertheless a spectacular scene, and I stood gazing at it for several minutes. Then I walked back along the little valley and out on to a terraced slope, thickly clothed with olive trees, some of them massive and gnarled enough to be a thousand years old. The path I followed took me down from terrace to terrace. And it was on one of these that for the second time that day I came upon a sight which has remained with me vividly ever since. Lying stark and stiff and deadly white, his legs curled up behind him, lay an Italian officer in full uniform. He must, I thought, have died from heart failure, he was so cold and white. And not 10 yards from where he lay were two unexploded 100 lb bombs. If they had gone off they would have killed him anyway, but as it was, I'm sure, the poor fellow died of shock.

I walked on downhill. It was now late in the afternoon. The bombing appeared to be over for the day, and by the time I reached the waterfront it was evening. When I came to the quayside, I saw a familiar sight and my second meeting with an old friend that day; but this time it was a ship – LS9, our Flotilla supply ship – come into harbour to evacuate troops.

The sight of Robin Fletcher and his Greek skipper standing on her narrow transom almost brought tears to my eyes (photo 22). There was now hope, real hope, that Stormonth-Darling and his boys would not be abandoned after all. Robin was hard-pressed but happy, bringing soldiers aboard and crowding them into every corner of his ship's deck and hold. I crept into the angle between the port side bulwarks and the break of the transom. There I curled up with my rucksack for a pillow. It was a warm night with a light south-westerly breeze. The sea was calm, and I was soon asleep.

★   ★   ★

22 'The sight of Robin Fletcher, with his Greek skipper, standing on her narrow transom . . .'

Robin Fletcher describes his part in these events as follows:

The 130-ton schooner *Agios Ioannis* (now LS9), spirited away more than a year ago from Samos by its courageous skipper and crew (photo 23), was working her slow and dignified way back up the coast of Asia Minor towards that very same island. Converted into a supply ship for the Levant Schooner Flotilla and carrying on board stores intended for caiques operating in the Aegean from their base in Alinda Bay, she had on board a Greek crew, an assortment of Allied service men, two journalists and myself as Naval Officer In Charge.

As we crossed the Gulf of Güllük bound for Port Vathy, we could see flashes of gunfire on our port beam and hear the crump of exploding bombs. The battle for Leros was on. What, I wondered, were the thoughts in the mind of our skipper as he returned to a Greek island in circumstances so different from when he had left it. Antonios Tsoutos

23   The crew of our HQ-and-supply schooner, LS9, with her coxswain, Leading Seaman White RN (top right).

was a small stocky man, untypically reserved. An occasional smile revealed a row of gold teeth, but the expression on his face gave nothing away as he sat cross-legged on the transom, his eyes fixed on landmarks ahead, his podgy hands holding the ropes controlling our enormous oak tiller.

Port Vathy is reached through a long inlet with steep cliffs on either side. We remained there, anchored close to the quay, for two whole days, while a strong Meltemi from the north-west whipped up a considerable sea, causing the timbers of *Agios Ioannis* to creak and groan as she yawed this way and that at her anchor. Along the quayside and in the offices behind there was little activity; an atmosphere of suspense, of waiting upon events, seemed to have descended upon the whole town and its surroundings.

On the third day the wind died and the sun came out. The boy Stamatis rowed me ashore, and I was interested to find there a remarkable change in scene and atmosphere. There was a great hustle and bustle of trucks, jeeps and hurrying men up and down the quayside; and, to my surprise, the military offices which had seemed so sleepy two days before were humming with life. When my own orders came through, they told me that Leros had fallen to the Germans and air attacks must be expected at any moment. I was to leave after dark and proceed to the nearest point on the Turkish coast, there to await further instructions.

Next morning, anchored close to the Turkish shore, we could see the Stukas circling over Port Vathy before diving to release their bombs, and the Ju88s coming up from Kos to glide in over the hills on to their targets. The attacks came over in waves. The crump of exploding bombs was unnaturally loud in the silence of our peaceful surroundings. It was depressing that there was no answering fire.

That afternoon we were ordered to return to Port Vathy after dark and tie up alongside, ready to embark troops. So for the last time, until happier days brought her back, *Agios Ioannis* chugged her way into a Greek harbour. Antonios let go the anchor and went slow astern with the skill of long experience; the boy Stamatis leapt ashore with the mooring lines, one after the other. Then we lowered and made fast the rickety gangway.

It was very dark. We couldn't see the damage caused by the Stukas and Ju88s, but we could just make out a crowd of silent figures forming ranks on the quayside. One by one they began to climb the gangway. I found myself next to one who, by the orders he was giving, must have been an officer. He had to be reminded (rather sharply, I fear) that the giving of orders aboard LS9 was my responsibility. Later I learned that he was a brigadier, but he made no protest and vanished.

Standing at the head of the gangway, I sent each soldier forward, telling him to fill whatever space he could find, leaving no pockets. The queue seemed endless, but at last the quayside was empty. Somehow or other room had been found above and below decks for more than two hundred men. Then the gangway was brought aboard, our mooring lines cast off, the anchor weighed and we headed for the open sea.

From Port Vathy we steered east-north-east for Kuşadasi, my main concern now being the possible presence of E-boats in the offing. Soldiers were packed shoulder to shoulder all over the main deck and hatches, so I had to pass my instructions by word of mouth for those at the bulwarks to load whatever small arms they carried and be ready to open fire when ordered.

There *were* in fact E-boats on the prowl that night; but they were lurking off the south coast of the island, ready to intercept vessels endeavouring to escape in that direction. My orders to the troops had one tragic consequence, however: a loaded revolver placed on a hatch rolled off with the motion of the ship and, on hitting the deck, fired a round which struck one of the soldiers. The men were so tightly packed that the only way I could reach the scene of the accident was outboard, with my hands on the rail and my feet feeling their way along the 4 in wide rubbing strake. But by the time I had barged myself inboard again through the mêlée to where he lay, the soldier had died.

We edged slowly and warily into Kuşadası harbour, anchored there and waited. It was daylight before there were any signs of movement ashore; then a platoon of Turkish soldiers marched down and halted on the quay. Next a launch full of officials came on board, but soon left again. We waited for another hour, when the officials returned with orders for the troops to disembark *without* their rifles or side arms, which must be left on board. The men were to be sent south via Syria and Lebanon by train, and looked very cheerful at the prospect. LS9, we were told, must remain at anchor.

The poor fellow who'd been shot was landed in our own boat; then we set about cleaning up the debris, stowed the weapons in the hold and waited . . . and waited . . . and waited. No one took any notice of us, no guard was posted, and when I rowed ashore to the harbour office to find out what plans the authorities had for us, I was simply ignored. When I tried to speak to them in French, they smiled or giggled and turned away. They probably couldn't speak a word of any language but Turkish.

Night came on. The Greeks rustled up a bit of supper, mostly tinned stuff, but there were three bottles of a very palatable red wine, which I'd found on my expedition ashore; so we didn't hurry over the meal. In fact it became a bit of a carousal, with songs and bazouki music and, in the end, a lively Greek dance on the main hatch; till at last when there was still no sign or sound from the shore, feeling triumphantly defiant and patriotic, we weighed and put to sea, heading for the Samos Strait and points south.

$\star$　　$\star$　　$\star$

I shared with Robin his first sad duty. We carried the dead soldier ashore and left him in the hands of the British Military Attaché, who had come down to arrange for onward passage of our troops. In the absence of his naval counterpart, he felt unable to approach the harbour authorities on Robin's behalf; he did, however, bring me a message from 'W', who had been informed of the situation by Cairo. As a result I was driven to Egrilar, a small port south-west of Izmir, where an RAF high speed launch (HSL) was stationed ready to rescue aircrew who had ditched or been shot down over the Aegean. Also on board her, when I arrived, was an LRDG sergeant, who would be able to identify Stormonth-Darling and his lads when we found them.

As soon as it grew dark, we slipped from the buoy and roared away into the night. The distance from Egrilar to the south coast of Mykonos is about 75 miles, which could have been covered by a caique in about twelve hours and by an HDML in eight. It took our HSL less than two.

The moon in its last quarter hung low over the hills as we entered a bay on the south coast of Mykonos, flashing the recognition signal for the day on a blue-shaded torch. The men ashore must have been surprised to see a speedboat instead of a caique or motor launch and were understandably suspicious. Their W/T batteries having long since run out, they hadn't heard about the most recent pick-up plan. So after making the correct reply to our challenge, they added '. . . And who the hell are you?'

The number of the HSL and the sergeant's name were flashed back and seemed to satisfy them, because a short while later we saw three folboats driving towards us down the moonpath. But just to make sure of their identity the sergeant bawled out, 'That you, Stormy?'

Some humorist replied in a falsetto voice and an exaggeratedly Oxford accent, '*Mr* bleedin' Stormy to you, sergeant,' and next moment the first folboat dropped alongside. The others followed, and all three boats were hauled aboard in a matter of seconds. Then the HSL's engines exploded into life, and away we roared to the north-east.

Sudden release from tension affects people in different ways. These boys, after three whole weeks of unrelieved anxiety, dodging about the mountains to avoid German patrols – with two devastating blows when pick-up caiques failed to reach them – must at times have been close to despair. Local Greeks had risked their lives to keep them informed of enemy movements, but not always in time. On several occasions they were nearly caught, and when the HSL found them at last, they were – as I had told the officer in Pythagorion – almost at the end of their tether.

Their relief now manifested itself in all sorts of ways, from long-drawn-out streams of violent obscenities to humorous backchat and joyous greeting. One youngster sat all by himself in silence, I think close to tears. I kept in the background, and I doubt if any of them knew I was there. The LSF had done its best, but in the end had little or nothing to do with their escape. My relief at seeing them safe at last was nevertheless as great almost as theirs.

It wasn't quite midnight when we arrived back at Egrilar. A British consular officer was there to meet the patrol and drive them away. But I decided, now the pressure was off, that it was time for a break. So after a few hours' sleep aboard the HSL I made my way by hired car up to Denizi and the small dockside hotel where they remembered me from the year before. I booked myself in for five days.

The girl behind the bar, who spoke English, said, 'We have no whisky any more. Will raki do?'

'Well, actually,' I said, 'what I long for is a large pot of Lyons tea and some ginger biscuits.'

I was being facetious, of course. It was rather a rest cure to be a bit silly and not have to regret it. Anyway she didn't really know what I meant by ginger biscuits; but later that day a packet of them arrived with a note from Gareth Evans, our vice-consul in Izmir, which ended with 'Glad you're back. There's something I'd like to speak to you about.'

Gareth had his spies everywhere and he was nothing if not an opportunist. 'Watching points', they sometimes call it.

---

[1]   Piloting Russian tankers escaping through the enemy blockade of the Aegean; see *No Stars to Guide* (Hodder & Stoughton, 1947).

CHAPTER THIRTEEN

Settled in Silence

I woke to bright sunlight streaming in at a side window of my room, and when I looked out I saw that it was going to be a brilliant day. Great! I'd have my coffee and omelette down at one of the quayside tables and watch the fishermen mending nets and working in their boats.

Stormonth-Darling and his boys had been taken over by the Consulate at Izmir for onward routing to Palestine and Egypt. I had been driven to Denizi, where I found my old room waiting for me at the little harbour hotel and a note from Gareth Evans to say he'd be contacting me. I wondered what was in his mind and rather hoped that he'd take a while to work it out; I felt like a few days' 'stand easy', and here at Denizi, where I knew some of the fishermen – and, of course, Yanni – would be as pleasant a place as any.

While I was on my third cup of coffee I saw Gareth's boatman hauling the Office[1] motor cruiser alongside and getting aboard. He busied himself for a while mopping down, bailing out a little and generally pottering. Then Gareth himself came sauntering by. He perched for a moment on the other chair at my table.

'What about a spin in the cruiser?' he suggested casually.

'Where to?'

'Have you ever seen Ayvalik?'

'You know I have. I was there with *Oilshipper*. One of the prettiest harbours on this coast.'

'Certainly is . . . so let's take a run up there, shall we?'

It was past noon when we slipped and stood away north up the coast, the boatman at the wheel under the spray hood, Gareth and I in the cockpit. It was hot. There was no wind, and the water was glassy in the Egri Liman Channel, with here and there a patch of roughening where a shoal of grey mullet came nibbling to the surface. But out in the open, north of Kara Burnu, the sea breeze had come in, and set us bouncing. I was glad then of the sweater and sports jacket I'd brought with me.

It was close on sunset when we came at last to the narrow pass between a high steep-sided island and the mainland, opening into the broad land-locked sheet of water which is Ayvalik Liman. The white houses of a small town were spread along the opposite shore. They were backed by low and partly wooded hills; and on their southern side, standing among olive groves, were a few isolated villas and beach houses. We turned in that

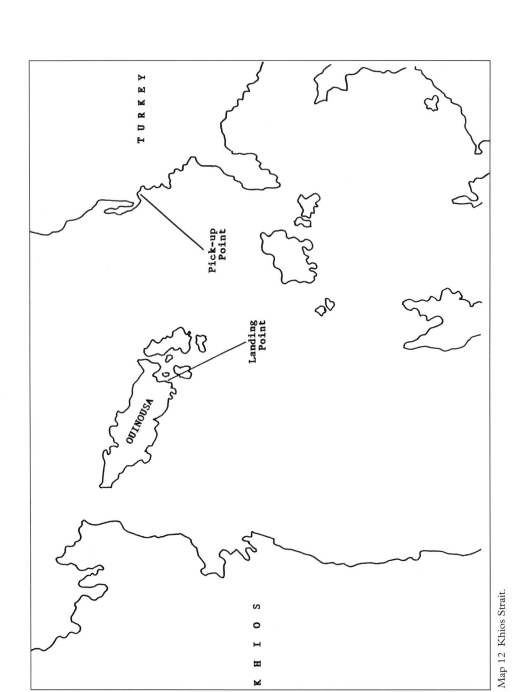

Map 12 Khios Strait.

direction and moored to a wooden jetty, with the tables of an attractive little restaurant dotted about the slope behind. Gareth and I sat down at one of these, and he called for raki and the menu.

'What'll you have?' he asked, when they came. But I hardly heard him. I was staring transfixed at the girl who brought them. It was not just that she was beautiful, with copper-tinted hair, pale skin, fine features and greenish eyes; it was the expression in those eyes – leopard's eyes, half closed yet sensuous and piercing – that held me.

She was a tall girl, with a slender, willowy body, emphasized by a close-fitting green cotton dress. And her hands . . . I think they were the most sensitive hands I had ever seen, with fingers that seemed to caress anything they touched, the glasses, plates, a knife, a spoon, the taper she used to light two candles on our table, as though it were the finest brush for painting on porcelain.

I came to myself and saw that Gareth had tired of waiting. It was growing dark. He pointed to three items on the menu and handed it back to the girl. She took it without a word and disappeared.

★   ★   ★

I don't remember what we ate – some sort of kebab, I think, with rice and aubergine – because what Gareth had to say was astonishing.

'I want you to land someone on Oinoussa,' he said, 'on your own . . . no one else.'

'What for?'

'You don't need to know that.'

'But why me? Can't your usual boats . . .?'

'You know already . . . you must have heard . . . that something's wrong on Oinoussa. Someone, I don't know who, and don't want to know, has been talking. Look,' he said, becoming impatient, 'I've got a first-class team, doing good work. I don't want to rock the boat by asking one of them to spy on another. I just want something settled, once and for all.'

He pulled out a sheet of tracing paper, on which he'd outlined the Oinoussa group of islands and nearby shores of Kara Burnu and Khios. 'Are you going to help me?'

'OK . . . if one of my old friends will lend me a boat.'

'Try Osman.'

'Yes. He's an obliging sort of chap.'

'Tomorrow evening, then? At nine-thirty?'

'All right.'

'Then you'll pick up here . . .' He pointed to a small bay close south of Egri Liman, '. . . And land somewhere here, depending on the wind.' He showed me a cove on the eastern end of Oinoussa with a tiny islet just off it. 'Then wait near this islet for the signal – the letter Q in groups of three, repeated continuously.'

'And how shall I know whoever it is you're sending with me?' He'd taken care not to mention any names, so I didn't ask for any.

'They'll show you this.' He picked up the menu from the next table, drew a rough fish on it and showed it to me. Then he got up and went into the restaurant to pay. When he came out, we left at once.

★ ★ ★

People always smile or wink when you want to borrow a flat or a car or a boat for an evening – which was as good an alibi for me as any other. All I had to do was to give Osman, the owner of one of the fishing caiques, a bottle of raki and ask for the loan of his motor boat till midnight, and look embarrassed when he nudged the chap he was drinking with and grinned. But he was a good friend, and spent quite a time showing me where everything was, and standing by while I warmed up the engine.

I was early at the rendezvous, but I didn't have to wait long before there were 'Qs' from a blue-shaded signal torch blinking at me from the beach. I ran the boat up on to the shingle and jumped down from her bow with the painter. Then I shone my masked torch on to the shadowy figure coming down the beach towards me. It was the girl from Ayvalik. She stood there impassive but watchful, dressed in a trouser suit of some dark material, her coppery hair caught up into a floppy beret. Her right hand was thrust down into the pocket of a greenish calf-length raincoat. In the left she held out to me the menu on which Gareth had drawn his fish.

I was so astonished at first that I simply stared at her. Then she shook the paper impatiently, bringing me to my senses. I took it from her and she clambered aboard, seating herself on the forward thwart. I shoved off and climbed in after her. Then I put the engine, which I'd left idling, into gear and headed out to sea. She sat facing aft. A sliver of moon had risen over the Turkish hills astern of us. It shone on her face, expressionless as ever, eyes narrowed, one hand still in her raincoat pocket, the other in her lap.

'Good evening,' I said.

There was no reply.

'Bonsoir.'

Still no sign of understanding. I thought she might be Greek. '*Kale spera.*'

She looked away, then half turned to face forward. I gave up and went back to a closer study of the chart which lay folded, and folded again, on the transom seat beside me.

I had the engine running at half speed, so as to make as little noise as possible. It therefore took us nearly an hour to reach the channel between Nisis Pasha and the main island. After that another fifteen minutes brought us to the cove Gareth had shown me.

I headed in slowly and rather gingerly, hoping to find a convenient landing place for the girl, and was just coasting along close in to some rocks when, all at once, she stood up, put one foot on the gunwale and leapt. The gap must have been all of 5 ft wide, but she made it, landing light as a mayfly on a spur of rock. Next moment she was gone.

I motored across to the islet, dropped a grapnel on a $1^{1}/_{2}$ in line and waited. It was a still night with the faintest of westerly breezes, bringing the distant sound of taverna music out to me in waves. Half an hour must have passed when I thought I heard a shot – a small sound, high pitched; it might have been the cracking of a branch quite close to me – it's difficult to tell at night, except that I knew there weren't any trees on that end of the island. Then two more shots rang out. Unmistakable this time – high pitched cracks, as from a small automatic.

I was on the alert now, but the shots were not repeated. I settled down to wait, watching the shore and the hillside above it. After a bit I brought my grapnel aboard, so as to be ready to take immediate action when . . .

There was the signal – the letter Q three times, and again, and again. I was closing the rocks now, and saw her, ready to jump. There was a shout from the ridge behind her. She jumped. I slammed the engine into gear and opened the throttle. A shot rang out, but it must have been well wide. And now we were out in the channel and surging along at our full 6 knots.

The girl was sitting on the forward thwart, as before, completely still and silent. I couldn't think of anything useful to say. She'd obviously been up to something that was no business of mine and all I really wanted was to get her safely back and be done with the whole business. Even so, as we approached the Turkish shore I couldn't resist shining my torch on her for a moment. Her face was expressionless as ever. The only difference in her pose was that she now had both hands folded in her lap, half open and at rest.

★   ★   ★

It was some time before I met Gareth again, down in Cairo, soon after the Greek Armed Forces mutiny which dislocated our lives and all our plans for a while. When we were alone I asked him for a bit of background to the escapade he got me involved in.

'There isn't much more I can tell you, and you know there isn't,' he said with a frown.

'What about that girl, then? I couldn't get a word out of her.'

'I'm not surprised. She's deaf and dumb.'

He must have seen the horrified look on my face, because he went on. 'As you know, we'd had disturbing reports from Oinoussa. One of your chaps made one.'

'About our fellows being betrayed?'

'Yes. So I needed someone absolutely secure to put things right – secure from my own team especially.' He paused, looking thoughtful. 'She's gone back to the Balkans. Her father and brother are Chetniks . . . some people say bandits. I think she feels safer with them.'

'But has she always been that way?'

'No. When she was fourteen, she and her mother were gang-raped by a bunch of soldiers, and her mother was killed. She's been speechless ever since.'

---

[1]   All embassy, consular and intelligence staff working under the diplomatic umbrella came to be referred to collectively as 'Office'. The motor cruiser was mostly used for picnics and such like.

CHAPTER FOURTEEN

A Set of Four

Lassen VC

Captain Anders Lassen VC, MC,[1] was, I think, the first, perhaps the only, foreigner ever to be awarded the Victoria Cross. Sadly, it was a posthumous award. But when I knew him he was a very beautiful young Dane, slightly built, with fair hair and piercing blue eyes. He led one of the raiding patrols we used to land among the Greek Islands to attack enemy shipping, garrisons and airfields, which had already earned him an MC with three bars.

Naturally, therefore, the background to a portrait of Andy will be filled in with glimpses of the light-hearted (and sometimes deadly) piracy that went on for nearly two years in those waters – where, to quote the rather dispirited letter of a German garrison commander to his superior officer (a letter we captured) 'the British come like cats and disappear like ghosts'. 'The British' he was referring to were Andy, his corporal (also, unorthodoxly, his personal servant) and six or eight other men of his patrol.

In character Andy was a fascinating mixture – quiet, sensitive, poetic at times and deeply sentimental, especially about children and dogs. He took with him everywhere a miserable little woolly-coated cur he had picked up in a back street of Beirut; it was mangy and bug-ridden and smelt abominably – by no means a pleasant shipmate in a 26 ft sailing boat, already crammed with men, stores and ammunition, on a ten-day voyage, creeping from island to island under cover of night, hiding under camouflage nets among the rocks by day. But it had pathetic eyes, and Andy refused ever to be separated from it.

On the other hand he was brave, possessed of a calm, deadly, almost horrifying courage, bred of a 'berserk' hatred of the Germans who had overrun his country and murdered two close and well loved relatives. He was a killer too, cold and ruthless – silently with the knife or at point blank range with pistol or rifle. On such occasions there was a froth of bubbles round his lips and his eyes went dead as stones.

Only once did I ever hear Andy raise his voice. We were lying hidden in a small cove on the island of Khalki, waiting to embark Andy and his patrol after a raid on a nearby harbour. Suddenly we heard the beat of an engine and, from the same direction, shouts, rising to screeches at times. We thought the game was up and prepared to repel boarders. But it was Andy.

He had captured a German boat and all her crew and was motoring round in her to the rendezvous. He was in a berserk rage – not with the cowed Germans, some of whom were wounded, but with his corporal, who had accidentally shot him in the leg.

We towed the motor boat back to our base in a Turkish fjord. Andy was in a great state of nerves; he refused to report sick, not because he wanted to make light of his wound (he was terrified of personal illness of any sort), but because he was afraid his corporal might get into trouble and be posted. He couldn't bear the idea of losing such a close friend and comrade in arms.

Andy also sailed with Noël Clegg, who tells of an afternoon when . . .

'We were still in Turkish waters, cruising down the Gulf of Kos in brilliant sunshine. Andy was sitting on the starboard side of the transom seat oiling his revolver. I came aft to discuss rendezvous arrangements, squatting on the deck in front of him with my back against the cabin bulkhead.

As we talked he went on industriously cleaning his weapon, and when he had finished he pulled the trigger a couple of times, to make sure that everything was in working order. He pulled the trigger the third time when, to everyone's surprise, it fired a round, which passed through the bulkhead and ricocheted around the cabin, scaring the pants off our "Sparker" who was down there listening to the afternoon routine from Cairo. I went below to make sure he was OK. When I came back on deck I found Andy, a thoughtful expression on his face, examining the bullet hole in the cabin bulkhead.

"Sit down, Noël," he said to me, "just vere you vas sitting."

I did so as well as I could, whereupon Andy took a pencil from the outer breast pocket of his tunic and ran it round my head and shoulders, tracing their outline on the bulkhead, and "Look at dis," he said.

I got to my knees and looked round. Andy's pencil trace passed within two inches of the bullet hole, at about the level of my right ear.

"You vas lucky," said Andy with a grin.

"Was it luck?" I said, trying to smile back. And to this day, knowing Andy's volatile and largely unpredictable temperament, I can't be quite certain that it was in fact an accident and not just Andy's way of keeping us all on our toes and ready for anything.'

★   ★   ★

When not on operations, Andy was scatter-brained and harum-scarum, usually penniless and, owing to his really god-like beauty and quiet devil-may-care manner, extremely attractive to women.

One morning he turned up at our base in Beirut in a great state of nerves. He was trembling, his face was white and his four front teeth (false – the result of a fight the year before) were missing. He couldn't remember where he had been the night before. But he was certain now that he'd swallowed his teeth and would die. He insisted on being X-rayed. He was as terrified as a schoolgirl.

While Andy was up at the sick bay, a smartly turned out and very deferential Arab servant, in fez and jellaba, arrived at the base with a small tissue-paper parcel. In it were Andy's teeth. They had been found under a pillow – quite the wrong pillow from a diplomatic point of view; there might have been international repercussions at a high level throughout the Middle East if the *wrong person* had found Andy's teeth.

But there was nothing, absolutely nothing, Andy couldn't or wouldn't do – swimming out to an enemy tanker anchored off the Cameroons and putting plastic explosive on her cable so that she would drift out to sea and fall into the hands of one of our submarines waiting there; walking round an enemy airfield, dropping hand grenades into the cockpits of a dozen or more aircraft parked there, then escaping by joining the German patrol which rushed out into the darkness to search for the attacker. His determination and enthusiasm for adventure – indeed for life – were only matched, in the end, by his enthusiasm for death.

Machine-gun posts and pill-boxes were holding up the Allied advance along a causeway through the marshes of Lake Comacchio, in Italy. Andy and his patrol were sent to silence them. They took two of the positions and were then confronted by a more formidable-looking blockhouse. Then, in the words of one of his men:

> Andy shouted to them in German to surrender. He was a ruthless man, but not brutal, and would sometimes offer a chance to surrender. Somebody shouted 'Kamarad'. So he stood up from the small rise we were using for cover, telling us to stay put, while he went forward in the darkness. As he neared the blockhouse there was a burst of machine-gun fire and then silence.
>
> When we got to him, he said, 'I'm going to die. It's no good. Look after the others. Get them out.' Then he collapsed unconscious, and when we got him to cover he was dead.

That brief account always affects me. Not only because I knew and admired Andy. But my own brother, Oliver, was killed in Northern France in the last few days of the war in Europe, in exactly the same way.

Restraint of Princes

Once you've learnt the way of the sea, there's a wonderful feeling of security about a sailor's life. He's safe from plague and pestilence, from the sins of yesterday and tomorrow's temptations. He's safe from himself, and above all – in the picturesque language of the old mercantile charter party – he's safe on the high seas from 'restraint of princes, rulers, peoples . . .'

In the LSF we used to land soldiers to attack a German or Italian

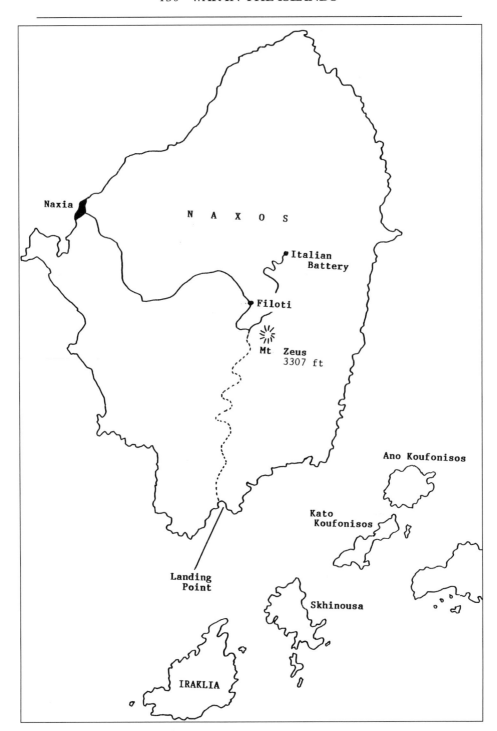

Map 13 Reconnaissance on Naxos.

garrison, and then cruise off on our own to lie up, or keep watch on enemy shipping. It was a wonderful life, in the sun and sheltered seas. But sad at times. Greek people have that extraordinary quality – not only of courage, but of complete abandon to an idea and, of course, an absolute certainty about the rightness and importance of their way of life on those brown, burnt rocks with white villages set in a fierce blue sea.

Many of them were starving, and we had to watch them starve; unless by chance we had just stored ship and had some food to spare. And yet, if ever we were seen, the islanders would come flocking with gifts and offers of hospitality . . . and talk about it afterwards, of course. Till eventually the Germans heard. Then there'd be hostages taken, and many shot. It happened repeatedly, so we tried to avoid the Greeks whenever possible.

Sometimes it wasn't possible; an island had to be visited and a reconnaissance made. I remember one on Naxos in the Cyclades, soon after Italy surrendered. The Aegean was fairly quiet just then – Italian garrisons like the one on Naxos had taken to the hills, and only a few German raiding parties were left to range about from island to island, bullying the people and stealing their food. Our job was to find out all we could about one of these, which was known to be working in the southern Cyclades; so an hour before dawn one morning we slipped into a cove on the southern side of Naxos and moored to some rocks, under camouflage nets, close to the shore.

★　★　★

I landed and scrambled up a steep hillside out of the cove; but I couldn't find any track in the darkness, and loose stones kept rattling down on to the rocks below me. Then a dog started barking, so I crouched in the bushes to wait for daylight. When it came, I saw a small farmstead beside a nearby stream.

I set off towards it, but had not gone far before a boy with red hair and freckles came out to meet me, leading a donkey. He spoke no English and I no Greek, so we stood smiling at each other for a while; then he motioned me to get on to the donkey and we started off along a rough track towards Filoti village, in the centre of the island.

Our journey took several hours through wild and mountainous country (photo 24). On the way we met groups of peasants, who rushed forward to shake hands, or even hug and kiss me when they knew I was British (photo 25). I was more worried than embarrassed by these performances. There's something rather majestic about a sailor on a donkey – I mean a big fat sailor, who has had a few drinks and doesn't mind making a fool of himself to amuse the crowd; but I was neither big nor fat and could only make trouble for these people. Besides, if trouble came they would see that I got away all right, while they, bound to their homes and families and their hills – what could they do?

24 '. . . through wild and mountainous country.'

25 'On the way we met groups of peasants . . .'

However, we came to Filoti at last, and I was relieved to hear that the Germans hadn't yet reached the island; so for the time being everyone was safe.

My visit followed the usual pattern. The mayor of Filoti – a tough-looking peasant with piercing black eyes and a great moustache curled up at the ends – took me to his house. A dozen others, men and women, crowded into the living room after us. The mayor's mother, dressed in black, with a black shawl over her head, hovered in the background watching me anxiously. And while we talked a young girl (about fourteen, I guessed) came in with eggs and oatcakes and a dish of olives. She'd got herself up in a flowered dress and silk stockings with high-heeled shoes which made her look strangely out of place in those peasant surroundings.

I wasn't hungry, but they insisted passionately that I should eat – the mayor, the girl in her gallant and rather moving finery (she had rouge and lipstick on her face as well) and all the others, nodding and smiling behind them. So I ate the food, and then began to ask questions.

'Are there any Italians here?'

The mayor pointed up into the mountains.

'Have they joined the Germans now that Italy's surrendered?'

'They fear them, they are very few.'

'And the German raiding parties? Have you heard about them?'

'A little.'

'How big are they?'

The mayor made a sweeping gesture which didn't tell me much.

'How many ships?'

He shrugged his shoulders, looking uncomfortable. Obviously he didn't want to talk, and I hadn't the heart to press him. In fact I'd almost decided to give up, when a young man burst in, gabbling excitedly. I heard the old mother draw in her breath. Then she rushed to a cupboard and brought out some maize wrapped in a cloth – all they had left, I dare say. She looked round wildly for somewhere to hide it. The others dispersed quickly. The mayor pointed through the window towards a low hill not far away.

'From there you will see,' he said, 'they have just arrived.'

We went out – the mayor, the donkey boy and I – and crossed the valley through groves of olive trees to the foot of the hill (photo 26). The sky was overcast and spitting with rain, so we climbed at a good pace up the stony slopes. When we reached the top, we lay down and I got out my binoculars. Below us the slopes curved gently down through scrub and pine trees to the sea. A strip of cultivated land with olives and carob trees ran along the coast as far as the town and port of Naxia, at the north-west corner of the island. I focused my glasses on the harbour and found the answers to most of my questions. A large landing craft was moored to the jetty, with two patrol boats at anchor nearby. Men and vehicles were coming ashore and disappearing into the town. We guessed there were a couple of hundred troops and that their first objective would be the Italians in the mountains.

We made off downhill again, and were approaching the outskirts of the

26 '. . . through olive groves to the foot of the hill.'

village (photo 27) when we heard the first vehicles coming up the road from Naxia. The Greeks stopped and glanced at me nervously. They were too proud, or too polite, to say anything; but I saw what they meant, so I took off my uniform cap and put it behind me. In my khaki shirt without shoulder straps, and grey flannel trousers, I looked like one of them. We went on and had just reached the main road when a German staff car, with two officers in greatcoats, came roaring through the village followed by a truck full of soldiers. As they tore past, we could see the sullen expressions on the men's faces, sitting in stiff rows, hands on knees, staring at the grey napes of each other's necks.

The mayor raised his cap and bowed. I thought I'd better do the same. One of the German officers glanced down as they passed and raised an arm in the Nazi salute. We gave a loud 'Hurrah!', but they took no notice, and next moment they were gone, with the white dust curling after them.

And now it was time for me to go too – as fast as possible, for all our sakes. The boy found his donkey, and we started off towards the mountains. For a mile or two we followed the dry bed of a stream through plantations of fruit trees and olives (photo 28). Then the track began to climb, and after about an hour we reached a saddle at the head of the valley. We looked back, but no one was stirring in Filoti, so on we went.

27 '. . . approaching the outskirts of the village . . .'

The track grew narrower and very rough, following the contours of the mountain. On one side the ground fell steeply away; on the other, grey cliffs reached up into the clouds. We came to a jutting spur from which we could see the trail snaking down into the valley behind us; suddenly, as we watched, a figure in field-grey uniform came out of the trees, climbing steadily up the track. I looked at the donkey boy. He was singing, as Greeks often do in the mountains. When I pointed at the man below, he only shrugged and went on singing. We plodded on, the donkey picking its way between the stones with maddening delicacy, round the shoulder of the hill and out on to the next spur. When I looked back again, the man behind us was less than a mile away and gaining fast. But that wasn't all, because behind him we could now see another man, in civilian clothes, also following us into the hills.

Well, you know, there are all sorts of rules in a situation like that; but I doubt if any of them really work. The true crux of the matter is 'when' rather than 'what' – *when* do you turn round and force a show-down? For form's sake I pulled an old Webley .45 out of my pack. But this only added embarrassment to anxiety. Because if there's one thing more ridiculous than a sailor climbing a mountain sitting on a donkey, it's a sailor climbing a mountain sitting on a donkey and waving a bloody great revolver which he's never fired in his life.

28 '. . . through plantations of fruit trees and olives.'

However, I won't drag out the agony. The first man caught up with us about a mile further on and turned out to be one of the local police constables – who also wore field-grey uniforms like German soldiers – and far from wanting to arrest me, he wanted to come with me. Then he pointed at the second figure, who was still a good way off, and said, with a touch of pride in his voice: 'Sergeant – Chief of Police'.

Night was coming on when we reached the cove. The sergeant joined us while we were waiting for the caique, and I was relieved to hear that he didn't want to join us as well; we were pretty crowded on board. Instead he produced a notebook, and in passable English (remembered, I dare say, from some boyhood visit to a mainland cinema) he said, 'Name and address, please?' And I just can't tell you how strange and almost thrilling it sounded – at dusk and miles from anywhere, on a mountainside in Greece.

'Name and address, please.' His expression and his polite but determined manner were perfect. Even the way he licked his pencil was just right. I could have hugged him, but he wouldn't have understood. Instead, I took his notebook and wrote down in block capitals 'MAE WEST, THE WHITE HOUSE, WASHINGTON'. Then the constable and I said goodbye and clambered down on to the foreshore. Ten minutes

29 'At sea, in our boats, we were safe as houses . . .'

later our caique stole out of the cove and stood south over a darkening sea.

The sergeant and the boy watched us go, together but a little apart, as befitted their stations. They grew smaller against the hills, which loomed behind them, massive with dusk and distance. The boy waved once. The sergeant saluted. He looked absurd in his brown civvy suit without a hat, and very brave. Till at last the night and the hills swallowed them.

*   *   *

We never went back to Naxos, to find out what became of them there. But one small incident gave us hope – for the sergeant anyway. When the Germans found out any of our names, they sometimes made capital of the fact in their local broadcasts. It was always the same old formula. You know . . . 'subversive elements under Allied orders attempted a landing on Naxos yesterday. They were repulsed due to the vigilance of the island's police force. The only casualty was one constable missing, believed captured' or words to that effect in Greek. And then, in dark and hollow tones, in English, 'Do not vorry, Mr Vest. Ve are ready for you. Ve vill get you next time, Mr Vest. Do not vorry!'

And of course we didn't. At sea, in our boats, we were safe as houses (photo 29) – much safer, really, in those bomb-happy times.

Moments of Decision

The south side of the island of Yioura, in the Cyclades, is rocky and bare, falling steeply into the sea from close on a thousand feet. There are no coves or inlets, except in one place where a small creek – little more than a cleft in the rock wall – forms the mouth of a narrow ravine. Just before dawn one day in 1943 we crept in and secured, with mast down and anchors out to hold us off the rocks. Then camouflage nets were hauled over, and when the sun rose the caique had 'disappeared'.

Throughout the day we took it in turns to keep watch from a small cave overlooking the entrance, while the others stripped off and lay down, stark naked, wherever they could under the nets. My turn was from eleven to two. It was very hot, and as the day wore on the sun beat mercilessly against the bare brown and yellow hillside, till it hurt one's eyes to look at it. Meltemi, the north wind, could not reach us; its bundles of white cloud, pouring over the cliff top high above us, dissolved at once in shreds and tatters. Little puffs of dust and the rattle of stones told of a family of goats picking its patient way across the screes.

One or two high-flying German aircraft passed over, and once an Italian motor torpedo-boat thundered by about a mile offshore. They posed no threat because our caique, under her rock-patterned nets, rigged on long bamboo spreaders to break the line of her hull, had become invisible. Even from where I crouched in the cave mouth it was difficult to make her out.

One of her Vickers guns was propped up on stones beside me. I reflected idly on the incongruities of war: if an enemy patrol approached, at what moment should I open fire with this puny weapon, giving our position away? And if Greek peasants stumbled on us, what then?

About an hour later I found out. A small rowing boat appeared round a nearby headland. There were five people in her, four youngsters and an older man, fishing for crabs and octopus among the rocks. I watched them working slowly down the coast towards us. When they came to the mouth of our creek they seemed to hesitate, then crept forward again, and I saw a lad in the bow stand up. They'd evidently seen something strange but weren't sure what it was, and in wartime anything strange can be frightening.

I heard them talking among themselves as they edged closer, until they were right under the caique's stern, when all at once a naked white body leaped up in her cockpit, and next moment Nicky's head poked out through the nets. There was an agonizing pause. Then I heard the Greek boy say, almost apologetically, 'You tell time, please?'

Nicky glanced at his wrist watch and, suddenly realizing that it was all he had on, grabbed at the first thing he could find to cover his nakedness, which happened to be the White Ensign lying on a thwart nearby. The effect was instantaneous. In an explosion of laughter and glad cries of 'Inglezoi,

30 Back row: the three sons and the nephew of the old man.

Inglezoi' the Greeks swarmed aboard, and our reserve bottle of *ouzo* had to be uncorked.

But this wasn't the end, of course. We couldn't let them go back to their village on Syros, to tell of their adventure and us. We were on our way home after landing a patrol of the Long Range Desert Group on the island of Kithnos. We might need the same hiding place again when we took them off in ten days' time. So after a meal together, the Greeks returned to their boat which was now made fast alongside. They must have realized that we were all in a difficult position. We heard them arguing and shouting for a bit, then back aboard they came and the English speaker said, 'We come with you, please . . . for join Greek Army in Egypt.'

The four boys (photo 30) were the three sons and the nephew of the old man who would be left to get the boat back on his own. And keep silent. We knew he would for the sake of his sons.

At dusk they came aboard and we prepared for sea. The old man (photo 31) cast off and lay watching us for a while. The boys called to him once. One could feel the agony in his answering call. Then he turned, and standing to his sweeps, rowed steadfastly out to sea towards the misty outline of Syros, 9 miles to the southward. We watched him growing smaller and smaller, till the dusk swallowed him. He never once looked back.

31 '. . . the old man . . .'

The Sea Loves No One

Men have striven in all sorts of ways for international brotherhood, and will no doubt continue to strive for it until the first invading force from outer space unites them unconditionally and at once. But seamen, already united against a power at least as formidable as an Army corps of aliens, find no difficulty in living peaceably together. As a uniting force the sea is above suspicion. It is also all-powerful. You may reinterpret your faith to suit a national emergency or the aspirations of your rulers; you can change your country; but you cannot deny the ocean or temper its demands; nor appeal for special dispensation to the stars, studying their mute reflections in the sea and giving not a damn for anybody. So you stick together. If you divide, the sea – listening always, knowing your thoughts, watching day and night for the smallest chinks of pride or sentiment in your ranks – the sea will have you. There's not the slightest doubt about it. . . .

Early one morning, just as a boat of ours was about to sail from Beirut, a junior staff officer rang up to say that an enemy submarine had been reported off the Lebanese coast. What were we going to do about it? He was a young man who had always been openly contemptuous of our 'dirty little false beard' flotilla, as he liked to call us; and the submarine, it appeared, was bound in the opposite direction from the one intended for our caique. So we, entirely within our rights (and yet a thousand times wrong, of course), said: 'You're the Staff. You tell us.' We must have known he wouldn't care to call out his superior at half past six in the morning to make a decision. In actual fact I doubt whether anyone would have stopped that sailing on so slight a chance of danger, or even that it would have been right to do so. But that is hardly the point. The point is that we had allowed ourselves to become divided, and the sea to know it.

'Nudge' Phillips, the skipper of the boat, who was an Australian and therefore happily unfettered by the chains of naval etiquette, told everyone within earshot and many who weren't, in the nicest possible way, to go and do things to themselves; he was sailing.

The sea smiled. And for many blue and sunlit days thereafter, as a gentle breeze barely ruffled the smiling – the damnably smiling – face of the sea, we waited for news of Nudge. Neither he, nor his boat, nor any of his crew were ever seen again.

Floating wreckage was later reported by an aircraft not far from the course he ought to have steered. It might have been the remains of his boat. There might, indeed, by some horrid coincidence, have been a second U-boat of whose presence we had heard nothing. Only the sea – the sea who loves no one and is forever unloved; who respects neither persons, nor aims, nor the hopes and fears of men – only the sea knows and knew.

---

[1] A Danish officer serving with the SBS, later promoted major and subsequently awarded a posthumous VC.

Tales from a Birmingham Businessman

CHAPTER FIFTEEN

Pongo at Sea

It was dark under the 3-tonner and it smelt heavily of diesel oil; but out in the open the rain was deluging down as only Sinai rain can deluge, scouring noisy rivulets through the red earth and down the rocky walls of the *wadi*. Jack wormed himself deeper into his bed roll and passed me the whisky bottle.

'Yes, it's something quite new,' he said, 'and top secret, of course.'

'Of course.'

'They asked for volunteers . . . men with nautical experience . . . so, as I've done a bit of dinghy sailing, I put my name in. That's where I'm bound now.'

'Haifa?'

'No, Beirut. They're fitting out there – pass the bottle – but I can't tell you all about it. You understand that, I'm sure.'

'Sure.' I lay back on my elbows, feeling relaxed and comfortable.

'Anyway you'd probably find it hard to believe.'

And as the night wore on and the level in the whisky bottle sank inexorably, accompanied by bursts of snoring from our two drivers asleep under the other truck, he told me all about it.

A fascinating tale it was too – about Greek skippers and crews who had escaped through the islands; others who had overpowered their German guards and sailed boldly down to Cyprus or Beirut, where they'd left their boats and travelled to Cairo to join the Greek forces re-assembling there. This had resulted in a build-up of caiques, large and small, which the Navy was now fitting with more powerful engines for secret intruder operations in the very waters from which they hailed.

The new unit was to be called the Levant Schooner Flotilla and was to be manned by volunteers from all three services. It was an intriguing prospect, and as soon as I got back from my course in Haifa, I put in a request to my CO to be considered for the LSF.

⋆   ⋆   ⋆

HMS *Mosquito*, the headquarters ship for Coastal Forces Eastern
Mediterranean, consisted of two or three small offices half-way down the
eastern mole of Alexandria harbour. The Senior Officer, Commander R.E.
Courage DSO, DSC, RN was a great red-faced bull of a man, with silky
red-blond hair and, in contrast to his powerful presence, a surprisingly
sensitive and understanding personality. His 'Sit down' had a friendly rather
than a peremptory ring.

'Where d'you come from?'

'Birmingham, sir.'

'Any sea experience?'

'Well, sir . . . that is . . .' Having never been to sea, except in the troopship
coming out, there was nothing I could do but reel off a series of half truths.
'I've sailed dinghies, sir.'

'Sailed *in* them, you mean?'

'No, sir, 12 ft Nationals and 14 ft Internationals.'

'Hmm . . . and what about navigation?'

I thought back to my days with a motorized battalion of the Rifle
Brigade in the Western Desert, navigating by the stars at night and sun
compass by day, with tables to tell me the exact bearing of every heavenly

32 A fine fresh breeze and no sea . . .

body. Commander Courage, affectionately known as 'Sweaty', waited patiently.

'In the Western Desert, sir, I was battalion navigator . . .'

'The LSF doesn't sail in deserts – so let's put it this way . . . do you think you could sail 70 or 80 miles in heavy weather, in the dark, across open water, to rendezvous in a cove on a Greek island, without shore lights of any kind to help you, except a blue-shaded torch signal on arrival?'

'It would need a bit of practice, sir,' I said hopefully.

'You're right,' said the Commander. 'It would. But what we need at the moment is an intelligence officer . . . how does that strike you? You could build on that if you've got it in you.'

He smiled encouragingly, and I felt the inner warmth, the quality of his leadership, coming through. 'Sweaty' Courage, who had commanded the destroyer *Havoc* at the Battle of Narvik, knew how to lead as well as to command.

⋆   ⋆   ⋆

On arrival at Beirut I reported at once to Adrian Seligman, who appeared to be in charge. He asked me, in view of the job I'd been sent to do, whether I was fluent in Italian, Greek or German, or maybe all three. When I told him that my only language was schoolboy French, he muttered something about 'another damn silly appointment'. But after a pause he added, more cheerfully, 'How about signals officer? Our signals bloke is coming up to the Aegean with us in a few days' time. Could you stand in for him here, d'you think?'

I was introduced to 'our signals bloke', a plump and extremely jovial captain in the Middlesex Yeomanry, Gordon Hogg by name, who asked me what I knew about W/T procedures. I told him I could operate a 38 set, the standard infantry equipment.

'The boys'll look after that side of it,' he said with confidence. 'What you'll have to do is keep the books and filing straight; although Betty, our Wren, is pretty good at that. So it's really just a question of keeping everybody happy. How are you on public relations?' We grinned at each other and went off for a drink.

The Flotilla office and stores were down on the dockside, surrounded by a hubbub of dockyard mateys, mechanics, contractors and workers of all kinds, including some astonishing women with fingers of steel who, with marlin spikes and hammers, were splicing eyes and long splices into heavy steel wire cables for the habour's boom defence system.

After a while I got to know my way around, and even began to take part in some of the activities, helping caiques and MLs to shift berth or taking the lines from others coming alongside. But the most entertaining sight, from half past eight to nine every morning, was Adrian and his great friend Nicky Benyon-Tinker (the current intelligence officer) pacing up and down the quay at high speed, hands clasped behind them, like latter-day Hornblowers on the quarter deck of their 74-gunner.

I also met a few fellow officers, mostly naval, in the wardroom of HMS *Martial*, the shore establishment. The more jocular among them referred to me and two other Army blokes as 'sea-going Pongos', but to Sub-Lieutenant Alec Thwaites RNVR we were always 'those f. . .ing brown jobs'. However, this did not deter him from inviting me to share his digs in the house of an elderly Russian lady called Bolgov.[1] And I hadn't been in Beirut for more than forty-eight hours before I ran into Geoffrey Kirk, also an RNVR sub-lieutenant, and Dick Harden, a subaltern in George Jellicoe's SBS, with both of whom I had been at a pre-prep school near St Albans, thirteen years before.

I soon realized that my knowledge of signals was, to say the least, marginal compared with that of the petty officers who actually ran the station. They were polite but clearly nonplussed at the presence of someone like me buzzing around them. Fortunately, however, the situation was soon relieved by the simultaneous arrival of three caiques, escaped from the Greek mainland, whose crews could hardly wait to moor them securely before disappearing down to Cairo to join their friends.

These boats would now have to be re-engined and re-equipped. But when the Flotilla left for the Aegean in a few days' time there would be no one to take charge of fitting them out – except me. So I got the job. And before he shoved off to our advanced base on the Turkish coast, Adrian told me to contact a Mr Spanner, the Admiralty Overseer, who in turn put me in touch with Joe and Riad Rizk, the contractors. They smiled.

Why is it that contractors always smile? I think it's because they know very well that *you* don't know very much, and whenever it comes to an argument *they* will have little difficulty in blinding you with scientific jargon – especially if it's in Arabic.

My own shortcomings were totally exposed at a last minute equipment meeting before the Flotilla left. There was a long discussion about strops and what should be done with them. I sat industriously taking notes, but didn't discover what strops might be until I was told much later that they were loops of rope. Then there was a debate about whether the boats should be provided with CQRs or Admiralty Patterns. The tide of argument went this way and that, and in the end I was asked for my opinion. In order not to look foolish (I had no idea what these objects were; they could have been anything from telescopes to plum puddings) I suggested that it might be wise for every boat to be equipped with both. I was looked upon with a new respect. 'Belt and braces,' said one old salt (of twenty or so) nodding sagely. I tried to look calmly confident, but the Flotilla had sailed before I discovered that what we'd been talking about were anchors.

It was the Buffer (Petty Officer Boatswain) who put me wise. He was an elderly fellow (not a day under thirty-eight, I guessed) with a magnificent physique, sandy hair and piercing blue eyes. He was, moreover, a God-fearing man, whose main aim in life, it seemed, was to bring up youngsters (of all ranks) in the way they should go – both morally and physically and in the lore of the sea. Most evenings he and I would go ashore together and sit drinking beer in one dive or another until late at night, while he took me carefully and kindly through the Admiralty *Manual of Seamanship* and talked in a nostalgic way about naval customs and the ships he had served in.

Eventually, after several weeks, two of the three boats were fitted out and ready, in spite of a stream of frequently conflicting advice from caique skippers like Geoffrey Kirk and Skipper Stipetic (a true Grimsby trawler skipper, of several years' experience though still only twenty-four). Noël Clegg, an RNVR Lieutenant, and John Charrington, an Army captain like myself, took over the two boats and in due course sailed them up to the Aegean. I redoubled my efforts to bring the third boat up to the mark.

This took another two weeks, and in the meantime her crew began to arrive from Alexandria. The coxswain, a Petty Officer called Lesley, was a South African – well built, obviously well educated and highly intelligent. The Leading Seaman, Dimitri Dikeos, was South African-born but of Greek origin and a fluent Greek speaker, which might well be a godsend in tight corners up in the islands. Then there was a seaman gunner, whose principal claim to recognition was that his sister had won the National Beauty Contest in Rhodesia. The complement was made up by a Scottish stoker, whose name I forget, and a W/T operator whose name no one ever asked for, because he was universally known as 'Sparks'.

They all fitted themselves fairly happily into bunks, lockers and duty stations, and after a few days of sea trials, which I allowed the coxswain and the stoker to handle between them, the good ship *Taxiarchis* (or LS5, as she was now called) was ready for sea.

I went up to report to Phillip Nicholls, the officer in charge of the base, and to ask whether a CO had been appointed. He came out of his office looking at me rather quizzically, I thought.

'You're a navigator, aren't you?'

'Only in the desert.'

'And they've sent up a first-class crew?'

'Yes.'

'Who can handle each other and the boat?'

'Ye–e–es,' I agreed suspiciously.

'OK. Then here are your sailing orders.' He handed me a sealed envelope. 'You sail at 0800 tomorrow. Good luck!' and he'd gone, leaving me gaping.

---

[1]   An exceptionally amiable old lady, who loved her 'boys', but found it difficult to pronounce some of their surnames. The nearest she could get to Alec's was 'Fleetoks'.

CHAPTER SIXTEEN

Learning the Ropes

The sea was wine dark and looked like oiled silk in the morning light. There was no wind, and all day it was incredibly hot. We rigged the main awning as we chugged along at a steady 6 knots, steering north-west by compass. Shorts and plimsolls were all we could stand – the plimsolls to protect our feet from the burning deck planking with pitch bubbling up in the seams. From time to time we'd slosh a bucket or two of sea water down between the port rail and the hatch coaming to cool things down a bit. When night came, I checked our course by the Pole Star. It looked about right. Lesley was steering and would be relieved by Dimitri at midnight. I laid out my bed roll on the main hatch.

Dreams can be violent and frightening, or they can be soothing. Mine that night transported me to a sun-swept glacier high up in the mountains, where the swish of my skis, as I floated down through deep powdery snow, was lulling me into a state of utter peace. The swishing slowly died, then ceased, and I was floating through the air above a tree-filled valley. To right and left of me the snow fields stretched away into the distance beneath a cloudless sky.

I woke to the reassuring murmur of our engine, with Dimitri crouched comfortably over the tiller aft, and brilliant moonlight flooding around us from a gibbous moon high up in the eastern sky. I looked over the side and could see through clear, bright water to ripple marks on a sandy bottom, with here and there a tuft of weed waving gently in the under-tow of purling wavelets. But stationary. Not moving past. We were gently but firmly aground.

In the distance to port, I could just make out what looked like a line of bushes with a tree or two among them, and at one point a group of pillars standing up starkly white in the moonlight, two of them joined by an architrave and cornice. We might have been Argonauts arriving on some ancient shore. Actually, however, these were the ruins of Salamis, in pre-Christian times the capital of Cyprus. We had grounded north of the entrance to Famagusta harbour, lying blacked-out and invisible 3 or 4 miles down the coast.

I cut the engine and woke all the sleepers. There was no astern gearing in those boats, so we put both our anchors into the dinghy, with ropes bent on to them, and ran them out, one off each quarter, as far astern as their lines would allow. Then we hove with all our might, half the crew on each line, but she wouldn't budge: the sea floor was so soft and nearly level that she was gripped all along her keel. Two of the bigger chaps jumped overboard to shove against her stem (the water came half-way up their thighs, no more) while the rest of us went on hauling on her stern lines. But it was no good. So all that was left to us was to radio for a tug to pull us off. We managed with some difficulty to get a signal off to NOIC Famagusta, via Cairo, by which time dawn was fast approaching, so we brewed up and settled down comfortably to breakfast.

We had only just finished when we saw an enormous steamer belching smoke as she bore down on us from a southerly direction. She was the ocean-going tug stationed at Famagusta, ready to go to the assistance of any vessel up to aircraft carrier or 15,000-ton merchantman in size. She came churning up to within a cable or so of where we lay and sent her boat to take one of our lines. Then with a thrust and pother of white water, which set us thumping on the bottom, she plucked us out, like a pig out of a thorn bush, threw the end of our line back to us, and made off at 15 or 18 knots back to her berth in Famagusta harbour. We followed at our stately 6 knots, passing through the boom at twenty past eight in the morning.

I was not surprised to see the famous 1908 Rolls-Royce, with 'Snow White' and the faithful Peter Pan (see fn. 4, p. 42) on the back seat, waiting for us on the quay. As we came alongside, the window of the Rolls wound down, and an angry red face topped by gleaming silver hair poked out.

'What the devil's the meaning of this?' he roared. 'Report to my office at 09.30.' And up went the window, as the Rolls turned short round and slid smoothly out of the harbour gates.

I climbed into my uniform, complete with cap and stick, and presented myself at the old man's office, snapping to attention in front of his desk and saluting. He was unimpressed.

'Are you the Commanding Officer of that boat wearing a White Ensign?'

'Yes, sir.'

He looked me up and down with evident distaste.

'Why the devil isn't there a naval officer in command?'

'Special Service, sir . . . volunteers from all three services. We ran out of naval officers – they're in short supply in Beirut.' I wanted to add, 'Don't you know there's a war on?' but thought better of it.

Snow White muttered darkly something about 'inexperienced youngsters in command of HM ships'. Then, in more matter-of-fact but not unfriendly tones, he went on, 'Your signal made no mention of any damage'.

'No, sir. We grounded softly on sand, and there was no sea.'

'Very well, then, see my supply officer for any fresh provisions you need, and we'll expect you in the wardroom at noon.' I thought I saw the hint of a twinkle in his eye, but I couldn't be sure.

*   *   *

At two in the afternoon we sailed – south about, past Limassol and Paphos, then up to the Turkish coast at Cape Khelidonia. We passed to seaward of Castelorizo, then steered north-west by north and closed the Turkish coast again off the Seven Capes. From there on we kept within Turkish territorial waters – inside Symi, round Cape Krio and up the Gulf of Kos to the land-locked bay of Yedi Atala, which the Flotilla had made their advanced base for current operations.

Sadly I still hadn't quite mastered the art of bringing LS5 to a halt by means of her stern anchor alone, especially in water as deep as this. As a result, a more direct method was employed, by which you ram your bowsprit into the bow of the vessel against which you propose to berth (in this case Jim Morgan's Fairmile ML 351), making a hole in it about 3 in square. When the rebound has spent itself, you go 'slow ahead, hard a'port', bumping and scraping your starboard rubbing strake along your neighbour's hull, until your stern line, which some kindly fellow aboard the Fairmile has taken and made fast, brings you quietly alongside. And there you are, safe and snug.

You then disregard, in a gentlemanly manner, the wild and highly personal obscenities levelled at you by the infuriated skipper of the other vessel, appealing to his better nature with the suggestion that he fit a copper tingle over the hole and let it be generally understood that a 40 mm enemy shell was responsible for the damage.

Jim Morgan was not appeased. But what will you? Life must go on. And in fact, a few days after our arrival, the Flotilla moved its base deeper into the Gulf of Kos, to Port Deremen where, for a change, we berthed without further incident alongside our HQ schooner LS9. I found it deeply satisfying to come to a halt in such a well bred and orderly manner.

Next morning, COMARO I – at that time Lieutenant Commander (E) J.H.P. Campbell DSO, RN – came aboard, and for a while we discussed various methods of berthing alongside other vessels without serious damage to yourself or them. In the end, he said, 'Well anyway, you must be beginning to get the hang of it, the navigation too, and whatever happens you mustn't lose confidence. So how about trying a simple operation? There's an LRDG patrol on Amorgos who are due to be picked up. They may have a few Greeks with them by now. D'you think you can handle it?'

I looked at Lesley and Dimitri. They both nodded encouragingly. 'We'd like to have a go, sir,' I told John Campbell.

We spent several hours that afternoon studying charts and planning the stages which would bring us to suitable lay-up islands before daylight each night. We were still busy at this when John Campbell came aboard again, bringing with him an elderly Greek in rough clothing, a 'gorblimey' cap and down-at-heel boots. He had no baggage of any kind; but cradled in the crook of his right arm, its head protruding over his elbow in a perky, enquiring manner, was a fully grown white hen.

'You're in luck,' said John, smiling. 'This chap was born and brought up

33 A quiet moment at sea – the author (left) and a passenger, Commander Hallaghan RN.

on Amorgos, and knows its coastline like the palm of his hand. He wants passage back there to visit his brother.' I must have looked perplexed, because he added, 'A Greek patrol boat from Alexandria dropped him off here yesterday.'

I made a sign to Dimitri, who came forward. The Greek set his hen down on the main hatch, where she settled herself without complaint, facing inboard (I dare say her legs were tied). Her rear end projected a little way over the hatch coaming.

Her owner and Dimitri were soon deep in animated conversation. I watched them and also the hen, whose rear end had begun to twitch suggestively. 'Here we go,' I thought. 'It's either an egg or a dropping that's coming out. In either case, there'll be a mess on deck.'

But I had reckoned without the close symbiotic relationship which evidently existed between man and beast. Without taking his eyes off Dimitri's face, the Greek simply reached out his cupped right hand to a point about three inches below the hen's anus, caught the excrement which emerged, flicked most of it overboard, wiped what was left down his trousers, and carried on talking as though nothing had happened. There was clearly a perfect understanding between that old man and his hen. Maybe they talked to each other when they were alone.

★   ★   ★

The distance from Port Deremen to the small island of Ophidusa, off the west coast of Stampalia, which we had chosen as our first lay-up berth, is about 100 miles – say seventeen hours at 6 knots. We sailed at noon next day, passing Cape Krio, at the end of the Dorian isthmus, soon after sunset. Three hours later, as we cleared the south-western point of Kos, we sighted a convoy out in the open, bound in an easterly direction; but they took no notice of us, probably didn't even see us skulking inshore close to the island. From there to Ophidusa took us another seven hours, and it was just getting light as we sidled into a small indentation in the eastern cliffs, where a rocky gully came steeply down to the water's edge.

The island, stony and barren, with only occasional patches of scrub and a little tough grass, is about 440 ft high. Nobody lives there; but Lesley and the stoker, who climbed up the gully to the top, found a discarded beer bottle, which suggested that Germans rather than Italians had visited the place.

Soon after sunset we slipped and stood north-west for the south coast of Amorgos, just visible on the horizon. As we approached the island at slow speed, silently, Dimitri kept in conversation with the old man, who assured us that we were heading straight for the agreed pick-up cove. But as we got nearer and nearer, the darkness was made darker still, it seemed, by mountains rising before us, blocking out the stars. I ordered 'Dead slow', which brought our speed down from 4 or 5 to less than 3 knots as we crept on, closer and closer. After a while I said to Dimitri, 'Are we really heading for a cove, d'you think? Ask the old man again.'

Dimitri turned to the old fellow, who was sitting on the main hatch stroking his hen crouched beside him. I saw him nod and say something in a confident voice.

'He says "Yes. We're getting closer".'

'I can damn well see we're getting closer; but are we on course? There've been no flashes or anything.'

Dimitri passed this on and came back with 'The old man says carry on'.

So we carried on, getting nearer and nearer to those menacing cliffs. It was impossible to judge our distance off in the darkness, till at last I decided something must be done.

'Stop engine!'

The stoker throttled back and disengaged. And now I had to think. There was clearly no cove ahead of us – just a bare cliff face falling sheer into the water. So which way should we turn? I had to take a chance – 'Hard a'starboard!'

But she had only just begun to answer her helm when there came an almighty crash, which threw me forward over the cabin top and Dimitri on top of me. We had hit the cliff. Our 7 ft bowsprit was smashed to pieces. Our clipper bow crumpled and fell apart. There was splintered timber all over the foredeck. 'What the bloody hell . . ?' I rounded on the old man, still sitting placidly on the main hatch. I couldn't see the expression on his face, but his hands were spread out in a deprecating gesture that infuriated me beyond bearing. I flung round again to Dimitri. 'Ask the old lunatic where we are!' I almost shouted.

Dimitri spoke to him in Greek, then turned back to me. 'You're not going to like this, skipper.'

'Well, what does he say?'

'He says "We've arrived".'

For once words actually failed me.

*   *   *

LS5 was already backing away from the cliff on the rebound, so Dikeos and our seaman gunner had no difficulty in getting her well clear with the sweeps. Fortunately, too, we hadn't re-stepped the mast after lowering it for camouflaging the evening before, so there was no damage there; our false clipper bow had taken the full impact of the crash, protecting our stem and hull. We were still, therefore, seaworthy; and after completing our turn to starboard, we stood eastwards along the coast at slow speed.

After a while we were overjoyed to see a dim blue light blinking at us in the correct series of dots and dashes from a small bay between two hills. The relief was overpowering: I found it difficult to restrain a shout of greeting. We ran in and beached the boat on shingle at the head of the bay. The LRDG fellows did have some Greeks with them, but we soon had them all aboard and their gear stowed. They showed great tact, I thought, in not commenting on the shambles up forward. One or two of them seemed even to assume that the wreckage had been piled there deliberately as a convenient stowage for their packs and weapons.

When they were all aboard and comfortably dispersed around the deck, we hauled ourselves off the beach and moved round to a secluded cove which the Army had reconnoitred. There we were able to secure close to the rocks under camouflage nets, with a sentry on the hillside nearby, so that the crew were able at last to get some sleep.

I, of course, couldn't sleep. But I managed to talk, through Dimitri, to one of the islanders who'd come aboard with the LRDG boys. I wanted to find out, if I could, the extent of the old man's knowledge of the island and its coastline. It turned out that he'd never been to Amorgos before in his life, but down in Alexandria someone had told him that one of his cousins from Ios, further west, had recently moved there. He thought it would be nice to meet up with his relative, so when the Greek patrol boat (originally bound for Amorgos) dumped him on the British at Port Deremen, he hit on the idea of appointing himself pilot of the first caique bound in the right direction.

I decided on the spot that we'd had enough of the old bugger. So next

evening, when we had motored quietly round to the main beach to embark
two more islanders who wanted passage to the Middle East, we put the old
fellow ashore with his hen under his arm. He seemed to assume that we
would soon return to pick him up and carry him back to Cyprus. I smiled.
We all smiled. Dikeos smiled and patted him on the shoulder. Then we
hauled off and stood out to sea, still smiling and waving. Now that we were
shot of him we really didn't bear him any ill will, and we frankly admired his
hen for her patience and good nature.

★   ★   ★

The passage back was uneventful. As soon as we reached Turkish waters off
Cape Krio, we made a damage report by W/T to COMARO I, but when we
arrived at Port Deremen, John Campbell was away on an operation. He had
left word, however, that we were to take our LRDG patrol on to Cyprus,
where they were due for leave.

It was a three-day passage to Limassol, but the weather held fair and we
were able to sail most of the way with a south-westerly breeze on the
quarter. After landing our passengers, we were ordered on to Beirut for
repairs. The passage occupied another full day, and we made harbour
shortly before midnight. But for us the night was young, and so were we.
And Beirut in those days was a playground to meet every taste. So it was
well on into the next forenoon before we surfaced, panting for tea.

'NOIC's on the quayside, for God's sake. What's the matter with you?' It
was the hoarse voice of Phillip Nichols – half shout, half whisper – at the
cabin hatch.

I struggled out of my bunk; dragged on trousers, shoes, jacket and scarf;
reached for my cap with one hand and the ladder with the other. When I
finally emerged on deck I found Rex Arnott on the quayside, with Phillip
beside him, staring gloomily at our tangled and cluttered foredeck.

'All makes work for the working man to do, I suppose,' he said with a
sigh, as I came up, 'and while they're doing it, you'd better take whatever
leave you're entitled to.'

'Thank you, sir.'

'And when you get back, how about a spell with one of our more
experienced ship handlers, say Stipetic or Barclay? Wouldn't do any harm,
would it? Eh? What?'

'No, sir.'

'I'll have a word with COMARO I when I see him. What shall we call it?
Post-graduate studies?'

'How about anti-demolition training?' suggested Phillip pleasantly.

There was really nothing I could usefully add, so I saluted and they
moved on down the quay.

The Bank Manager's Tale

CHAPTER SEVENTEEN

Land and Sea Meetings

Who are you, Sea Lady
And where in the seas are we? . . .

Why drops the moonlight through my heart,
And why so quietly
Go the great engines of my boat
As if their souls were free?

'Santorin – A Legend of the Aegean'
James Elroy Flecker

Dear Enemy

With stores for a week on board, and an SBS patrol of six men under Captain Clark, we sailed at noon one day, early in April 1944, down the Gulf of Kos towards the channel between Kum Burnu, the north-east point of Kos, and Turkey. Since there was a battery of 75 mm guns on Kum Burnu there was every incentive to hug the Turkish shore on this stage of the passage. But the trouble was that Nature had planted an obstruction known as Magpie Rock right in the path of vessels taking that route; it had less than 3 ft of water over it at low tide, and would undoubtedly rip the bottom out of any caique unlucky enough to pass over it. We always tended, therefore, to keep closer to the Turkish coast in that area than anywhere else.

We passed about two cables off Arkialla Point and were half-way to Pasha Rock when rifle shots rang out from the hills above. Fortunately they were not very well aimed or they may, in fact, have been just warning shots. By now, however, we were well clear of Magpie Rock; so we hoisted our Flotilla flag and following its stirring injunction (see p. v) stood boldly on to the westward.

It was a warm night for early spring, with a light breeze and very little sea; but we felt rather conspicuous under a waxing moon, already well up on our port quarter, and looked forward to reaching the darker background of

Pserimos Island, now fine on our port bow and about 3 miles distant. My intention was to pass north of Pserimos and cut down through the Kalimnos Channel, then due west to Amorgos, where our brief was to discover, if we could, the strength and disposition of the German and/or Italian garrisons.

Now that the guns of Kum Burnu and the Turkish coastguards' rifles were astern of us, we were able to relax for a while and enjoy the balmy night air and peaceful surroundings. We enjoyed them for all of twenty minutes, when suddenly there was a loud splash and a great spout of water a little way off on our starboard bow. Then another to port. I put the helm hard a'starboard, to give us time to think. We were being fired on, but whether by a ship or a shore battery there was no way of knowing, until a flash on the northern horizon well clear of any land, followed by a 'crump' and another water spout a few hundred yards away, told us (though we still couldn't see anything, even through night-glasses) that it was a low-profile vessel, probably a German R-boat or F-lighter armed with a 75 mm or 88 mm gun, that was attacking us.

The enemy gunner didn't appear to have us bracketed, however, so I put the helm over to port, further to confuse his aim and range-finding, while we had a brief discussion on immediate tactics. We had the luxury on this trip of a first lieutenant – Geoffrey Kirk – who had recently joined the Flotilla. He came to us from special service gunboats in the English Channel, used (among other more offensive tasks) for landing agents on the Brittany coast; so he was already accustomed to our kind of work, though in a harsher climate than the Eastern Mediterranean. His advice was to seek the shadows offered by the north coast of Pserimos, now almost abeam to port. But I felt that once the enemy had us cornered there, he would simply close in and wait for us to emerge into the moonlight, a sitting target to be picked off at his leisure. So once again we obeyed the Flotilla motto. And it worked. After a few more rounds of enemy fire, which didn't come too close, the firing ceased.

The next day the local German radio broadcasts (we learned later) claimed the sinking of an enemy craft north of Pserimos by one of their F-lighters – which were indeed armed with a single 75 mm gun. How they lost us, and whether they really thought they had sunk us, remained a mystery. But the outcome was that we kept going, and reached our intended cove at the south-eastern end of Amorgos soon after first light next morning.

We spent the day under nets, and in the evening moved round to a deep and well sheltered inlet close east of Alato Point. But not entirely without incident en route; as we came round the north-eastern end of the island and were approaching Cape Langhadia lighthouse, we saw, in the failing light, the characteristic outline of a large warship – a cruiser at least – close inshore and less than half a mile ahead.

We slipped back behind the nearest headland and waited, to see if she would move away. But when we tried again, twenty minutes later, she was still there. We noticed, however, that there was no activity of any kind on

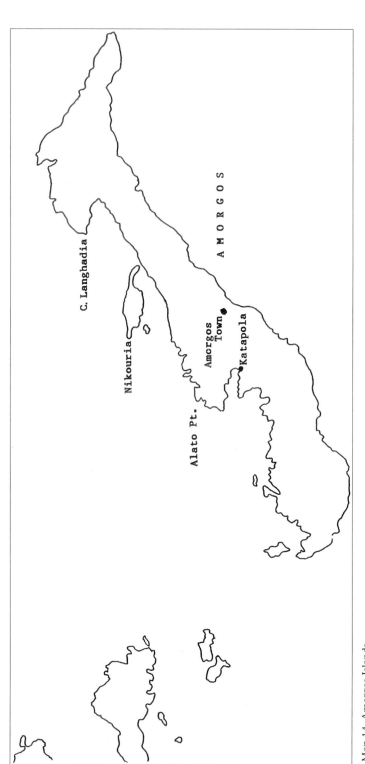

Map 14 Amorgos Islands.

board or in her immediate vicinity – no boats, no people, nothing. We crept closer. Still no signs of life. But the outline was unmistakable – the single funnel just abaft the bridge and the characteristic bulges of gun turrets forward and aft. Until all at once, the coxswain, who was up forward, called out, 'It's a fuckin' island!' And so it was. It was Nikouria Island, 2 or 3 miles down the coast, which we had taken for a cruiser 600 yards or so ahead of us.

By the time we reached the inlet we were aiming for it was dark. So we set watches and the rest of us turned in. Next morning, just as we were finishing an early breakfast, a small crowd of Greeks came down to the cove with messages of welcome from the mayor of nearby Katapola. Geoffrey, who, it turned out, was a classical scholar and also spoke passable modern Greek, discovered from our visitors that the garrison had been withdrawn from the island nearly a year ago. The only German still on Amorgos was a solitary sergeant, who had been left behind with a radio set and charging motor as a lookout post. A large quantity of stores and provisions had also been left against the garrison's possible return at any time.

However, the batteries and fuel for the charging motor had in due course run out. So the sergeant – a Rhinelander called Heinrich – had concentrated instead on cultivating the friendship and trust of the islanders, handing out German Army rations fairly liberally from the store left by the retreating garrison. He had also learned to speak Greek by billeting himself on a family in Katapola, to whose eldest daughter he had since become 'engaged'.

Heinrich was by now, in fact, a great favourite, especially with the children of Amorgos; and when we met him and his 'fiancée' next day, it was easy to see why. Quite apart from his generosity with German Army rations, Heinrich was a likeable enough fellow – soft-spoken, short and rather tubby, with a ready smile, dark hair and brown eyes. He fitted comfortably into his surroundings; at first sight one might even have taken him for a Greek islander.

Our SBS patrol found him and his girlfriend sitting quietly in the little church and explained to him that he would have to come with us as a prisoner. He showed no surprise, but when he told his girl there were tears and supplications. Heinrich took them calmly and sympathetically but without any show of emotion. The SBS boys couldn't understand what they said: he may have told her that he would send for her from Cairo. She calmed down anyway.

'And my boat?' he asked me, when he was brought aboard. 'You take him also?' I must have looked surprised, because he added in a friendly, rather than a lofty, manner, 'I pay freight after'.

When evening came and it was time to leave, a small fishing boat with a short mast and lug sail was brought round to where we lay. We passed a 5 in mooring line through a strop in her bow and secured it to her main thwart. The boy Niko, who had relatives in Alexandria and wished also to join the Greek Army, was coming with us as well. His family were very proud of him; but there were, of course, more tears and fluttering of handkerchiefs when we finally left. Niko and Heinrich stood in the stern, side by side, waving back.

We headed first for the island of Levitha, towing Heinrich's boat. But soon after midnight a fresh northerly blew up, reducing our speed from 6 to less than 3 knots. It was essential that we reach our hide-out on Levitha before daylight, so there was nothing for it but to cut the boat adrift. Heinrich watched impassively and then said, 'Ze var is soon finish. No? In Cairo many vill vish for trading here . . . I soon coming back.'

My last memory of Heinrich is of him sitting on the main hatch chatting with the crew and handing out cans of beer and tins of sausages from his rucksack. By the time we got back to Balisu Bay in Turkey, two days later, he had become almost as great a favourite on board as he had been on Amorgos.

Berthed on a Volcano

We left Balisu again at noon ten days later, in company with LS1 (Skipper Stipetic) who carried Andy Lassen and nine of his fifteen-man patrol. Stefan Kasoulis and the other six SBS lads, plus three Greek Sacred Company men, were with us in LS11. The two boats, loaded down with rubber dinghies, folboats, mortars, machine-guns, radio sets, rucksacks, ammunition and fairly hefty looking soldiers, in addition to all the usual naval gear, were bound for the island of Santorin, where Andy and his boys were to stick limpet mines on the hulls of any ships they found there.

It was a glorious day. We cruised at half speed along the southern shore of the Gulf of Kos, enjoying the afternoon sunshine, so as to reach Cape Krio at dusk. From there we steered west-south-west past Yali Island, then south-west to Sirina,[1] where we spent the next day under nets. The following day we hid in a creek on Anedro and, when night fell, set out for our first objective, which was to land Stefan Kasoulis and two of his men on the east coast of Santorin, near Perissa monastery. They hoped that the monks would be able to give them up-to-date information about the German and Italian garrisons.

They returned after an hour, disappointed. The monks had left the monastery, which was now inhabited by peasants, who seemed to know nothing of interest about the enemy. So we sailed on round the southern point of the scimitar-shaped island into the great central bay or crater. For Santorin is a volcano whose explosive eruption in ancient times is said to have destroyed the Minoan civilization on Crete, some 60 or 70 miles away to the south.

Santorin and Thirasia Islands, 4 miles to the westward, with 1,000 ft cliffs on their inner sides, are all that remain of the crater's rim, while the core of the volcano emerges as the two central islands of Palaia Kammeni and Nea Kammeni – no more than massive piles of black pumice and reddish-brown rubble – which still show signs of activity, with an all-pervading smell of

Map 15 Santorin Island.

sulphur and wisps of smoke or steam issuing from cracks between the
heated rocks.

It was dark. There was no moon, and the surrounding cliffs seemed to
hem us in, making it darker still. The white houses of the two main Santorin
villages, sprinkled along the cliff top, were barely discernible. We crept in
towards the 400 ft bulk of Nea Kammeni, the larger of the two central
islands. On its western side, the chart showed an inviting inlet 'where no one
will dream of looking for you', John Campbell had told us.

The chances of finding this inlet in the dark were slim, so Skipper Stipetic
and our own coxswain paddled off in folboats to search for it. They were
away for nearly an hour but found no sign whatever of any inlet; so, with the
sky already greying in the east, we were forced to haul ourselves as close to
the rocks as we could get. LS1 then worked her way in beside us, and we
both set about spreading camouflage nets.

But now another problem arose. The nets we carried were designed to match the limestone of most Aegean islands – an ochreous yellow with darker patches and a dark green fringe at the bottom, to blend in with the band of darker rock formed everywhere by the rise and fall of Mediterranean tides. Here, however, the rocks were black or dark brown; so our nets were useless, and in the end we spread our brown foresails across the two decks, so as to break up, as far as possible, our boat-shaped outlines from the air. And there we had to lie throughout a hot and humid day, with sulphurous fumes blowing over us in waves, setting us coughing and sometimes making our eyes water as well.

Geoffrey Kirk and Andy now clambered ashore and made their way up to the crest of the island, where they found a small central crater surrounded by large black boulders, the fissures between them leaking acrid smoke and a few of them containing yellow puddles of sulphurous liquid. From the top, through binoculars, they searched the cliffs and shoreline of Santorin, 2 miles away to the east, but could see no shipping of any kind. So the plans had to be changed and the rest of the day was spent by Andy and his patrol preparing for a direct assault on the garrison ashore.

In this they received unexpected assistance from a solitary fisherman who came across us as he worked his way round the island, searching for sea urchins and octopus through his home-made water glass – a 10 litre petrol can with a glass bottom. At first, when we grabbed him, he was too frightened to speak, but a few ouzos soon put him at his ease and he became positively garrulous. He told us that the garrison consisted of about twenty Germans and double that number of Italians. Most of them were billeted on the first floor of the Bank of Athens at Thira, on the western cliffs. The lighthouses at both ends of the island always had guards of two men, while another dozen or so manned and guarded the radio station at Marovigli.

This was just what Andy and his men needed to know, and as soon as it grew dark we dragged and bumped ourselves clear of the most uncomfortable berth we had so far experienced and proceeded round the north end of Santorin to land them on a beach on the north-east coast of the island. Then both caiques withdrew to the south-west and reached the Khristiani Islands as dawn was breaking.

⋆　⋆　⋆

It was a calm and most enjoyable sail, before a moderate northerly breeze; and we were especially pleased to observe that the speed of our boats under sail had been materially improved; we discovered later that this was due to their hulls having been swept clean of any weed by the sulphurous volcanic waters in which they had spent the previous day. On arrival at the larger of the two Khristiani Islands, both boats secured in a steep-sided cleft in the rocks known to Skipper Stipetic, which was well protected from the north and east, but rather open to the west.

The first day passed idyllically. There was plenty of room on board now that the troops were gone, and we slept and ate and wandered happily over the island, which had one solitary inhabitant – an ancient and jovial shepherd, who told us he always brought his flock across from Santorin during the spring and summer months.

Geoffrey and the coxswain made a rough fishing net out of spare camouflage netting, and tried to catch some of the fat red mullet swimming deep down in the rock pools. Their crude attempts were easily thwarted by the contemptuous fish.

That night we all slept soundly. But just before dawn we heard the noise of an engine growing louder as a ghostly craft glided by, travelling westward about a hundred yards offshore. It quickly disappeared. But with full daylight a sharp westerly breeze sprang up, making our berth distinctly uncomfortable. On two counts, therefore, I decided to shift to an apparently ideal sea-cave further down the coast, whose mouth I had sighted the previous afternoon during a short exploration by folboat.

When we reached it, it turned out to be more cramped and darker than I had hoped. And despite the apparent flat calm outside, a surprising amount of swell entered its mouth, which sent us into a perpetual roll; indeed, as Geoffrey put it, 'threw us around like a pea in a bottle' and kept us all busy with bearing-off spars. It was evident that a more comfortable berth must be found, and quickly; so Geoffrey and the gunner paddled off in the folboat to find one. Within a few minutes they were back again, looking worried.

'What's the trouble?'

'Unknown inflatable with three men aboard,' said Geoffrey, as he reached for grenades and tommy-guns. 'Must be from the boat that passed by this morning.'

Then off they went again, the gunner paddling. Geoffrey with binoculars at the ready and a tommy-gun across his knees. When they got back nearly an hour later (having found no suitable berth), Geoffrey told us what had happened.

'It was a sort of Stanley/Livingstone situation,' he said. 'When we got round the corner we saw them much closer. Two of their fellows had binoculars on us while the other paddled . . . but the swells kept coming between us: when we were up on a crest, they'd be down and so on . . . till suddenly we both hit a crest at the same time, and I saw they'd got bigger guns than we had. But I also saw a face I knew – Beckinsale of MO4, and he recognized me. Their *Armadillo* is moored to rocks round the corner, and they're looking for a better berth like we are. Lucky we didn't shoot each other to ribbons!'

We hung on in that cave for an hour or so more, then managed to struggle out and get back to our original berth, which now seemed quite cosy by contrast. And the rest of the afternoon passed peacefully enough, apart from some heavy explosions from the direction of Santorin. Our radio link with the shore party wasn't working, so we worried about who was winning.

Everyone was glad when evening came and it was time to get under way. But the sunset had looked ominous, and once clear of the land we met a stiff northerly wind with a lumpy sea, that brought our speed down to 5 knots, no more. The night was black and we soon lost sight of LS1 who seemed to be making better weather of it than we. The wind continued to freshen and the seas to grow steeper and shorter. Soon we were making less than 4 knots against them. After three hours at sea, Santorin appeared little nearer; but occasional glimpses through the spray and the gloom showed the high, dark bulk of Mesa Vouno still lying ahead. The seas were coming over fairly solid now; and with binoculars saturated, eyes bleared and smarting, we were unable to pick out any other feature on which to get a bearing, to fix our position. We might be outside or inside our course line; we had no way of telling.

I left Geoffrey in charge of the deck, and went below to study the chart. After a bit I noticed that the ship's motion was steadier; the sea must be calmer. That could mean only one thing. I rushed up on deck just in time to see the bows rise a bit as we came to a standstill. We had run aground on a sandy shelving beach bordering the low-lying vine-covered plain of Perissa – so low-lying and flat that even now it was difficult to see, in the darkness, where the land ended and the sea began. Fortunately, though, no damage had been done to the propeller, though the rudder was jammed fairly hard into the sand.

For the next four hours we tried everything we knew to get her off. Geoffrey and Guns ran out an anchor astern, chain cable and all, against a stiff breeze and rising sea, the wind having now backed to south-south-west. Twice they were all but capsized. And when we finally hove on the cable, the anchor came steadily home through the soft sand.

We then threw everything of any weight over the side, and went overboard ourselves to shove and heave and try to rock the boat in the hope of loosening the sand's hold on her keel. But all to no avail. And with less than two hours to daylight the situation looked unhealthy, to say the least. . . . Were raiding forces in control of this part of the island or not? From the explosions we'd heard there had clearly been heavy fighting, so air reconnaissance and possibly reinforcements could be expected at any time. And if the SBS happened to be in difficulties, having to wait another day to be taken off could be a serious matter for them.

Geoffrey and I had a hurried conference. Two things seemed essential: first, to get local help in towing or shoving the caique off; and secondly, to make contact somehow with Andy and his patrols. It was decided that Geoffrey, since he spoke Greek, should try to achieve these two aims. So he strapped on some webbing with holster and revolver, put a section of chart and a tin of corned beef in his pocket, slung a pair of rubber-soled shoes round his neck and waded ashore.

Hard Slog through the Mountains

Geoffrey now takes up the tale:

My first objective was the village of Emborion, a couple of miles inland. Walking through vineyards in the dark was no fun at all; for the moon, which had been all too brilliant on our trip to Amorgos, was now entirely absent. The soil was sandy and loose, and every fifty yards or so there was a ditch or a wall to trip over. Eventually I made out the white glow of houses, and soon came upon a rough track which in due course became the village street.

The place seemed to be full of dogs, who barked furiously every time I stumbled over one of the large stones which were apt, at that time, to encumber village streets in Greece. I prayed fervently that no patrolling or fugitive enemy troops had reached this place. Choosing what appeared to be one of the larger houses, I climbed its three rough steps and knocked softly on the door. No sound came from within. I knocked harder. And again, harder still. At last a frightened voice asked who I was. '*Enas philos* [a friend]', I replied, in the best theatrical tradition, 'who needs your help.'

The door was slowly opened by an old man in a nightgown and I stepped inside. Crouching behind him was his ancient wife. They were clearly relieved that I was not in German or Italian uniform. They accepted my assurance that I was '*Inglezos*' without question and with evident joy. I was seated in the best chair – damp and scruffy as I was – and given a glass of some primitive liqueur, which did me all the good in the world, for I suddenly realized that I was extremely tired.

We now got down to some tortuous conversation. My Greek was not too bad at a simple level; but being country folk they found it difficult to accept that a foreigner could have any knowledge at all of their language, and simply did not listen or try to comprehend. That still happens all over Greece, even today. Gradually, however, I gathered that there were no enemy troops in the immediate vicinity. There was no definite news about the fighting in the villages, though rumour had it that the garrison had been almost annihilated, with scattered remnants wandering round the mountains in a state of confusion. I told the old man that our caique had run aground and that we needed help to get her off; but here language difficulties cropped up again, since he refused to believe that I could mean 'caique'. British commandos, it was universally assumed, came in nothing humbler than a submarine, or perhaps a cruiser.

He decided that he must call in a young man of the village who spoke excellent English, and nothing would dissuade him. There was an interminable wait. Eventually the young man arrived, said 'Goodbye' in polished American and relapsed into silence.

I addressed him encouragingly in slow English, but he only smiled apologetically. Yet he did consent, after a while, to talk to me in simple

Greek, and gave me important news . . . our raiding party was no longer at their landing point, but at the monastery of Perissa itself, which was not far away. I accepted his offer to guide me there, and also his promise that as soon as daylight came he would collect some friends and launch a fishing boat which would try to tow us clear, and maybe drop a kedge anchor further offshore as well for all of us to haul on.

⋆   ⋆   ⋆

We set off together, my companion chatting volubly as we tramped along dusty lanes between fields of vines. Just as dawn was breaking we reached the monastery, a handsome and quite extensive complex of buildings with two or three domes. It appeared to be deserted, but as we approached closer an English voice shouted a challenge. I replied hastily and a tired-looking sentry emerged to escort us into one of the outhouses. There I found most of the raiding party spread over the stone floor, their bodies flung down in attitudes of extreme exhaustion. Against the wall were half a dozen German sailors, staring apprehensively into the barrel of a Sten gun wielded by an SBS sergeant.

Andy Lassen was awake. From him I learned that there had been a pretty stiff fight, which ranged all over the mountains and lasted for some thirty-six hours; that delightful Stefan Kassoulis and their medical sergeant had been killed, the latter finally passing out after a four-hour march over the hills with half a magazine of Schmeisser bullets in his stomach. This was a tragic loss, but the enemy had suffered far worse: at least thirty killed, ten captured and the rest scattered over the island in a state of panic. The radio station had been destroyed and its confidential books captured, but not before a signal had been sent to the mainland for help.

They had no food left because some of their stores had had to be abandoned, so my tin of bully provided a rather scant breakfast for fifteen hungry men. Meanwhile a signal had been sent on an Army set asking for a relatively high speed vessel to evacuate some of the party; it had been hoped at that stage to save the sergeant's life. I promised to keep them informed on progress with our stranded caique, and confirmed that the pick-up beach for the second night would be at Perissa itself. Then I started back to the point where we had run aground. By now it was full daylight. My legs were heavy and unresponsive, and both my pairs of shoes were torn almost to shreds; so the journey took nearly three hours. I could see no sign of the caique; and as I continued along the shore I began to think that I had miscalculated her position altogether – until, on rounding a bend in the coast, I came upon the exact spot, marked by floating debris in the sea from the stores we had jettisoned. And paddling knee-deep in the water were three stalwart Greek women salvaging what they could.

I asked them what had become of the caique. After fervent embraces they told me that when they arrived soon after dawn they had seen her disappearing up the coast. That eased my mind to some extent; there were as yet no aircraft around, and with any luck the boat would reach Anedro without being spotted. So I started back for the monastery, but collapsed into a ditch after an hour and fell asleep at once.

Discomfort eventually conquered exhaustion, and an hour or so later I got going again, reaching the monastery at midday. Andy Lassen and his men were in better shape now, and the food situation had greatly improved, since the peasants from round about had been bringing in gifts of tomatoes, fruit and cheese.

An excellent fellow called Niko, who had attached himself to the SBS during the fighting, was the self-appointed reception centre for all reports coming in about what was happening in the rest of the island. Shortly after my arrival he told us that two Arado seaplanes had landed in the harbour during the morning, but had recently taken off again; also that a destroyer had been observed lying stopped just south of the island.

Nothing could be done before nightfall, so Andy and I went out to look at the remains of a little circular Hellenic temple just outside the courtyard wall. It was my first sight from close to of an ancient Greek building in its natural setting and, for me, it was an emotional moment.

The afternoon sun was so hot that we fell asleep under a fig tree, only to be woken by the roar of engines. Through the leaves of the tree above us, we saw four Ju88s sweeping overhead at less than 1,000 ft. They circled the monastery for about five minutes, then flew off northwards still searching. It was now four o'clock, and the hours till nightfall were passed with a certain degree of impatience. When it came, the whole party moved down to the beach, together with the prisoners and a handful of Greeks who had been loyal helpers and wanted to join the Greek Army. My young Emborion friend was one of them.

We stared to seaward for ages, devoutly hoping that nothing this time would prevent the caiques from turning up; the weather, at least, had abated. Then just before midnight not two but three dark shapes were dimly discerned – two smaller and one larger – all converging on our beach. The larger boat was a puzzle, but eventually I was able to identify her as an HDML, which had (it turned out later) been not far away on a different operation and had been diverted to meet Andy's appeal for a faster vessel.

Identification signals were flashed to and fro, after which the caiques anchored a little way offshore, while the ML (having astern gear) was able to come in closer. The prisoners were embarked first, then the rest of the party. There was a good deal of confusion, not least because half the male population of Santorin seemed to have turned up on the beach, in addition to the legitimate evacuees, and were climbing into the dinghies in the hope of being taken to Egypt. They were reluctantly turfed out, and in the end the rest of us got away, about half in the ML and the others divided between the two caiques. For my own part, I was glad to climb aboard LS11 again, my one day as a soldier having convinced me that the naval life is best.

Our skipper, Noël Clegg, filled me in on what had happened between my leaving the caique and returning to her. 'We'd given up hope of refloating her ourselves,' he said, 'and were resigned to waiting for you to come back with reinforcements, when suddenly, for no apparent reason, she floated off of her own accord. I'd heard of these small tidal surges in the Med, but didn't really believe in them till now. Anyway, we sailed up to Anedro in full daylight without any trouble.'

'What if you'd known there was an enemy destroyer in the area?'

'We had nowhere else to go. . . . Damned lucky we didn't try Khristiani again. We'd have run right into her.'

It was at Anedro that the three craft met again after the pick-up at Perissa. An exhausting but relatively cheerful day was spent there, though the shadow of the two dead men hung over us. Then by stages we went back to Balisu Bay in Turkey, where both John Campbell and David Sutherland (commanding the SBS detachment) seemed pleased to see us. Despite alarms and excursions the operation had been extremely successful. And a few days later we learned that on the very night we left, the German destroyer, seen lying stopped south of Santorin, had landed a considerable force, which had spent several fruitless days searching the island for the SBS raiders.

---

[1] Now called Agios Johannis Island.

The Professor's Tales

CHAPTER EIGHTEEN

Ancient and Modern

Our route lay further to the north this time than on previous operations, which had interesting consequences. We carried seven members of the Greek Sacred Company on board, four of them officers, as well as their 'Intruder' rubber dinghy and a quantity of food for the islanders. In the evening of 20 August I anchored in Aspat Bay, on the Turkish coast about 4 miles beyond Bodrum, where it was noted in the log that the Turks were exceedingly friendly. That night and the following morning were spent there.

The next port of call was rather different. We had decided to anchor for the night some 30 miles up the Turkish coast, in a shallow sandy bay east of Tekeğaş Burnu on the northern side of the Gulf of Güllük. For some reason the patrol had to waste a bit of time before arrival in Mykonos, and it was better to do this, we thought, in the relative safety of Turkish waters.

The bay was peaceful enough and the weather calm, so I was taking supper down below with the senior Greek officer, who was sharing my little cabin. It was a very pleasant occasion – until suddenly there was an almighty crash as a bullet embedded itself in the woodwork just above my head. I needed no further invitation to hasten up on deck.

At the head of the bay, only a couple of hundred yards from where we lay at anchor, two soldiers could be discerned crouching behind a rock. I waved my arms and shouted angrily. They shouted angrily back. Eventually one emerged and made gestures that plainly indicated I should come ashore. There seemed little point in arguing, since they could shoot at us from behind good shelter and we were fully exposed if we tried to weigh anchor and put to sea. Moreover, being in neutral waters in daylight, we had nothing rigged in the way of weaponry. So the dinghy was shoved overboard and I got into it, together with my Greek officer friend Yiannis, who spoke not only good English but, it transpired, adequate Turkish.

As we landed, two fairly desperate-looking characters emerged from behind their rock. The younger one was a corporal, the other – a grizzled old curmudgeon – a private. We explained that we were waiting for minor

34 The people of Heraklia with Robert Ballantine (back row, centre, with fair hair) and two Greek Sacred Company men (third from left and extreme right).

engine repairs to be completed, and would be delighted to leave in an hour or so. The corporal asked what the devil we were doing flying a Turkish flag: this seemed to annoy him, although I explained through my Greek colleague that it was intended as a courtesy, which was not entirely true. In any case, he was unimpressed. I then suggested that one or both of them should come aboard, where we would contact their higher command in Ankara on our radio and confirm that we had permission for our visit. This was a regular ploy (involving a charade with the transmitter and the reporting of totally fictitious messages out of the ether) which, incredibly enough, normally worked with the zealous but usually illiterate Turkish militiamen. Unfortunately, these two were of a different calibre, and the invitation aboard was rejected with contumely.

The older one was now despatched inland by the corporal, who kept us carefully covered with his rifle. In twenty minutes or so he returned, accompanied by an officer on a large white horse. We repeated our story to the officer, who was clearly unimpressed and told us we must follow him to his headquarters some 3 miles away. There was little alternative, so I shouted across to the men in the caique that they should wait for our return. Then Yiannis and I followed the rider and the two soldiers across the sandhills and along a rough track.

The terrain was featureless and relatively hard going. I indicated to the officer that he ought to give me a lift on the back of his horse, but he declined. As we proceeded, the elder of the Turkish soldiers kept addressing his officer in distinctly surly tones. After a time a thoughtful Yiannis vouchsafed the cheerful news that he was trying to persuade him that we should be peremptorily disposed of – murdered, in short – thus saving a tiring and unnecessary journey. It appeared that this gnarled-looking character was a Gallipoli veteran who had no particular liking for the British, let alone the Greeks. Fortunately for us, however, the officer, although he listened carefully to these pleas, took no notice of them, evidently deciding to play it by the book.

As the journey proceeded my morale improved, except that I had come ashore in gym shoes and was finding the path, such as it was, extremely uncomfortable. Eventually we arrived in a small town called Yoran. It had a dishevelled open square, at one end of which stood the remains of an enormous Greek temple! It was the temple of Apollo at Didyma, and I had been hoping against hope that this was where the Turkish HQ might be. At first no one took much notice of us, and we sat on the ground for half an hour or so, watching a group of fairly primitive soldiers being instructed in how to take a German machine-gun to pieces. Eventually we were interrogated at some length by the man with the white horse and a more senior officer, after which we were given a plate of soup and put to bed in the nearby police station.

The night seemed long and uncomfortable. But early next morning things took a turn for the better. Instructions from on high had come through by telephone, to the effect that we should be returned to our ship and told to leave Turkish waters forthwith: just what we wished to do. The atmosphere became almost friendly (despite the Gallipoli veteran still lurking around from time to time and casting baleful glances in my direction), so I asked if I could spend half an hour wandering round the ruins. Permission was granted, and almost everyone in sight came with me.

In theory I knew quite a lot about this huge, unfinished marble temple, Hellenistic in conception but containing within it an earlier shrine (rather like the great church at Assisi). My informal lecture as we went round was translated after a fashion and evidently much appreciated; for me, it was deeply exciting to see my first major Greek antiquity, especially after very little sleep and in somewhat bizarre circumstances. All in all, it was a fascinating morning, after which we walked back to the coast in a far more relaxed state of mind than on the journey inland the previous day. This time I was offered a ride on horseback, which I accepted out of politeness until it became too uncomfortable. The crew and the rest of the Greek raiding patrol were touchingly relieved to welcome us back. They thought they had seen the last of us, and were on the point of radioing to base for further instructions. As it was, we sat out the rest of daylight and headed off at dusk, with feelings of rejoicing, into the wine-dark sea.

Course was set south of Gaidaro, and south again of the Furni Islands.

But by 2 a.m. the weather began to deteriorate and we were making slow progress. By dawn I decided to close the southern shore of Ikaria – a long, mountainous island – and hope for some shelter from the north-westerly gale. Actually the gusts from the mountains, the so-called katabatic winds, grew fiercer as we approached the coast, and we were forced to take shelter right inshore, in St Nicholas Bay, where a small crowd of locals gathered to greet us. I rowed ashore with a couple of boxes of food, and stayed awhile practising my Greek on an unexpected new acquaintance, a sophisticated and extremely pretty girl who was redolent neither of garlic nor of the nunnery. By dusk the weather was improving a bit and I had to cut short for ever this burgeoning friendship as we headed westward for Dragonisi, a useful little islet close up against the eastern coast of Mykonos.

In the event we decided to press on and land a recce party at night, in St Anna Bay on Mykonos itself, from where we moved south at dawn to Kalofata Bay. At midday a Greek arrived with a note from the recce party saying that the Germans in Mykonos town were barricaded in and short of food; we could leave them to their own devices, taking off our own party without further ado that same evening and moving on to land them on Andros to the north.

All went according to plan. We picked up our men, augmented by three Greek refugees, then cruised up through the concealing darkness past the sacred island of Delos and along the western coast of Tinos, landing our party just before dawn in Plaka Bay on Andros, where we berthed alongside the rocks after establishing that there were no enemy in the immediate vicinity.

That day we made two forays out to sea to intercept and question large passing caiques. The Germans had commandeered a certain number of local craft, but many others chugging slowly between the islands were innocently trying to carry on a bit of residual trade, mostly in much-needed foodstuffs. Our intercepts proved to be two of these, so we let them proceed on their way.

By evening the weather was deteriorating again – this was late August, and the dreaded Meltemi or Etesian wind was still blowing up strongly from time to time. Next day all lines were out to hold us in our half-sheltered bay. The reconnaissance party returned in the evening, but there was no possibility of leaving. They reported that local guerrillas were watching out for Germans, in case they sent patrols out from town in our direction.

Next morning found us still weather-bound, though the weather showed signs of moderating. This was just as well, since in the late afternoon a bandolier-laden character came on board to say that the German garrison had been informed of our presence. I got the underlying message, which was that we had better leave *instanter*, and that the people who wanted us to do so were precisely the local guerrilla bunch, the ELAS gang, who did not like our interest in Andros affairs and passing shipping, which was interfering with their own steadily tightening grip on local affairs in the interests of international Communism.

However much the Germans knew, there was little point in delay, so we left at once in a moderate but uncomfortable sea, to anchor for the night in nearby Marmara Cove. There we were weather-bound for a further day, and the same sort of guerrilla problems arose. My log records that at 1815 we had to send an armed party to the nearby village to retrieve a Greek officer and his telegraphist, detained by Communist guerrillas from Evvia. At the same time the release of two caiques operated by ISLD was negotiated. Once again I was quite glad to extricate us from shore-bound complications. This trip was revealing a great deal about the complexity of Allied relations, both with Turkey on the one hand and the increasingly obstreperous Greek resistance groups on the other. The good old days, when one could count on the support of almost any Greek islander, were coming to an end, at least in the chain of islands running down from Evvia and the mainland into the central Aegean.

Our course was now eastward and home by way of Dragonisi and Sirina. The approach to Dragonisi around midnight looked unappealing in a moderate to rough sea, so I headed for Delos – not a regular port of call, but tempting in this weather, not least on a personal level for its antiquities. In the early hours we first secured alongside the mole in the tiny boat harbour there, but were urgently asked to move by a slightly built man who emerged from the darkness to identify himself as the resident MO4 agent. He conjured up a motor boat which led us into a small bay some 3 miles away, on the south side of the deserted island of Rheneia – famous for its tomb groups, since in ancient times no one was allowed to die on Apollo's sacred island of Delos; so the moribund (along with expectant mothers, a different source of pollution) were ferried over to Rheneia to complete the job.

My new friend, who had a radio operator on Rheneia and lived in a shepherd's hut there, explained that Delos was too conspicuous for a boat even of our size, and might compromise his own operations. Incidentally he was able to give us a good deal of the kind of information – at least about Rheneia – which we ourselves had been sent out to obtain. I was determined to see the antiquities of Delos none the less, and persuaded him to accompany me back, soon after dawn, to the sacred isle.

That day was absolutely marvellous. Delos, as everyone knows, is still exciting, even with cruise ships anchored in the channel between Delos and Rheneia and landing tourists by the hundreds in the tiny harbour there. It is still, in a way, solitary, since there are no hotels and everyone has to be away before dusk. But *then* it was still more secret and undefiled, with a certain spice added by the knowledge of enemy-occupied islands visible all around it. And the great sanctuary, which (together with Apollo's other shrine at Delphi) dominated the minds and imaginations of Greeks from long before Homer, was the first really extensive site I had seen. Now the guardian of the museum and his small family were its only inhabitants, together with a goatherd or two in summer.

It was a brilliant and wind-swept day. I was shown everything, in the

35 An afternoon ashore near the top of Mount Cynthos, on Delos. Caique skippers (left to right): Sam Barclay, Alec Thwaites, Robin Fletcher, Bill Turnbull. In the background are the ruins of the ancient city.

monumental area at least. My agent friend was by now extremely relaxed, and we climbed together to the top of little Mount Kynthus to see the whole of the central Cyclades laid out before us, with Mykonos close by to the east, Tinos to the north, Syros to the west, and the great bulk of Naxos visible through a slight haze southwards. Below us the ruin-strewn, barren soil of Delos itself, with the rocky islets of Rhemmatia Channel and the arid brown flatlands of Rheneia, were set off against a brilliant blue, streaked with white, as the wind blew the tops off the serried waves of a typical short Aegean sea.

But such magical interludes do not last for ever. Descending to the museum around lunchtime we found a messenger waiting with a note from the radio operator on Rheneia to say that something of an emergency had arisen: HDML 1381 had been caught by the Germans on Sirina, and all Aegean operations were compromised by the capture of her code-books.

LS12 certainly could not leave much before dark, so we waited an hour or so more (refreshing ourselves with coarse bread and a little *retsina*) before crossing over in the motor boat back to Rheneia. By 5 p.m. I was back on board, and was shown the following signal by Sparks:

To: All Ships Aegean   From: FOLEM[1]

SECRET

Various codes and code-books including AGOX and current MINOR WAR VESSELS and CAIQUE recognition signals all believed compromised as result of capture of ML 1381 by enemy. Above mentioned SPs[2] are only to be used if no other available, and then with great caution.

Sparks, with characteristic competence, had already appended the following pencilled note to the signal:

I.   Our signal sent this morning was in 'one time pad' and is perfectly secure. I received FOLEM's signal before transmitting your signal and consequently altered the code.

II. If AGOX is compromised all our signals except this morning's are liable to have been read by the enemy.

III. Germans *cannot* decode our signal sent this morning.

IV. Call-signs are probably compromised, but that will not affect us immediately.

I have passed to Cox'n your instructions re lookout towards Syros.

Sparks.

Thus it was clear that, although my last report had been sent out by unbreakable one time pad, earlier signals had been sent by a code that would reveal us to be in the area. This, together with possible collaboration between ELAS and the German garrison on Andros about our position and intentions, persuaded me that an early start would be desirable – in other words, we should get the hell out of the Cyclades and make best speed towards the Turkish coast. Our mission was, after all, accomplished, and we were on our way home.

So we departed in full daylight at 6 p.m., marginally supplementing our engine speed with full sail and, I hoped, making ourselves look even more like a Greek fishing vessel than usual, for the benefit of the German lookout post some 2 miles away on the south coast of Mykonos. Course was set for Gaidaros, far to the east of us, passing between Patmos and the Furni islands. With a stiff north-westerly wind and a following sea we made good progress, regaining Turkish waters by breakfast-time and, after a brief stop in Phariah Bay, in the Gulf of Güllük, reached our base in Deremen some twelve hours later.

---

[1]   Flag Officer Levant and Eastern Mediterranean.
[2]   Secret Publications.

CHAPTER NINETEEN

Friends and Enemies

When ML 354 relieved us at Syros we took their five German prisoners on board and that evening headed back for Khios. The weather was none too good and rapidly became worse. As we emerged from the Steno Pass around midnight the wind was south-easterly, force 7, sea moderate to rough. There was a longish open sea crossing to Khios, so I decided to seek temporary shelter in Korthi Bay, Andros, not least because the German passengers were adding to the discomfort of life on board. As the caique lurched sickeningly from side to side, with the wind howling through the rigging and seas tearing over the gunwale, they huddled despairingly on deck, burying themselves under a tarpaulin.

To port, through the spray and the darkness, I could see the dim outline of Andros. It could only be 4 or 5 miles off. I leant on the tiller to alter course for Cape Ayios Kosmos, the eastern point of the bay. This brought the seas abeam. The rolling became heavier, the gunwale under every time. Conditions were nearly dangerous, not quite. The prisoners evidently thought otherwise, since one of them extricated himself from the tarpaulin and crawled down the deck towards me. I recognized the blond one who spoke English, and told him to get back amidships. Instead of obeying he collapsed on the deck and clawed at my legs in supplication. He sobbed and implored me to save him and his companions, accusing me *en passant* of ill-treatment and breaking international agreements. They had no lifebelts, he said. He was a bedraggled, pathetic object and evidently no seaman.

I told him that if he continued to disobey orders I would be forced to lock him up down below, where conditions were much worse. Furthermore, there *were* no lifebelts. If he kept his friends quiet they would share no worse a fate than the crew. Then I called over to the coxswain to take the tiller, and made my way to the waist of the caique where the prisoners were lying. They had spewed all over the place and were wet and frightened. I told them through the blond that with luck we should find shelter in an hour or so. Feeling slightly sick myself, I returned aft. The coast was drawing close and we were getting some shelter from the north, but there was still no sign of the expected bay.

Eventually we found it, and motored cautiously in, sounding with the lead as we edged towards a small jetty. At three fathoms we dropped anchor – only to haul it up again as the boat dragged fast at the first heavy gust from the hills. Three times more we dropped it before finding good holding-ground. Then we went to sleep.

When dawn came I went out on deck and saw that the caique lay about two hundred yards from the shore, around which clustered a score of low white cottages. A small fishing boat was shoving off from the beach to have a closer look at us. As it approached I leant over the side and shouted good morning to its four suspicious Greek occupants. At this they nosed closer, and one of them stood up in the boat to see what our caique – which was then flying a Greek flag with the German red-and-white pennant beneath it – was carrying on deck. One of the first things he saw was the heap of sodden field-grey uniforms that concealed the prisoners, and above them, seated on the main hatch, a seaman on guard with a tommy-gun. The Greek looked relieved, and behind his heavy beard appeared to smile.

'Germans?' he asked. 'Then you must be English: *prepei na sisthe Inglezoi.*'

'English, English,' the other three shouted, and climbed over the canvas sidescreen to shake me warmly by the hand. Three of the crew had appeared from below to see what the commotion was, and they too were affectionately greeted. Fortunately the man with the gun was left with an unimpeded view of his charges, not that they had much spirit for deeds of resistance.

Some tea was on the boil and I offered our new Greek friends a mug each, which they accepted with delight, tea being almost unknown in those years of dearth. I enquired about the situation on the island. Bad, very bad, they replied. The Germans had all left, they had been sunk at sea it was hoped, but in their place were the Communist guerrillas.

'False Greeks,' they said. 'Ah, Captain, they terrorize our lives.' Admittedly the Germans had been worse – they were fiends in disguise. Couldn't I see this from the degenerate faces of the prisoners there? (Actually they had recovered a bit from their craven stupor, but looked unhappy again, and fearful, when they saw the Greeks on board.)

I had no special desire to discuss the prisoners, and turned the talk to the question of the best place to moor. They indicated a small buoy that was strong enough to hold us, and would enable us to secure the stern to the end of the little ruined jetty. So we set about shifting the caique to the new berth. Then the occupants of the houses, mostly women, came down to the water's edge to stare at the strange and evidently benevolent *Inglezoi.*

It was not long before they, too, spotted the prisoners. At that moment the cook was just dishing up breakfast, and I noticed without too much surprise that the prisoners' ration was the same as my own. 'Cox'n,' I said, 'don't you remember my saying that while these men are on board they are to be treated as enemies, not pet rabbits? That means they have to be given enough plain food to keep them healthy, and no more. You'd be surprised how little that is according to international law. Now they're lapping up the last of the fresh tomatoes. If you must waste fresh food, I'd rather it was thrown overboard, or better still, given to these half-starved Greeks.'

Leading Seaman King, normally no softy and certainly no enemy lover, leant against the tiller and looked aggrieved.

'Look, sir,' he said. 'If this was a big ship it would be different. Then the prisoners would be down below and they'd have their food by themselves, and I should be happy enough to know that they were on a diet of bread and water for a change. But as it is, they have to be up on deck within five yards of where we're having our own dinner, and we couldn't enjoy our food, after what you'll agree was a sticky old night, if they were sitting there gazing at us with their eyes popping out.'

'Personally speaking, I agree with you,' I said. 'They're a depressing enough bunch already, and would be worse on empty bellies. It would put me off my food just as much as you; I'm not really so tough, it's just that I think one ought to try to be! But the real point now, in any case, is that all these half-starved Greeks are watching. None of them has eaten as much food as this for three years, and it's hardly fair to expect them to understand our arguments about cramped conditions on board. As long as they're here, the prisoners will have to feed on the stuff the Greeks have to live on.'

'Aye, aye, sir,' the coxswain replied, 'but I'll just go and chase those bloody Greeks away so that we can get down to our grub in peace.'

Unfortunately the damage had been done, arousing a storm of resentment against the prisoners. They had already started their food. Squatting on deck, they shovelled it down as though they had not eaten for a week. With every mouthful their gloom lifted and they regained something of the status of human beings, their apathy and apparent degeneracy dropping away from them. It was something of a relief, really, to the rest of us on board, but not to the tragic chorus of Greek matrons peering angrily over the stern. They were standing on tiptoe, craning their necks, leaning this way and that, to see what food the prisoners were eating now. One of them managed to stand on the gunwale for a moment to get a better view, jumping down again with a cry in which delight and horror were mixed – delight at the appearance of the food, horror that these hated men were allowed to eat it. A buzz of excitement rose from the group as they realized what the prisoners were having; scattered phrases reached me . . . 'potatoes' . . . 'tea with milk in it' . . . 'meat' . . . 'meat'.

They were completely silent for a minute or so, and then, after some urgent whispering, one of them – the oldest, judging by her withered face and prominent moustache – climbed on board over the stern where I was sitting. Like all her race, she was a democrat, and under the impulse of righteous indignation the scrupulous respect she would normally have felt for my calling and nationality totally disappeared.

'Look here, young sir,' she said, 'why in the name of the all-holy Virgin are you feeding these pigs as though they were kings? If you have food to waste, then give it to us, whose children are growing up deformed because they starve. If you had lived on this island, and seen the way these swine behave, you wouldn't be giving them your titbits. Hand the pigs over to us, that's what you should do and we'll tear their fingernails out one by one, before we kill them.' The gesture that accompanied this advice was blood-curdling in the extreme, and the other women joined in with fierce movements and raised voices. That they knew how to treat prisoners was the gist of their response.

I decided to deal with the matter once and for all. 'All right,' I replied. 'You can have the prisoners, and do to them exactly what you want.' The result was inevitable: they looked sheepish and confused, muttered together and slowly withdrew along the little jetty and ashore. The prisoners themselves, fortunately for them, did not follow this particular exchange, and started trying to dry out their saturated clothing. We were stuck in that particular bay for another thirty-six hours, during which international tensions gradually relaxed.

The Oxford Don's Tale

CHAPTER TWENTY

Priests in Peril

The sheltered waters of Port Deremen, in the Gulf of Kos, wore the glazed, dark blue sheen of morning calm, waiting for the first cat's paws of the sea breeze to ruffle their surface. Ropes and cables hung loose from the decks of a crowd of caiques and motor launches huddled together round their parent schooners, incongruous in these idyllic surroundings of clear, clean water and rocky, scrub-covered or densely wooded hills. Although I didn't know it, I was looking for the last time upon this paradise; we were under orders to sail that day – 1 September 1944 -- with a patrol of soldiers to be landed on the island of Lemnos, and before I got back, raiding forces flotillas would have moved with the tide of war to the urban setting of the port of Khios.

We sailed in the early afternoon and adjusted our speed in order to reach the narrows between Kos and Turkey after dark. As the sun set, the mountainous outline of Kos Island sharpened and seemed for a while uncomfortably close. We edged in nearer to the Turkish shore, passing inside Magpie Rock. But nothing stirred. Even the searchlight on Kum Burnu, which usually swept the straits when a ship was heard approaching, failed to appear. We rounded Pasha Rock and stood north inside the Karabaghla Islands to the Gulf of Güllük. When we reached it there were no more dangers ahead of us for more than 40 miles, so I was able to turn in for a few hours.

★   ★   ★

I woke to the strains of a Beethoven symphony. Norman, the W/T operator, must have finished his early morning watch and tuned to a broadcasting station somewhere. I lay awake listening for a while, gazing up through the cabin hatch at the sky and the coxswain sitting comfortably on the transom seat, the tiller cradled in his arms. After a bit I managed to summon up enough energy to roll out of my bunk. I gave myself a shake, then clambered up on deck hoping for breakfast.

Down in the hold amidships the spare hand rose somewhat grudgingly

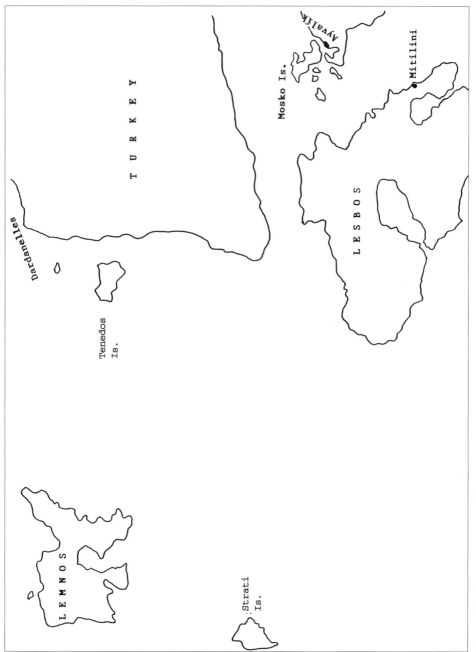

Map 16 North-eastern Aegean – Lemnos to Lesbos with Strati Island.

from his card game with three of our soldier passengers to get me a mug of tea and a slice of spam on bread. The patrol we carried consisted of a second lieutenant, a corporal and five men, all serving with the SBS.

My thoughts wandered to the straits, less than a mile wide, between Samos and Turkey, through which we would have to pass that night – '*rivages enchanteurs ravissants, ou a pourtant souvent retenti le fracas des armes*'. Less than a year had passed since those shores had witnessed the most recent clash of arms, when the Germans, after recapturing Leros, had descended in force, with massive air support, upon Samos. Then a small fleet of caiques had crossed to and fro, evacuating British, Greek and Italian troops from the island. I myself, in charge of Headquarters schooner LS9, had transported the bulk of the British garrison to Kuşadasi, the nearest Turkish port. Then, with their arms and equipment still on board, I had passed through these same straits on the way to Cyprus and Beirut.

When we reached the narrows they looked quiet enough. And apart from one or two rifle shots from the Turkish post on Bayrak Adasi, and the plop of a bullet or two nearby (the customary greeting from all Turkish lookout posts to passing vessels, warning them to keep their distance) our passage through the straits was a peaceful one. At dawn on 3 September – the fifth anniversary of the outbreak of war and my mother's sixty-first birthday – we entered the Gulf of Kuşadasi and stood north-west into open water.

★   ★   ★

Strati Island, 6 miles long from north to south and 4 miles wide, lies in the open Aegean, some 40 miles west-north-west of Lesbos and 15 miles south of Lemnos. It is more than usually barren, with a hilly spine along its eastern side, rising to nearly 1,000 ft at the highest point. We closed that side of the island shortly before daybreak, searching for a deep-water cave in which we had been advised to lie up during the day. We found it eventually and, with our mast down and stern anchor out, edged our way inside.

A low swell followed us in, running past us into the echoing darkness, out of which an eerie murmur of wavelets on shingle, rising and falling, came

36 A deep-water cave in which a caique would be safe from aerial observation.

back to us. The water was deep but the walls of the cave smooth, without any clefts or jutting rocks to which a grapnel or the bight of a rope might be secured.

After an hour or so, the wave murmur from inside the cave rose to a growl, and then to a roar: wind and sea were getting up. The caique began to yaw uncontrollably from side to side, bringing up with a thump against her fenders, first on one side then on the other. It was time to get out, and fast. Luckily we had a long scope of line on our stern anchor, so we were able to haul ourselves well clear without much difficulty.

The only other shelter shown on our chart was a small bay with a village at its head on the north-west side of the island. We made for this. With a freshening easterly wind we had no alternative, and must risk the unlikely presence of Germans on so remote and unimportant an island. We expected, however, that our arrival would bring a crowd of curious villagers down to the waterfront, as we entered what turned out to be a snug little harbour. Imagine our astonishment, therefore, when we secured to the single jetty, to find no sign of life whatever. No boats, no people, not even a cat or chickens or a barking dog to greet us. And when I went ashore with the SBS officer and the coxswain we found every house (there were a dozen or so, and a small church) completely empty. Doors hung open. A shutter banged in the wind. There was crockery in a few drawers and on some of the tables, occasional pictures on the walls and rectangular patches where others had been removed. Bits of clothing lay about, in drawers, on chairs or on the floor. In one house rumpled sheets had been left on two of the beds, and a dog's or cat's bowl in a corner still held some scraps. A weird, unearthly atmosphere hung over the whole village, reminding one of Castelorizo Island, from which the entire population had been evacuated by the Allies in 1941. No doubt the Germans had removed these people in the same way.

⋆　　⋆　　⋆

We wandered back aboard, where I stretched out on deck. In the bright sunshine, sheltered by our canvas bulwarks, it was pleasantly warm and I was soon asleep. I must have slept soundly, because it was nearly four o'clock when the coxswain's shout of 'Hey, Skips! There's something coming our way' woke me with a start. He pointed out to sea, and there, sure enough, was a small caique making for the harbour from the north-west – the direction of Mount Athos and Salonika. The wind had dropped, and the 'pop–pop–pop' of her single-cylinder engine was just audible. I called down to the SBS boys in the hold to come up on deck. One never knew. It might just be villagers coming back for a night or two in their own homes; or it could, of course, be an enemy patrol on reconnaissance. There was no way of telling until they got closer. And now, as we watched, another larger caique, a schooner, appeared on the horizon, also steering towards us.

Our total armament was a .303 Vickers machine-gun on either quarter, a 20 mm single-shot anti-tank gun in the bows and two 2 in mortars which could be sited anywhere. To this the SBS could add a Bren gun, sub-machine-guns and two dozen hand grenades. They brought their weapons up from below, then spread out along the jetty and the land beyond, taking advantage of any cover they could find – bushes, an old rainwater tank on its side, discarded crates and so on. The officer and the corporal stayed on board.

The small caique was now entering harbour. We could only see two figures on her deck – the skipper steering and a boy up forward. She rounded the end of the jetty and dropped her anchor about three ship's lengths from it, then came astern and the boy jumped ashore with a mooring line which he passed through a ring on the jetty. The engine was now stopped and a gang plank rigged. Then, with no more than a glance in our direction, the skipper and boy both disappeared below.

We waited, wondering what to do next and feeling, if anything, rather foolish. Then to our amazement, there emerged from the caique's cabin two bearded priests dressed in the traditional cassocks and 'chimney-pot' hats of the Greek Orthodox Church. One was an old man with a bushy white beard, the other much younger – almost a boy – with a sparse black beard and side whiskers. They stepped ashore, the young man leading, and came straight along the jetty to where we lay.

37 Priests of the Greek Orthodox Church.

The younger priest came aboard first and was obviously in an agitated state of mind. My knowledge of Greek in those days was sketchy, but I could understand it a good deal better than I could speak it, and it soon became clear that the approaching schooner – now less than a mile away – was the cause of his agitation. '*Kakourgi* [bad men],' he kept repeating, with a wave of the hand in her direction.

He seemed to be trying to warn me – perhaps to tell me that we were in danger from those bad men, or so I interpreted the few phrases I could understand. Were they Germans then? I wondered, and focused my binoculars on the man at the wheel. He looked much the same as any other Greek seaman, with his peaked cap, bare feet and rolled-up trousers; but down on the main deck I could now make out dark-bearded fellows wearing black scarves round their heads, with bandoliers over their shoulders and across their chests – *andartes* for sure, and probably Communists, who at that time were known to be anti-British.

'*Kakourgi! Kakourgi!*' The old man joined in, pointing at the schooner, and then, '*Prostasia* [protection] . . . *prostasia! prostasia!*'

I tried to reassure them by pointing to our weapons and the soldiers ashore. 'We do not need *prostasia*,' I said, slowly and deliberately, shaking my head to reinforce the point.

They looked puzzled and started talking, with insistent gestures, to each other. The old man sat himself on the cabin top, fingering his beads and looking unhappy. He was, I think, trying to reason with his young friend.

'Peace, my father,' the boy said in Greek. 'The holy brothers on Lesbos will welcome us.'

The old man looked up with tears in his eyes, smiling gratefully into the boy's face. 'We have come a long way,' he said. 'We must not hesitate now.'

The boy turned again to me, speaking now in broken English. 'We coming from Macedonia, on travel for Holy Land . . . Caiqui going for Rhodes . . . you carrying us for Mitilini?'

I smiled – reassuringly, I hoped. No doubt his presence on board would give us some protection by making a quarrel with the *andartes* less likely; the Greeks, I thought, were a God-fearing people. But LS6 was not a large boat, and we had twelve soldiers and sailors in her already.

'You carrying for Mitilini?' the young man repeated.

'OK,' I said. 'But now we must go.' It would be out of the question to have Greek civilians with us when we landed our patrol on its secret mission. 'Tomorrow morning we'll be back,' I assured him, 'and then we can take you to Mitilini.'

While I talked, the coxswain and I were shepherding them gently but firmly to the gangway and down on to the jetty. They left us reluctantly and, I thought, sadly – with one or two final '*kakourgis*' and '*prostasias*', and frequent backward glances as they wandered disconsolately along the jetty back to their caique. But now we had to concentrate on reassembling our patrol and getting to sea. They must be landed on Lemnos well before midnight, to give them the best possible chance of finding a safe hide-out in the mountains by dawn.

By the time we eventually left harbour, the schooner had come in and was moored alongside. Her people – twenty or more *andartes* – were gathered on deck watching us. We waved to them as we passed. They stared back unmoving and in stony silence. A sullen, unfriendly lot we thought them, but we had other more pressing preoccupations on our minds just then.

★   ★   ★

The passage to Lemnos was uneventful. The patrol was landed without incident, and we got back to Strati at dawn.

The harbour was empty! There was no sign of the schooner or the priests' caique, nor any other sign of life. The place was deserted, as we'd originally found it. And silent – a silence marked by the occasional banging of that single shutter in the wind, which seemed somehow to emphasize the utter desolation of the scene.

A misunderstanding over signal codes left us hanging about for two more days without orders, and when the wind turned westerly we went back to our cave on the east coast. A day or two later, however, the muddle was sorted out and we were told to proceed to Port Mitilini, on the east coast of Lesbos Island, from which the Germans had just withdrawn. When we arrived there I asked the harbour authorities and the crews of local caiques for news of the two priests and the Communist schooner, but no one had heard of them.

I was also told by our people on Khios, when we returned to our new base there a week later, that the withdrawal of German forces had sparked off hostilities between Left and Right all over Greece. The Communists had set up People's Courts, where suspected collaborators and anyone else they didn't like – notably priests and school teachers – were being tried, and usually executed. The Mitilini Communist Party had a particularly bad reputation in this respect.

I thought back to our meeting with the two priests in Strati harbour, and all at once the episode took on a different and more ominous complexion. What if they had not been warning us that *we* were in danger from the Communists, and had instead been pleading for protection rather than offering it? Had we unwittingly thrown two innocent and holy men to the wolves? It was a deeply disturbing thought which remains with me still.

Tales from a Greek Shipping Company Director

CHAPTER TWENTY-ONE

The Mountains of Epirus

When the Italians invaded Greece I joined the Army. I was nineteen and in my first year at Athens University, reading law. We volunteers were put in the charge of a corporal, whose duty it was to lecture us on military matters. But most of the time he preferred to harangue us on the virtues of Communism.

A family friend, Colonel Vendiris, who had left the Army when Metaxas came to power, gave me instruction in the arts of war: how to use my weapons and, with the help of cushions scattered here and there on the drawing room floor, how to take advantage of the lie of the land. 'Do not fear,' he used to say. 'One bullet won't kill a thousand men. It's usually the other way round.'

It was late December 1940. Without further instruction we were sent by train to Patras, then across the Gulf in an ancient Scottish steamboat, called *Caledonia*, to Kryoneri, where we were loaded into cattle trucks (forty men or four horses) and carried on the Western Greek railway to the railhead at Agrinion. From there we climbed by Army truck into the mountains. It was now dark and very cold, but at every village the women came out with gifts of cakes, coffee or fruit to cheer us on our way. Sometimes we had to disembark with shovels to clear a snow-blocked pass or gully, until finally in the early hours of the morning we reached Ioannina, the capital of Epirus. Here we rested for a while, but early next day drove on to Metsovon in the Pindus range.

Our mountain warfare training now began in earnest, with formation skiing and long treks over rough country, fully equipped and carrying heavy loads – including enough ammunition for our Mannlicher cavalry carbines, as well as hand grenades, mortar bombs, mortars, tents and groundsheets, with iron rations to last us for a week or more in the mountains.

When we returned at the end of each day to the Metsovon High School, where we were billeted, there would be girls waiting outside. And whenever

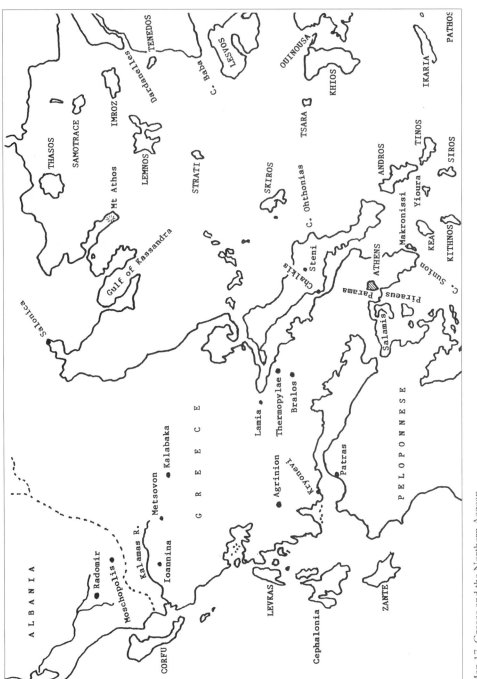

Map 17 Greece and the Northern Aegean.

any one of us came out, he would be approached. But not for love – the inbred dignity of the mountain people demanded chastity above all else from their women folk. However, they were desperately poor, some families near to starving, and all the girls wanted was to earn a few drachmas (or food if we could spare any) in return for washing our clothes.

They were charming and some of them very lovely. One, called Katerina, was fifteen. Her sister, Elektra, eighteen, was tall and graceful, with raven-black hair combed tightly back and fine dark eyes. In her peasant's pleated skirt almost to her ankles, embroidered bodice and short jacket, she looked very beautiful. My best friend, Nikos Nikolaidis, a student at the Academy of Art, was entranced. 'George,' he said, 'I have never seen a lovelier woman. You must not let me . . . you must prevent me from falling in love with her.'

Her younger sister was shorter and plumper, but with a sweet open face – the face of a child – which smiled with genuine pleasure. And like most country girls, neither of them looked at us boldly, or with any hint of coquetry, but with eyes cast modestly down. And when we asked, 'How much will you charge to wash our clothes?' the elder girl replied at once. 'Anything . . . whatever you care to give us. But first you must come home and meet our mother. She will decide.'

Nikos and I looked at each other with some disquiet. What were we letting ourselves in for? Would Mother turn out to be a stern old dragon who would question our motives, perhaps even our intentions towards her daughters? She turned out to be nothing of the sort. She was a robust but kindly looking country woman, in her early fifties, one would have said. Her dark hair was flecked with grey, and her smiling eyes twinkled merrily as she came towards us. She greeted us with a natural grace which many a society hostess would have envied.

Their father, a woodcutter, was away in the mountains. Their house consisted of a single room in which they all – there were six of them – lived and slept. At one end there was an open hearth. We were offered *tsipouro*, a drink like *ouzo* without the aniseed, made from grapes or mulberries and served in small glasses. Then to establish their status (it was, I think, in the nature of a 'hands off' warning) we were shown the girls' trousseaux of national dress, heavy and elaborate, carefully folded away in large wooden boxes.

The older girls, Sophia and Persephone, joined us, Persephone bringing an ancient oil lamp to light the room. 'In Athens do you have lamps like this, or pressure lamps?' she asked. None of them really understood when I answered, 'No, we have electricity.' But for politeness' sake Sophia, the eldest, nodded. 'We've heard of that,' she said thoughtfully. 'Does it give a good light? And how do you light it?' I tried to explain, and was surprised to find how difficult it was. They asked us then about life in Athens. We described it as best we could, but I doubt if they really got the picture – especially when it came to lifts (rooms which you enter, and then, when you push a button in the wall, they rise from floor to floor of the building).

We spent many happy evenings in that little house, whose people became our friends. Their life, which we occasionally shared for an hour or two, was a hard one – chopping and carrying wood from the forest, drawing water from the village well, tilling and harvesting their small patch of garden.

★　★　★

Meanwhile, in our training we learned to ski on the steepest slopes and on the flat with our carbines slung across our shoulders. After three weeks of this, we were sent by truck into Albania, where we were billeted in a fourteenth-century monastery at Moschopolis.

It was an austere and sparsely furnished building of rough-hewn stone. I remember lying on my stomach on the floor of a large empty room, with the others sitting or jostling around me, while I wrote in my diary by the light of a stub of candle stuck on top of my steel helmet, and later, sitting on the monastery garden wall to eat some of my bread ration. . . . Then the cramps, vicious stomach aches. We all suffered from the runs, but there was only one loo and it was strictly reserved for officers. The rest of us had to find a corner somewhere out in the snow.

That night I was seized with a violent stomach pain. But the thought of clumping downstairs and out into the freezing night and snow was horrifying. Anyway there was no time. In the wall beside me was the mouth of a corridor. I rushed down it, turned right, and there, in front of me, was the open door of a loo. I leaped in and let go – just in time!

But then I realized I was in the officers' loo. In some trepidation I pulled on my trousers, and was just leaving when, in the mouth of the corridor, there appeared the tall and elegant figure of our battalion commander, Major Janis Paparolou.

'Good evening, Mr Paparolou,' I said – a most unmilitary way of addressing one's CO, but it was scarcely a military occasion.

'Good morning, Mr Bisbas,' he said politely.

He was killed during the German flank attack upon us three months later. He died heroically, revolver in hand, blazing away at the advancing Germans, several of whom he brought down. We were all very proud of him.

★　★　★

From Moschopolis, our training completed, we were sent at last to the front. But this in itself was a battle more ferocious than any we had yet encountered. For the front was receding fast, as the Greek Army, counter-attacking strongly, forced the enemy back mile after mile.

Our platoon was commanded by Costas Thialos, a 24-year-old cavalry officer. The rest of us were all 19- or 20-year-olds; and on that six-day march over mountain trails in freezing weather, bivouacking at night under our groundsheet capes, we found him an inspiring leader. Day after day, carrying great loads of weaponry – rifles, grenades, ammunition, picks and shovels, tents, groundsheets, sleeping bags, clothing, rucksacks, skis and ski sticks – 40 kg per man in all, we followed the goat tracks across snow- or scree-covered hillsides; in and out of gullies choked with boulders; over plateaux where bitter winds sweeping up the valleys brought the sound of gunfire which never seemed to get nearer.

The routine was fifty minutes' march or climb and ten minutes' rest in every hour. On and on we went, with each changing gradient up or down producing new points of chafe in boots which must never be removed, the only relaxation being an occasional brush with the remnants of an Italian rearguard.

I can feel again the relief, the positive elation, at being told that in half an hour we would stand and fight, followed by disappointment bordering on despair when we found the enemy already gone, and we must struggle on again. We came to realize that for the soldier the battles themselves are no hardship compared with the exhaustion, the hunger, the thirst, the aching and blistered feet of the marches in between. And I would never have believed, if it hadn't happened to me, that you could sleep where you fell, in snow or on icy ground, and dream long dreams between the whistle blast for 'halt and fall out' and ten minutes later the two blasts for 'fall in and move off'.

★   ★   ★

Here, George Bisbas paused in his tale, to dwell for a while on the background to the war. 'At 4.00 a.m. on 26 October, 1940,' he began, 'Count Grazzi called on General Metaxas, who was asleep in bed, and delivered Italy's ultimatum to Greece, which would expire at 6.00 a.m. But at 5.00 a.m. Italian planes were already bombing and strafing Patras (where I was born), while at the same time Alpini formations were attacking Greek positions on the Kalamas River with Ioannina as their objective.'

George regarded me gravely, but the warlike glint in his eye told a different story. 'Within a week,' he said quietly, 'Greece had brought her Army to full strength with reservists and conscripts. And they had driven the Italians back almost to the sea when, on 11 April 1941, six German divisions invaded from Macedonia, on our northern flank. And even then . . .' (his eyes were blazing now) 'Even then the Greek conscript battalions, containing many recuperating wounded to bring them up to strength, fought back with great ferocity, holding the invader for twenty-three days on the Rupel line of forts facing Bulgaria.'

'But now, of course, we in Albania were obliged to fall back to straighten the line with the British Expeditionary Force advancing through Thessaly. We reached the road leading to Radomir village, with the Radomir Heights beyond. There we halted, and were told to seat ourselves round the sides of a cup in the hillside – a natural amphitheatre – for our CO to address us.

Colonel Sinioris, CO of the 1st Infantry Regiment, was a man of commanding dignity. He spoke to us, after five days of continuous retreat, in a voice of courage and determination:

"To the 1st Battalion of the 1st Regiment of Infantry and the Machine-Gun and Alpine Companies," he said, "has fallen the honour of defending the Heights of Radomir and the road down which the 9th Division and the major part of the 2nd Corps must pass. I shall use no heroic language to say that you will cover and protect to the last man the retreat of your brothers in arms, so that they in turn may re-form and defend our country against the invader. God be with you and with your arms."

'Then, on a lighter note, he went on, "Each man will receive one *kouramana* [loaf of rough bread]." Our eyes gleamed. None of us had had a proper meal for days. The last of my private possessions (a piece of scented soap, I remember) had been bartered with an Albanian peasant woman, near whose house we had halted, for a very small piece of maize bread. We all looked like scarecrows, with sunken cheeks and staring eyes.

'We were marched to a small roadside monastery, where each man was issued with his *kouramana*. Some tore off chunks and started eating, though the bread must last throughout tomorrow's battle – "if my belly's still in one piece to receive it," growled my next door neighbour.'

★   ★   ★

It was when we had almost reached the position we were to hold, on a plateau overlooking the main road, that I realized I'd left my steel helmet behind. I was too tired to go back for it, and in any case it was too late.

As darkness was coming on, Lieutenant Costas Thialos began to read the orders for the night, giving each of us his arc of fire. Our Mannlichers dated from the Greco–Turkish conflict of 1921–2, some of them, perhaps from the Balkan Wars of 1912–13. Many of our men also carried machine–pistols of Steier (Austrian) make, transferred to us from the police who had just been equipped with them. 'But we're short of ammunition,' Costas Thialos told us, after showing us our positions on the plateau.

Immediately in front of us was a deep ravine, and over on the opposite side was another mountain, somewhat lower than our own, which was occupied by the Italians. On our left was a range of hills, one of them fairly close and potentially threatening, should the enemy reach it. To our right the ground sloped gently away from our position to the road along which our main body was to retreat, and which we must deny to the enemy pursuing them.

Other elements of our company had taken up positions between ourselves and the road, while the machine-gun company covered the road itself. Our hill was of particular importance tactically, because in order to reach the road and cut off the retreating Greek forces, the Italians must first dislodge us, so as to be able to cross the river without sustaining massive casualties.

When it was dark, we were told to dig slit trenches; but the ground was very hard and stony. Our shovels were of little use, and I admit that I was too lazy to dig. Instead I made myself a small rampart of rocks and stones beside a tree, and placed my pack behind it.

During the night I was sent with three others on a reconnaissance patrol. There was a deathly hush over the valley, through which the splash and thunder of the torrent rose and fell, sometimes swelling to a roar, then dying away in the uncertain gusting of a cold wind sweeping down the ravine. Nothing seemed to be moving. One imagined small creatures lying in the long grass or under bushes, eyes staring, muzzles twitching anxiously. There was a feeling of expectancy in the air, but no alien sounds. We clambered back uphill as dawn was breaking. When we reached our lines I lay down behind my barricade, gnawed off a crust of bread and fell asleep.

★   ★   ★

A mighty explosion brought me up on to my knees. Looking behind me, I saw that a large bush screening my position from the rear had disappeared. Soon 4 in mortar bombs were raining down around us; not all of them went off, but those that did sent stones and shrapnel flying. We pressed ourselves to the ground and hoped. The bombardment must have lasted about half an hour. On my left were two young men from the mountains of Epirus – hardy peasants and good friends. I called to them. They were OK. And so, surprisingly, were the rest of our section. Costas Thialos came round and spoke to each of us in turn. Then he levelled his binoculars at the mountain opposite and, after a moment, said quietly, 'Ah, here they come.'

We could see movement over there. Some 300 metres away it must have been – figures dodging from bush to bush and advancing steadily.

'Hold your fire . . . wait for the command,' Costas Thialos ordered, and added 'How is Vatsikourides?'

Vatsikourides was the only man in the platoon who did not have either a machine-pistol or a carbine. Instead he was given a huge old Lebel grenade-throwing rifle – probably dating from the 1914–18 war, but he had only three grenades. So the platoon joke throughout our time on the mountain was the endless repetition of Vatsi's voice saying: 'Shall I shoot? Shall I shoot now, sir? Shall I shoot now?' and the gruff reply, 'No, Vatsi, . . . hold your fire . . . hold it, Vatsi.' As can be imagined, there were a number of more or less salacious variations to this refrain.

Vatsi was a simple fellow and we all loved him. The last time I saw him, as I moved into my own position, he was standing with his back to the wall of a shepherd's bothy between us and the next section, his Lebel at his side, shouting to us, 'This time, you see . . . I'm going to get them . . . see if I don't.' The unaffected glee of anticipation lit up his broad and shining face.

The next time Costas Thialos came round, it was I who asked, 'How is Vatsikourides? Has he fired his Lebel?'

'Not yet. But he's going to.'

Soon after that, more ammunition was distributed all down the line – 100 rounds per man – and it must have been about 9.00 a.m. when we heard the first bursts of machine-gun fire from across the ravine.

'Watch out,' called Thialos, 'they're on their way again. That's their covering fire to make us keep our heads down.'

But once again nothing happened for nearly an hour, when all at once a hand grenade exploded close by, and I heard the two Epirus boys shouting. 'We can see them, sir; shall we get them, sir?' And Thialos replying, 'Don't move. . . . Don't fire. . . . Steady there . . . steady . . . I can see them too.'

But a moment later came the order 'Open fire! Kill the swine!' Then I could see them – wave after wave of Italians, charging at us from the left and throwing their little red hand grenades which burst all round us. And I too began to shoot, load and shoot, load and shoot. The Italians dodged and weaved. Then all at once they were gone, and the order came: 'Cease fire . . . rest. . . .'

★　　★　　★

That went on all day. Charge after charge from left and right and straight in front of us. And the enemy were suffering casualties. Some lay where they fell, some crawled away, some were carried back by their comrades. Whether we also had our casualties, I couldn't tell. But Costas Thialos and the platoon sergeant passed up and down the line without pause throughout the battle, encouraging, supporting, advising continuously. They were brave men, inspiring great admiration and loyalty in us all.

The firing had been so intense that the bushes and saplings before us were stripped bare of leaves. Bullets and shrapnel had whistled about our ears, yet by some miracle none of us was hit. At one stage my carbine had jammed. I crawled over to my Epirus friends, who knew more about weapons than I. They took the gun and after a little while called to say that it was fixed; so I crawled over again to fetch it. Familiarity was beginning to breed contempt. But as Colonel Vendiris had said: 'Never fear. One bullet won't kill a thousand men. It's usually the other way round.'

The Italians showed courage in this engagement, but perhaps rather less determination. With their superiority in numbers, they should have been able to over-run our positions with ease. In the meantime, looking to our right, towards that vital road, we could see the trucks, staff cars and field artillery of our main body, plus a strange assortment of civilian vehicles pressed into service, moving steadily southwards. It was an encouraging sight that gave us all hope. We settled down to slog it out.

And then, about the middle of the afternoon, word was passed along the line that the unit holding the vital hill on our left had withdrawn. If the Italians occupied it now, they could eat us for breakfast. We tried not to think about it. And at 5.00 p.m. Thialos came round again, to each section in turn with a final exhortation: 'Hold on at all costs till 8.00 p.m. The main body will be through by then. So come what may, we won't withdraw till then.' Rifle and machine-gun fire from the Italians grew fiercer, as they came on again. We had almost exhausted our ammunition, but Thialos promised us that more would be issued.

Eight o'clock came. It was getting dark and the firing had ceased. But in the dusk my imagination conjured up eerie sounds and shadowy figures moving here and there in the gloom. We knew by now that the hill to our left had been occupied in strength. The Italians must be moving to encircle us. But maybe they would wait till daylight to attack. A slender shaving of moon hung low in the western sky.

At last our platoon sergeant, Sergeant Thampsas, came along the line with the order we'd been waiting for – 'Boys, start to move back, past the shepherds's hut, there. But don't rush . . . one by one.' He then told the corporal, who was in the line with us, how far we should move and where we should re-form. To me he said, 'When the lads to your right go, wait for thirty seconds then move. But mind you don't stumble or break any twigs . . . we must withdraw in absolute silence.'

It was nearly dark when the boys to my right moved off. I counted up to thirty, then humped on my pack, slung my carbine across my shoulders and crawled through the bushes. When I judged that I was well screened from view, I got up and walked towards the shepherd's hut.

As I approached, I was surprised to see Vatsikourides still standing there with his trusty Lebel beside him.

'Aren't you coming with us?' I asked in a low voice.

There was no reply. I moved closer. His three grenades were still there – one on the Lebel and two in the rack. Vatsi was standing stiffly erect, leaning back a little against the wall of the hut. In the starlight he looked serene but determined, as always. Then I saw it – a neat little hole in his left temple. Vatsi had gone on ahead.

CHAPTER TWENTY-TWO

A Hard Road Home

When we reached a small stream I threw myself face down in the water, gulping it down. My lips were cracked, my throat parched and burning. One of the boys ahead shouted, 'There are dead mules in the water upstream! You are drinking their blood.' But I was too far gone to care. Then, with a swoosh and a whirring, like diving birds, a flurry of mortar bombs fell around us. The Italians had heard and were replying. One bomb burst quite close to us and I was hit in the ankle, but surprisingly felt no pain.

We walked all night, sometimes above the tree line, where patches of late snow lingered in hollows or under rocks; sometimes through thick forest or over open grassland. Early next morning we reached battalion headquarters in a farm beside the road. We were the last to arrive.

The roll was called, company by company. When it came to No. 3 Company, it went something like this:

'Arnopoulos, Andreas.'

'*Paron* [present].'

'Bisbas, Giorgios.'

'*Paron.*'

'Houinas, Alessandros.'

Silence. Then the voice of the sergeant-major in charge: '*Epece yper patridos* [He fell for his country].'

'Rizos, Demetrios.'

'*Epece yper patridos.*'

It began to look as though half the company, perhaps more than half, had been killed in that desperate rearguard action.

'Tombros, Theodros.'

'*Paron.*'

'Giorgiopolis, Emmanouil.'

'*Paron.*'

'Hadjinicolaos, Aimelios.'

'*Epece yper patridos.*'

This was a heavy blow. Aimelios Hadjinicolaos and I had been at school together, and I remembered our joy at meeting again in Ioannina. We had spent most of our pocket money buying presents for each other, and had even planned to go to a brothel together, but when we saw the length of the queue outside, we changed our minds. Instead we bought ourselves 'pasteli' and ate them on a bench in the municipal gardens.

And so it went on: '*Paron*' . . . '*Epece yper patridos*' . . . '*Paron*' . . . '*Epece yper patridos*' . . . on and on, until last of all:

'Vatsikourides, Anastasos.'

'*Epece yper patridos.*'

The loss of Vatsi, our beloved court jester, whose cheerful buffooneries had so raised our spirits and were such a powerful uniting force among us, affected us all. Whatever our differences (and they were many) we could all laugh at or with Vatsikourides – from the company commander down to the youngest recruit. And it was now, at last, that the true horrors of war came home to us. When the roll call was over we sat or stood around in small groups, saying little but taking comfort in each other's company.

★   ★   ★

Once more Colonel Sinioris was addressing us. 'Today, April 20th, is Easter Day,' he told us. (Few, if any, had kept account of dates.) 'We must put our sorrows behind us and think only of the future. Every man will receive half a red egg and double rations of bread and meat. Report to the quartermaster sergeant in the barn over there with your mess tins.'

This cheered us all considerably. We had still not had a proper meal for a long time, and nothing but *kouramana* to help us through the battle. I took my place in the queue, and had just got back with a full mess tin to where my companions were sitting, when a formation of five Stukas dived on us out of the sun. I and my two friends, who had already received their rations, were determined not to let the Germans spoil our dinner. And they didn't. At the first screech of a diving Stuka's siren, we put our mess tins on the ground and fell flat beside them, with our faces touching the tins. And between each dive (they followed one after the other) we grabbed a comforting mouthful of bread and lamb, then lay flat again while we masticated with care.

But others were less fortunate. Two were killed and half a dozen wounded. There was a river nearby, and I remember men running to it to bathe their wounds – some had to be helped, one carried – then sharing among them any rations which their dead comrades had not had time to eat.

After the meal, two men from each platoon were sent off to collect water bottles and fill them at the river, ready for the evening's march. By a lucky chance, the mail orderly found us while I and another man were collecting water bottles, and we both had letters. We read them as we strolled down to the river, each festooned with a dozen bottles hanging from both shoulders. And when we reached the river bank, we rolled up the pages we had read into funnels which we stuck into the narrow mouths of the water bottles, so that we could fill them quickly and easily with our mugs.

In the middle of the afternoon we were marched off again on the long road south. The enemy were still some way behind us, but must be catching up fast. We had little or no ammunition left, and several of our machine-guns were out of action. There was, of course, no transport any more; all that was still serviceable, including any civilian vehicles they had chanced upon along the way, had been requisitioned by the retreating main body, which it was still our duty to protect with all our remaining strength. So there was nothing for it but to soldier on and hope for miracles.

It was now that I realized at last that my own wound needed attention. There was still no pain, but my right foot was sloshing and sliding about inside its boot, so I knew that it must be bleeding. There was no doctor or medical orderly around, but a dentist, who happened to have joined us somewhere along the way, took a look at my foot and removed two small splinters of metal, then bound it up with a field dressing from my pack.

Next day, about noon, as we were crossing an open hillside, the company sergeant-major's whistle sounded the alarm, and we all dived for whatever cover we could find under bushes or behind boulders. But it was one of our own aircraft which came over quite low, following the road and dropping leaflets. These told us that a cease fire had been signed. For us the war was over.

*   *   *

We scrambled back on to the road in some sort of order and moved off. But all semblance of discipline soon left us. Men fell out when they felt like it, to rest or speak to peasants in the cottages we passed. Others formed into larger or smaller groups, chose their own pace and tried to establish some kind of companionship among themselves. We abandoned any heavy gear we no longer needed, and sometimes bartered it for food or even shelter. Our weapons we gave to farmers and shepherds or to peasants in the villages, who would soon need to defend themselves against a growing tide of lawlessness in the countryside.

We had by now crossed the Albanian border into the Greek mountains, with stony hillsides falling away to sparse and then denser forest in the valleys. Patchy snow lay here and there on the higher slopes. Cliffs rose grey and forbidding above them, pocked with caves or clefts and gullies.

My foot had become infected and was paining me now. I limped heavily, but was still able to struggle on at a slower pace, with frequent stops by the roadside. A comrade did his best to help me, but we were falling behind all the time, and soon found ourselves alone in the mountains. After three more days of painful plodding we came at last to a fork where a side road led steeply down through dense pine forest to Metsovon in the valley below. And whether it was the relief of finding myself so near to journey's end or plain exhaustion, I don't know; but I must have collapsed – passed right out. And when eventually I opened my eyes I saw that we had been joined by an old man leading a mule loaded with timber from the forest.

'We'd better get him on to the beast,' I heard him say.

'We'll never manage it alone,' said my friend, who was also weak from exhaustion and lack of food.

'We must do our best,' said the old man, and I saw him casting off the cords which secured his precious load of timber to a rough wooden framework on the mule's back. He flung the whole contraption, timber and all, to the ground, then helped me to clamber to my feet. In the end, between all three of us, we managed to settle me on the back of the mule; but it was a tremendous effort, and for me excruciatingly painful.

We set off down the hill, the old man leading the mule and at the same time helping my friend to hold me steady on its back. I was in a daze, and barely conscious of my surroundings, until all at once I recognized the house belonging to the Averovs, an illustrious family, one of whom became Minister of Defence in more recent times. Their house had been a landmark to us boys during our training period. But something else I now remembered was that Katerina and Elektra's house was almost next door. And to my joy we stopped outside it. The old man was the girls' father.

My comrade, who had supported me throughout our long march, now said goodbye and left us. He had other friends in Metsovon who would welcome him. The old man helped me down from the mule's back and over to the door of his house. 'Sophia! Persephone! Elektra! Katerina!' They came out one by one, but none of them recognized me. Three months' growth of stubble on cheeks drawn in with hunger and fatigue; eyes sunk deep in their sockets and red from exposure; long straggling hair; my own mother would not have known me. But more than that, I had looked Death in the face and Death had stared back at me. I had become a man.

★   ★   ★

Three or four stone steps led up to a rickety wooden door. The girls helped me up them, supporting me on both sides till we got through into the house. And then, at last, they saw who I was. Katerina, with a gasp of horror – mingled with love, it seemed to me – put her arms round me and sobbed. She was, after all, only fifteen. And yet, in her sobbing and the convulsive grip of her arms about me I sensed a new maturity, born of suffering and pity – pity for me and for the human flotsam, bedraggled and beaten, trailing with me and after me through the town.

Sophia changed the cover on one of the *onda* near the fire and begged me to lie down. They asked no questions, they were only concerned to make me comfortable, and after a little while the mother brought me a bowl of chopped macaroni with tomato sauce, but no oil.

'Please eat this,' she said. 'It is not, I fear, as nourishing as we would wish, but it is all we have.'

She put away the bag of macaroni. It was less than a quarter full, I noticed, and wondered how long it would have to last them. Then Katerina came and changed my dressing, which was soiled and ragged and soaked in blood. There were tears in her eyes once more as she bathed away the surrounding scum and poured a little of their precious olive oil into the open wound. She bound it up with strips from a white kerchief, torn but spotlessly clean.

When she had finished, she gazed into my eyes for a moment. Then cool hands caressed my burning forehead and remained there, pressing my head gently back into the single pillow. 'Sleep,' she said softly. And then, '*Sagapo* [I love you],' and she slipped quietly away. I lay for a while open-eyed but at peace. It was wonderful to be here among kind people, friends who cared about me. I could hear the murmur of hushed voices from the other side of the room. The sound was soothing, calming. . . . And '*Sagapo*'? Did she, could she really mean it? She was growing into a lovely young woman, more graceful, and more self assured than I remembered her, and I could still feel in my imagination those cool, caressing, soothing hands on my forehead as I drifted away into sleep.

⋆   ⋆   ⋆

Next day I felt better. I was given a cup of warm goat's milk and a small piece of cheese, and had just finished eating and drinking when there came a loud crash on the door, and a German corporal with three or four men behind him burst in. They were looking for Greek soldiers.

I was grabbed and flung into the street, then marched off to the town square where, under the oak trees, they had a whole sheep roasting on a spit. A small crowd of German soldiers sat round it, laughing and joking and cutting off hunks of meat to cram into their mouths. I watched in astonishment until I was jerked back to reality by a heavy kick in the backside which sent me flying. When I'd picked myself up I was given a broom and told to get sweeping, along with a bunch of dejected-looking 'other prisoners' on the far side of the square.

It was then that a young German officer – tall, handsome, with a kindly expression on his face – came over to us. The corporal snapped to attention, wooden-faced. The officer looked him up and down. Then he said to him in German (which I speak), 'By what right and for what purpose do you maltreat this man?'

His voice was stern, but not hard. He struck me as a well educated and gentlemanly fellow. He took the broom from me and tossed it to the corporal. Then said to me in English, 'Come. I've just been collecting my mail. When I've read it, we'll have something to eat. What is your name?'

I told him, then asked for his. 'Egon Rapner,' he replied. 'I come from Heidelberg, and as soon as Germany has won this war I'm going back there to finish my studies.'

He led me, limping, to a bench on a small rise overlooking the square and motioned me to sit down. He sat beside me and passed over a bundle of periodicals which he was carrying with his letters. 'Look at these,' he said, 'while I read my mail.' And while he was reading he also spoke to me, as though to keep me company.

He was a young man, about my own age, and I wondered what made him treat me so kindly. He spoke in rather hesitant English, and sometimes in French, asking me first of all what I did in civilian life. When he heard that I was at Law School his face lit up; he was also a law student, at Heidelberg University, and from then on I felt that there was some kind of bond, a bond of understanding, between us.

When he had finished his mail, he turned to me with a smile. 'And who do *you* think will win the war?'

'May I be frank?'

'Of course.'

'Then I'm sure the Allies will win. They must.'

'Why do you think that?' he asked.

'Because the Allies command all the approaches to Europe, and will never run right out of supplies, whereas Germany, completely surrounded by her enemies must surely starve in the end.'

I was afraid that I had gone too far – that our new-found friendship was as yet too fragile to withstand such plain speaking. But I was wrong.

'I hope that you are mistaken,' he said gravely. 'Because if Germany loses the war I shall never see Heidelberg again. . . . I'll never go back.'

He was an impressive young man. He impressed me anyway, and I knew what he meant about returning to a defeated country. Perhaps what he had just seen in the square had brought things home to him. For a while there was silence between us. Egon looked serious, and a bit sad at times. He seemed to be thinking deeply.

Then all at once he shook himself, took a deep breath, and got up from the bench. 'Come,' he said. 'We must do something useful while we can.' He took me to the Greek Army depot (now guarded by German sentries) which was full of food and other stores. 'Take whatever you need,' he said, and gave me two large bags, the size of large suitcases, which I proceeded to fill with abandon. There was bread of several kinds; cakes and biscuits; sugar, dried milk and cheeses; a large leg of salt pork as well as tins of meat, soup and various sauces, potatoes, lentils, beans and peas; rice, macaroni, dried fruits and apples; even a bottle of *ouzo* and a few of wine. I filled both my bags till I could only just lift them. He watched me with pleasure and occasionally tossed in a few items of his own choosing – dark chocolate, coffee, a tin of peaches, olives and a whole side of *bacalão*, which I have always loved.

My foot was less painful since Katerina had bathed it again. I felt ready to attempt the journey to Athens. Egon escorted me back to the woodcutter's house. 'Meet me in the square at six in the morning,' he said as we parted. 'I want to be sure that you get away unmolested.'

*   *   *

My return to the house was a moment of triumph for all of us. The family had never expected to see me again, nor I them; yet here I was in good health and laden with luxuries. The mother and the older girls bore these away and started at once to prepare a feast.

The old man had managed to rescue most of the timber he'd left by the roadside to make room for me on his mule. They now built the fire up till it roared, while Katerina and Elektra fetched pots and bowls of many sizes, filled them with water and placed them round or on top of the blazing logs. Both then took buckets and brought more water from the well. When the pots on the fire began to steam, Katerina said in a masterful tone of voice, 'Come on! Off with those filthy clothes . . . all of them . . . we won't eat you.'

I stripped to my underpants, feeling that I must retain some defence, however slight, against her autocratic manner. 'You don't trust us then,' she said laughing, as she led the way down into the basement where an enormous wooden washtub stood in the middle of the room. They found a piece of soap from somewhere and I had the bath of a lifetime, with Katerina sitting on the floor beside the bath, my wounded foot in her lap, and Elektra scrubbing my back. Every now and then Sophia or Persephone would come along with a basin of warm water, which she tested carefully with her elbow to make sure it wasn't too hot, before pouring it gently over me.

When there was no more warm water, I got up and dried myself on a piece of towelling which the girls' mother handed me. Then I got the safety razor out of my pack. It was blunt and a bit rusty, but still just usable, though it took a good twenty minutes to make any real impression on the stubble fields covering most of my face.

The meal, when it came, was eaten in an atmosphere of deep and powerful emotions – of joy and great gusto by the younger ones, including me; practised restraint by the parents and the two older girls. We started with a large cauldron of pea and lentil soup, with chunks of pork floating in it. We scooped it out with our mugs, catching a chunk of meat at the same time, and dunking pieces of bread into the cauldron itself. This was followed by rice and macaroni with a mixture of three different sauces. We drank two of the six bottles of country wine I had brought back. The old man and I had a swig or two of *ouzo*.

We all stayed up late, talking and sometimes singing a little. One or two neighbours joined us after a while, and Sophia brought me a parcel of bread, olives and cheese to take with me in the morning. When her mother saw this, she said at once, 'But what about the *bacalão*, his favourite? Wait, I will work on it . . . all night if need be. . . .' And that was what she did. All night long she soaked and boiled and changed the water, to get the salt out of the fish and make it edible.

As the night wore on, I noticed that Katerina was becoming more subdued and wondered what this meant. At one point, when we happened to be on our own – as far as one could be in a single room – she asked, 'What will you do when you get to Athens?'

'Go home to see my mother and father.'

'Are they very wealthy?'

'Not especially.'

'But you live in a large house?'

'Large enough for all of us.'

'How many?'

'Four when we are all there.'

'And a large garden?'

'There is a garden.'

'I would love to live in a house,' said Katerina wistfully. 'We're getting too big for this room. And when father can't work any more. . .'

'You must come to see us,' I said eagerly. 'When the war is really over, you must come to stay with us in Athens.'

'And then come back here?' Her wry smile made me feel a brute; but just then the mother called to us, and the moment passed.

★   ★   ★

I met Egon in the square, as agreed. He gave me an Italian Army bicycle to help me on my way home, and walked with me to the outskirts of the town, where we said goodbye.

'I know where you spent the night,' he said. 'You must trust me not to pass it on.' He looked at me seriously for a moment, then said quietly and deliberately. 'And I'll see that they get food as long as my unit is in the area.'

I thanked him and started on my way. But no sooner had I got well clear of the town than two German motorcyclists came roaring after me. They threw me off my bike, and the bike itself into the ravine, and then roared off without another word. Soon afterwards, however, a Greek Army truck carrying prisoners of war under guard came by and picked me up. But when we reached Kalambaka on the road to Athens, orders came through that all Greek prisoners were to be released. So we were dumped in a field outside town and told to find our own way home.

That was a march I shall never forget. Stumbling and limping, with my wounded foot now a constant agony, I could barely manage 10 miles a day, and that only with the help of friends, who would stay with me for a while, then pass me on to another or leave me sitting by the roadside to rest till some other willing helper came along. Soon I was at the tail of the column – if one could call it that – and falling further and further behind, with three or four others in a similar plight. There were compensations, though. It was now late spring; the clumps of pink *mathiola* with their haunting scent were nearly over, but in the fields, on hillsides and close to the road lay swathes of pink or purple anemones and scarlet poppies. Dwarf iris and campanula flourished in rocky places, and now and then a wavering line of geese or cranes passed talking overhead, bound for their northern nesting grounds.

We were on the main trunk road to Athens, down which came a steady stream of German military transport, supplying their formations further south. We tried to thumb lifts, but without success, even when, with great difficulty, we held up heavily bandaged limbs. Indeed, on one occasion a truck swerved deliberately at a group of three of us, forcing us to jump for our lives to avoid it. But in the end, after a full week of continual struggle in all kinds of weather, we reached Lamia.

Two days later we came upon a nightmarish scene so horrific that it pains me still to think of it. This was the battlefield of Thermopylae, where for the second time in history a desperate rearguard action had been fought in defence of Athens against a ferocious and vastly superior invader. Two infantry brigades and a few batteries of 25-pounders from the British Expeditionary Force under General Scobie had confronted two German divisions supported by field artillery, and held them for three full days, suffering heavy casualties before they were finally overwhelmed.

The battle was over some four days before we passed that way. Yet the carnage and destruction which still remained there stunned the senses: corpses and parts of corpses, blood everywhere in pools and patches, bloodstained clothing, both field-grey and khaki, smashed vehicles, tanks on their sides, guns without wheels, and here and there a few shallow graves, where there had been time to dig them – some marked by German helmets, some with pairs of British Army boots. And the stench was overpowering.

We hurried past as quickly as we could, and took the next road south to the railhead at Bralos, where thankfully we found a troop train waiting. I remember clambering aboard one of the familiar 'forty men or four horses' wagons before an eruption of desperate young men crowded in after me, jamming me against the wagon side under a high window through which I was barely able to look. I was just in time to see a quick-witted bystander kick a gap in a trail of cordite, on which some fool had dropped a lighted cigarette end. The trail, which must have been made by powder falling from a torn bag on its way to the ammunition dump close by, was well alight and running fast towards the dump. In a few more seconds, but for that timely kick, all our sufferings would have been over. Just then, however, the train started, and quite different sufferings on a bumpy track, in a wagon jam-packed with hot and smelly bodies, began.

It was torture, pure unrelieved torture for eight solid hours, held bolt upright in the crush, swaying back and forth or pressed hard against the ridged, unyielding wagon wall. Sometimes I was lifted off my feet by the press, for a few brief moment's relief from actual pain in my wounded foot; sometimes I was forced down till I could hardly breathe. This continued all night, prolonged by repeated halts and even some reversings, until we finally reached Athens in time for a late breakfast (though none was provided) at ten o'clock next morning.

As can be imagined, my return home was a tumultuous affair, full of tears and rapturous embraces. Even my father, himself an old soldier, was visibly moved. Luckily, though, I had had the foresight to get a good haircut and shave, following a luxurious bath at my grandmother's house, whilst she broke it gently to my mother by telephone that I was around and in generally good health. So we were all able to enjoy an excellent dinner, after which my parents went to bed early, leaving me to sink quietly back into surroundings from which I seemed to have been separated by a whole lifetime.

And in many ways this was so. Although barely a year older, I was indeed very different – a different generation altogether – from the lively youngster who had gone so eagerly to war. I wondered whether my sister and all my friends (those who were still alive) had changed as well. And I couldn't help thinking again of Egon Rapner and his strange befriending of a stray enemy. Why had he picked on me? And then the blunt question within minutes of our meeting: 'Who do you think will win the war?' I came to the conclusion that Egon was a dedicated German with a passionate love for his country and her standards of scholarship, scientific research and philosophical thought, but deeply unsure about the objectives, the morality and the whole future of the Third Reich.

And me? What had I learned from my brief but bloody experience of the brutality of man? This was difficult to answer. I had lost much-loved friends, but I had made new ones. I had seen many of the standards I'd been brought up to honour turned upside down, but I had been shown new and different standards. A promising career had been interrupted; but, heavens above, at twenty there was time enough to start a new one.

Next morning I went to the University Club, which was now a military hospital. They kept me there for a month, until my wound, which was more serious than I had thought (due mainly to neglect), slowly healed.

CHAPTER TWENTY-THREE

Escape into Turkey

When I was able to walk again, Maria took me on outings to the parks and gardens, and one day she suggested a picnic over at Vouliagmeni, where we used to go swimming before the war. Maria and I were engaged. I was always getting engaged in those days, but more frequently and for longer periods to Maria than to any other girl.

I brought out my bicycle and we set off; me pedalling, Maria on the carrier. And after a few stops to rest (it was 25 kilometres from the centre of Athens to Vouliagmeni) we came at last to our well remembered beach, and were getting into our swim suits when I noticed a gang of young fellows in the water calling to each other in Italian.

As one of them was wading ashore, he looked up and saw me sitting there with my military hospital jacket still on. 'Greek soldier on our beach!' he shouted to the others, and came towards me in an obviously threatening manner. I scrambled to my feet ready to defend myself – and Maria too, if necessary – when a lanky young German broke away from a group standing nearby and barred the Italian's path.

'Get back to your play-pen, baby face,' he said scornfully, 'if you don't want your little bottom smacked.'

He spoke in German, so the full weight of his insult was lost on the other, but there was no mistaking his obvious contempt. I could see the Italian trembling with rage. He stood there glaring and muttering, then turned on his heel and went back to his friends, who had now come out of the water. We saw them arguing and gesticulating for a while, with furious looks towards the German and us. But in the end nothing came of it, and they drifted away.

I went over to the German to thank him. He was a scholarly looking young man, dressed in fatigues and wearing pince-nez spectacles; very different to look at from Egon Rapner, and yet in his attitude he reminded me of Egon.

'It was kind of you to come to our rescue,' I said, 'and we're very grateful.'

He looked at me for a moment, then nodded dismissively. 'Those Italians need putting in their place at times,' he said as he turned to rejoin his companions.

I felt humiliated. His main concern, it seemed, had been to show his contempt for the Italians. And maybe he had similar feelings about us, the defeated foe. I went back to Maria, rage boiling up in me. Our own contempt and hatred for the Italians, whom we had beaten and driven into the sea, and who now returned, riding on the backs of the Germans, to lord it over us, were emotions which ruled our lives just then. We hated the Germans too, of course, but we did not despise them. Yet the two together made life in Athens – for me at any rate – well nigh unbearable.

'I really can't stand it here any longer,' I said to Maria, and she understood. We had spoken before about the impossible situation we found ourselves in, she as well as I.

'It's no fun having your bottom pinched, or being leered at by arrogant youngsters who won't stand aside to let you pass,' she told me once, and we'd had a long talk about leaving for the Middle East, I first, she later when things had settled down a bit. The incident at Vouliagmeni brought matters to a head.

A census was being taken of demobilized soldiers who needed help to return to their homes. A label bearing the name of his home town or island was pinned to each man's tunic when he reported to the demobilization centre. Being an Athenian, I needed no such assistance, but I was very keen to escape and join the Greek forces in Egypt, so I had a word with Senior Nursing Sister Alexa Karpouzoglu – a pretty young VAD who was a friend of my sister's. She arranged for my tunic to be labelled 'Samos', which was the closest Greek island to Turkey.

I presented myself to one of the desk clerks at the demobilization centre, and was instructed to join the schooner *Evangelistria* which would be sailing from Piraeus in two days' time. Maria was very brave about it. There wasn't much food to be had. Up in the mountain villages many were starving. But she managed to collect some olives and a few bits of goats' cheese, as well as a bag of assorted pieces of bread. I put the food in my Army pack, along with a woollen scarf, a jersey and an extra pair of underpants. We looked at each other for a long time, holding hands. Then we said goodbye and I went off down to the harbour.

★　　★　　★

We sailed next day, bound for Mykonos. It was high summer, with a strong Meltemi gusting down over the hills. We made good progress down the coast to cape Sunion, with its temple of Poseidon on the cliff-top above it. I waved goodbye to the old devil as we passed. For me this was a moment of pure exhilaration, of release and of great expectations. The sun was blazing hot in the lee of the deckhouses; but standing beside the helmsman or up forward, the cool Meltemi swept you fresh and clear. It was a glorious day.

As we rounded the cape the wind increased to gale force and the sea rose mountains high against us. Men were moaning and shouting around the deck. Some were very seasick; others suffering from half-healed wounds. One or two had lost limbs and found it impossible to steady themselves against the violent plunging of the ship as she bucketed into a fierce head sea; they slid helplessly into the scuppers and lay there as though unconscious, swept by every second wave that came pounding over the rail on top of them. But all were Samiots and ready to face any hardship that brought them nearer home.

Close-hauled on the port tack, with close-reefed fore and main sails, we stood across for Kea Island, then came about on to the starboard tack, laying north-west by west for Makronisi. There we tacked again, and this time were able to weather the northern point of Kea and stand boldly out into the Aegean with the wind well free to port, passing between Yioura and Syros to reach Mykonos soon after sunset. Next day we left for Samos and entered Pythagorion, on the southern side of the island, before nightfall.

But this was by no means the end of the story. Italian soldiers, assisted by Greek gendarmes and port authorities, were checking everyone, to make sure that they were Samiots. All the other passengers were greeted by relatives or friends, who were able to establish their bona fides; but I knew no one on Samos, except for an old friend, Andreas Pouliadakis, whom I hadn't seen since schooldays. He might have left the island; he might even be dead. However, I was sure that he had once lived here, so I slipped ashore with the crowd and made for a taverna where I hoped to get lost in the mêlée. I was lucky. The taverna owner knew my friend and directed me to his home on the coast, about a mile east of Pythagorion.

I set off along a rough track which curved round an open hillside dotted with olive and carob trees. It was now high summer and already most of the arbutus was in flower amongst the scrub. After about half an hour I came to a small farmhouse nestling among olives and oleander at the mouth of a dry gully, and to my joy there was Andreas himself working in the garden beside it.

He was delighted to see me. In those days you were delighted to see anyone you had known before the war, but usually hesitated to ask after people, in case they had been killed. So this was a happy meeting for both of us. But when I told him I wanted a boat to get me across to Turkey he looked thoughtful.

'I have a small rowing boat,' he said, 'but she hasn't been in the water for more than a year. She'll leak like a sieve.'

'Only at first,' I said cheerfully. 'Her seams will soon take up. We must launch her at once.'

We found the boat in a lean-to shed at the back of the building and hauled her down on to the beach. She was an odd little craft with a very low freeboard, and certainly needed a good soaking to make her seaworthy. Andreas went back to the shed for the oars. He was a well built lad of my own age, but with curly dark hair and the beginnings of a beard. I'd always known him as lively and full of ideas. It looked as though he was turning a few over in his mind as he came striding back down the slope from the house, grinning all over his sunburnt face, with the oars on his shoulder.

'I believe I'll come with you,' he called, when still a little way off. 'It's just what I've been waiting for . . . something worth doing . . . something for Greece. Would they have me in the Navy, d'you think?'

'I'm sure they'd jump at you,' I said. I knew nothing about the Navy but it would be good to have a companion.

We ran the boat down into the water and swung her round. Then we tied her stern line to a large stone and dropped it a little way offshore, bringing her painter to another stone on the beach. Water poured in through her gaping seams, and we helped with a bucket and an old saucepan, till she was just floating with her gunwales awash.

★   ★   ★

Andreas' mother and father were equally welcoming. Especially his mother, who came out of the house to greet us as we came up from the beach. But when Andreas told them he was thinking of joining me, they were aghast.

'How can you even think of leaving us, Andreas, at a time like this?' His mother looked shocked. 'Who will do the garden? Harvest olives from the high branches?'

'And who will see to the goats?' said the old man. 'And lift the potatoes?'

'The bees? The chickens?' added his wife.

'The planting for next year? I shall need help,' insisted the old man.

The discussion went on until late in the evening and all the next day. About mid-morning on the third day, while I was diving to let go the boat's stern line and bring her to the beach, Andreas came out of the house and down the slope towards me. He looked downcast, confused, kicking at stones as he came.

'What shall I do?' he asked me, looking truly perplexed.

'You must stay,' I said. 'You can't leave them. I'll be all right on my own.'

To me it was obvious. My own mother had been desperately unhappy when I left, but she had my sister, relatives, friends and family in Athens. With these people it was different. I knew a little about their background. She was the daughter of a well-to-do Athenian doctor who had once had a holiday cottage on Samos. That was how she had met her husband, a successful young fisherman at the time; but before he was thirty – with a little help from his new father-in-law to get him going – he had started a small business in Pythagorion, bringing in hardware, fishing gear, building materials, tools and equipment, and had done very well at it – well enough to send his son (they had only one) to school in Athens. Before the war, moreover, a village girl had come in three times a week, and there'd been a man and a boy to run the farm. Now there was no one.

'You can't leave them, Andreas,' I insisted. 'They need you.'

After the midday meal, we hauled the boat out and painted her topsides black. I had been warned that an Italian motor launch patrolled round Samos between dusk and dawn, keeping a close watch on the straits, which were half Greek, half Turkish, with an island – Bayrak Adasi – three cables out from the Turkish shore. There was a lookout post on that island, whose soldiers were in the habit of shooting at anything that moved on the water.

As soon as the paint was dry we got the boat ready for sea. A large water melon, a bottle of water, some bread, Feta cheese and a jar of olives were the provisions I needed, with a good rough blanket to cover them and me against spray, in case the wind got up. And an anchor. I had to have an anchor, in case the current was stronger than expected and I was forced to rest a while before striking out across the straits. We searched around for the lightweight grapnel which had belonged to the boat, but there was no sign of it anywhere. All we could find was a rusty old caique anchor, with about ten fathoms of chain cable shackled on to it, lying half hidden in grass and scrub near the beach. It was much too heavy and clumsy, but better than nothing, so we stowed it in the bows of the boat with its cable ranged fore and aft over the floor boards.

At the last moment old Mrs Pouliadakis came hurrying down to the beach with an enormous honey cake which she had baked for me specially. Her smile was kindly and warm, but I'm sure she was relieved to see the back of me.

★   ★   ★

At dusk I set off. The weather was calm, and I only had 2 or 3 miles to row, so I was full of hope. At first I kept close inshore, working eastwards along the coast towards the narrows, waiting for the patrol boat to go by. After about twenty minutes she appeared, passing westwards through the straits, her searchlight sweeping ahead of her as she came. I crouched down into the bottom of the boat, and she passed without seeing me. Or if she did, her people must have thought I was a piece of wreckage; the boat was old and fairly shapeless, without much sheer.

But now another problem was presenting itself. The extra weight of the anchor and cable was pressing the boat down in the water, causing her to leak more heavily than we had bargained for. Already there were 4 or 5 in of water sloshing around my feet, and the boat's gunwale couldn't have stood up more than 6 in or so out of the sea. I set to with the saucepan which had been stowed under the transom seat, and after ten or fifteen minutes energetic baling had her dry enough to start rowing again.

I now struck out straight across the narrows, to pass west of the Turkish island, and struggled on for another twenty minutes. But right in the middle of the straits, in full view of anyone who cared to look, I had to stop and start baling again. And so it went on – twenty minutes rowing and ten minutes baling – again and again, on and on.

After about an hour I could see that I was more than half-way across, and therefore now in Turkish territorial waters. I stopped rowing and sat quietly baling, as I waited for the patrol boat to come round again. A half moon sailed out from behind a dense rain cloud, high up over the dark mass of

Samsun Dag, which stood before me, black and forbidding, like a prison wall.

Presently the patrol boat appeared, her searchlight sweeping the narrows. I crouched down again until she had passed – she was unlikely to attack me in Turkish waters, but one never knew. Then I took up my oars and battled on. All I remember about the next hour or so is an aching weariness in my arms and back, as I slogged away at those oars, dragging my waterlogged boat through the sea with the current against me. I was safe – or thought I was – from attack by the Italians. But now the Turks in the lookout post on Bayrak Adasi had to be reckoned with – and they were reputed to have extremely itchy trigger fingers.

I turned a bit south to give them as wide a berth as possible, but this didn't increase the range very much. Yet for some reason they left me alone, and soon I was within a cable or less of the shore. The boat, however, was sinking fast. I put all my strength into one last agonizing effort. Then one of my oars broke. I did what I could with the other oar, shifting it from side to side at every second stroke. And just as I'd made up my mind that I'd have to swim the last few yards, there came a wonderful, blissful crunching and bumping, as we nosed up to some rocks on the edge of a shingle beach. I was in Turkey.

⋆   ⋆   ⋆

It was pitch dark – darker, it seemed, than out at sea. The moon had vanished again behind clouds, leaving me in deep shadow under the black bulk of Samsun Dag, now standing right over me. From habit I tried to haul the boat clear of the rocks on to a strip of shingle higher up, but she was stuck fast and half full of water, so I had to leave her. I made my way up the beach to where an overhanging rock would give me a little shelter from the light rain, which (surprisingly for summertime) had begun to fall. The wind was northerly, and dark clouds massing over in that direction told of more to come. I was wet and very tired, but also in a state of some anxiety. There had been ugly rumours of Greeks who had landed in Turkey being tortured and even killed by hostile peasants, who found them before the police or military arrived. I crouched there in the shadow, looking about me and wondering what to do next. Fortunately I had been able to rescue from the boat my blanket and most of the food, including the remains of my honey cake, so for the moment I was reasonably comfortable, and after a while I dozed off.

How long I slept I couldn't tell, but all at once I was wide awake. Something had woken me, but what it was I had no idea. A sound, no doubt. But what sort of sound, how loud and where from, to bring me bolt upright with such a start? The moon had come out again and was high in the sky. I could see the whole foreshore quite plainly, and the scrub-covered bank behind it; and beyond that a stony hillside with a scatter of trees and bushes.

Apart from the rhythmic swish of the sea lapping the beach, the silence was complete. I felt a prickle down my back and realized that I was breathing too fast. I must control it, calm down, get a grip of myself and . . . there! – a light scuffling sound from the other side of my rock! This was it, I thought, and drew my working knife from its sheath, prepared to defend myself against whatever it was, human or animal.

The scuffling began again, but seemed to be coming no nearer. I crept forward to peer round the side of the rock. Then froze. Something touched my leg. I spun round, and there, cringing and cowering in the moonlight, tail between its legs and whimpering piteously as it pressed itself against my calf, was a small brown dog.

My relief at the sight of the unhappy creature, in need of protection like me, was overpowering. It gave me heart. There were now two of us instead of only one on his own. I tossed it a lump of cheese and a crust. It snatched them up, one after the other, and gulped them down. It must have been starving. I gave it two more pieces, then settled back under my rock, the dog pressing against me, its head in my lap.

The night wore on, and soon the dark outline of Samsun Dag began to harden as dawn approached. But I must have dozed off again, because when I next opened my eyes it was broad daylight, although the sun itself was still hidden behind the mountain. I got to my feet and set off up the beach, the dog beside me. I could see it better now – a small brown creature with a terrier's head and a few patches of white on its face and body. I stopped for a moment to give it another piece of cheese, which made it squirm with pleasure, and actually wag its long uncropped tail.

After scrambling up the rocks at the back of the beach I found a goat track, which soon joined a broader pathway leading off to the right. In the distance I could see a few hovels and one or two larger houses grouped around what looked like the mouth of a gorge. The landscape all around, with its stony hills covered with scrub and occasional olive trees was achingly familiar, reminding me that in the not too distant past the whole of this coast had been inhabited by Greeks.

I hadn't gone very much further, however, before I came upon a surly-looking peasant sitting beside the track, with goats foraging in the scrub behind him, who clearly took a different view. He eyed me stonily. To him I was just another foreigner – Greek or Serb, or possibly Croat – and therefore up to no good.

'*Astinomous?*' I asked him. His stony stare continued unblinking. . . . 'Police?' I tried. Not a flicker. '*Polizei?*' Without taking his eyes off me for a moment he pointed up the track. I nodded and set off again. I could feel his eyes following me as I moved away.

At the next bend I suddenly became aware that my dog friend had left me. And when I looked round, I was just in time to see him disappearing into the scrub. I wondered why, until I observed two men with a large and aggressive-looking mongrel coming down the hill towards me. My friend must have decided, at sight of them, that he might after all receive less than a hero's welcome in that village. It's a hard world, I reflected sadly, if not with much originality. I would miss my friend who, at a black moment, had made me feel that I wasn't alone in adversity, and had given me courage at a time when it was most needed.

The two men now came up to me; one of them spoke reasonably good Greek, so I was able to explain my position. They took me to a house which apparently did duty as a police station. I was immediately handcuffed and submitted to a rigorous interrogation, in which the Greek-speaker took a leading part. He turned out to be a plain-clothes policeman, attached to the post for this very purpose.

'They were watching you from the island,' he told me when the interrogation was over. 'You were lucky not to be shot. It was fortunate for you also that no escapers have come over for some time, so we're in need of up-to-date intelligence.'

I found it difficult to believe that my guarded answers to all his questions had done much to meet this need. But now that I was at last in official hands – a 'source' for his next report – I really had nothing to complain about, even when I was taken down to a cell in the basement, which I had to share for a few hours with two lugubrious Turks, who said not a word even to each other, during the whole of that time.

In due course I was brought up again and put into a car, in which I was driven round the coast to Cesme, via Kuşadasi and Ephesus. The drive itself, however, was a somewhat informal affair. My guard sat in front with the driver, who appeared to be the owner of the car (an ancient Renault), while I shared the back seat with half a dozen trussed chickens – a present for the guard's mother who lived in Kuşadasi. We stopped at her house for coffee, which must have been routine procedure, because she seemed not to notice my efforts to drink her coffee as elegantly as possible with both hands clamped firmly together by handcuffs.

And there the story really ends. The Greek Consul in Izmir arranged for my release from police custody and my journey by train to Aleppo. From there, after fifteen days in a transit camp, I was sent down to Cairo, where I joined the 1st Battalion of the 1st Greek Brigade and became involved in a whole new series of military experiences, both ashore and afloat and in the air.

CHAPTER TWENTY-FOUR

Death March to Steni

It was close on midnight on a calm night in late October 1943, when we started signalling the shore: 'KQ . . . KQ . . . KQ . . .' in groups of three every two minutes. The moon had set an hour or two before, and a light overcast was spreading from the north-west. It was very dark. Under the lee of Cape Ohthonia, on the island of Evvia, we were sheltered from the north wind as we edged in towards the land.

A pale strip of beach, barely visible along the water's edge, was backed by low hills, which might be dunes; it was difficult to judge height and distance in the dark. We lowered a kedge from aft on five fathoms of light line. When it took the ground we'd be able to check our speed, or haul off in a hurry if challenged. We crept on with little more than steerage way on the boat. 'KQ . . . KQ . . . KQ . . .' in different directions, up and down the coast, for half an hour . . . for an hour . . . for an hour and a half, and still no reply.

This was my third operation as conducting officer of a Greek Sacred Company caique sent to the Greek mainland to pick up military and civilian escapees and transport them to the Middle East. We had been using Port Rafti, at that time a remote fishing village and caique harbour, as our pick-up point. But an undercover agent in Athens had warned that Communists – the notorious EAM – had rumbled us, so on this trip we had chosen a deserted beach on the seaward side of Evvia, with convenient islets less than 16 miles offshore, where we could hide under camouflage nets during daytime. There would be a party of twenty-five soldiers and civilians to bring off, we had been told. But we knew from experience that there would almost certainly be more, perhaps even double that number, when the time came to embark them.

'KQ . . KQ . . . KQ . . .' We had three lookouts up forward, each concentrating on a different sector, but not a flicker came back to us out of the darkness. Something could have gone wrong, of course, and there might be nobody there. Or they might be hiding for fear of a trap; bogus pick-up caiques had been used, especially by the Communists, who were tougher than the Germans on Greeks trying to escape to Egypt, where capitalist forces were building up. Or had the party been caught by coast watchers and marched off for trial and probable execution?

At last we could wait no longer. In another three hours it would be getting light, by which time the caique must not only be well clear of the coast but, if possible, hidden under nets at one of the offshore islets. I turned to the skipper.

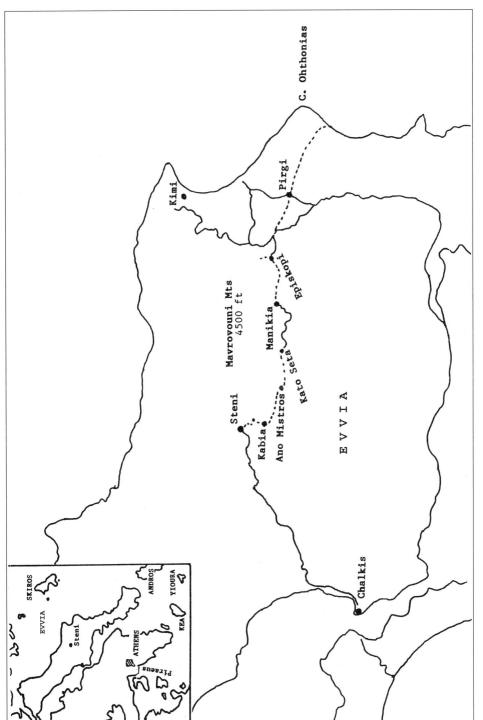

Map 18 Evvia.

'Put me ashore in the dinghy,' I said. 'If I'm not back within an hour you must leave and come back at midnight tonight.'

★   ★   ★

The beach was sandy and backed by dunes. The boatman swung the dinghy round, and I stepped over her stern into the shallows, then turned and gave him a hearty shove. He disappeared into the darkness. The splashes of his oars grew fainter, then ceased. The silence, except for the faint gurgle and hiss of wavelets nuzzling the sand, was complete. I waded ashore and set off northwards up the beach, flashing the recognition signal down on to the sand, where only someone actually looking for it would see it. Now and then my feet crunched through a patch of shingle, sounding unnaturally loud in the stillness. Occasionally, too, the bell-like note of Athene's owls sounded from the scrub inland.

After about half a mile (ten minutes by my watch) the beach ended in rocks. I turned and started walking back, but hadn't gone more than a hundred yards or so, when I was brought up short by what sounded like a laugh. I crouched down, listening with baited breath . . . yes, there it came again, and more, the unmistakable murmur of people talking. I turned, still crouching, and clambered as silently as I could up the face of a sand dune topped by coarse grass and bushes. Keeping under cover I peered over the crest – and there they were, the whole party, sitting or lounging among stunted trees and bushes in a grassy hollow, chatting and smoking as though they hadn't a care in the world.

For a moment I was too astonished to speak. Then I stood up, gave the agreed password, and walked down to join them. They scrambled to their feet, and their leader, Commander Tassos Alexion, whom I knew, came forward. But before he could speak, I cut in with 'What on earth are you doing down here, sir? We've been signalling for nearly two hours.'

'That was very foolish of you,' said the Commander, not in the least put out by my somewhat petulant attitude. 'We expected you to come and find us.'

'It was agreed, sir, that you would watch for our signal and answer it.'

'I countermanded that,' said the Commander coolly. 'Signals from out at sea can be picked up by anyone along the coast, including the enemy.'

'But how could we find you when we had no idea of where you might be?'

'Well, you did find us, didn't you? So all's well.'

'No, it damn well isn't.' I was furious now. 'Two vital hours of darkness have been lost, and unless you're ready to come aboard at once the caique will leave without you.'

'Calm down, my friend. And mind your manners,' said the Commander sternly. 'We're all ready to move.'

But of course they weren't. They argued. They dawdled. Someone had lost a jersey. A young school teacher wanted to drag a complicated kind of boiler suit over her two-piece outfit. Two young infantry lieutenants, whom I also knew, were quarrelling over some past disagreement. Both had been at school with me. I tried to reason with them, asking for their help; and after a bit one of them joined me rather shamefacedly.

The party consisted mostly of ex-soldiers and NCOs, with a sprinkling of civilians, three of them women. One was an old lady going to join her son who had escaped earlier and was now serving with the Greek Army in Egypt. Another was the wife of a regular officer also in Cairo. The third was the school teacher, rather a plain young woman with straight brown hair. The officer's wife wore heavy trousers and a sweater under a thick tweed jacket. The old lady was wrapped in a long dark green cloak, which completely hid the rest of her clothing.

My school-friend and I moved about among them all, listening to their talk and putting in a word or two where we could; but we were quite unable to convince anyone of the seriousness of our position. I knew that the Communists had patrols out every night, watching for escapees, whom they looked upon as traitors; but I dared not stress this, for fear of causing panic which could only make matters worse. Yet at any moment one of these patrols might come along. At last the Commander himself became impatient: 'Come now, all of you. . . . Follow me.'

'*Iassos!*' The cheerful greeting, followed by the appearance of two men carrying shotguns emerging suddenly into the starlight from the deeper shadow of the surrounding scrub, brought those already on their feet to an abrupt halt. Those about to join them sat down again.

'Who are you and what do you want?' asked the Commander sharply.

It wasn't possible in the dim light to make out colours or facial expressions, but one of the two newcomers was bulkier and slower moving than the other, and it was clear that he was the older man. It was also he who spoke.

'You're out after duck, maybe – the dawn flight?' He spoke in a friendly conversational tone of voice. 'May we join you?'

The composition of our party and the fact that none of us had guns made obvious nonsense of this, but for the moment there was little we could do about it. The Commander, who was standing next to me, glared but said nothing. The school teacher, who felt perhaps that she understood the peasant mentality better than the rest of us, was the first to speak. 'We're on a picnic,' she said pleasantly. 'It's Mr Kanellopoulos' name day.' She pointed at a middle-aged gentleman in the background, probably a retired Army officer.

A young naval rating, recently released from a prisoner-of-war camp, who happened to have brought a fish-spear and goggles with him, backed her up. 'I'm going to see if I can get some octopus for a barbecue. How's the fishing along here?'

'You'll need a torch. Have you got a torch?' One could tell from his faintly mocking tone that there was a smile on the older peasant's face. The atmosphere of suspense deepened. Everyone was on edge. Only the old lady – dignified, composed, serene – remained calm and aloof.

The 'peasants' seemed friendly enough, nodding and, one felt, smiling at the somewhat feverish efforts people were making to engage them in conversation. But I could tell from the way they spoke and some of the expressions they used that these were not true country dwellers. Moreover, the older man's bantering comments from time to time showed that he was none too impressed by our charade.

We were all seated now, but I managed to get the Commander to one side, and spoke to him urgently. 'This is a Communist patrol,' I insisted. 'They're only waiting for a few more of their mates to turn up, so that they can grab the whole party. We must act at once.'

'You may be right,' said the Commander calmly. 'But don't get too worked up. There are thirty-two of us, including at least twenty able-bodied men. They wouldn't find it easy to take us.'

I was far from reassured. And when I saw the older peasant whisper something to his companion, who then got up and left us, I knew there was going to be trouble. 'Now!' I demanded. 'We must leave at once and,' pointing to the remaining peasant, 'take this beauty with us.' I stood up and drew the Italian revolver I carried in case of emergency.

But it was already too late. Armed men were appearing out of the darkness all round us. Other shadowy figures could be seen moving about in the background. There must have been twenty or thirty of them, some carrying automatic weapons, some shotguns.

I dropped my revolver, shuffling it into the sand with my foot. It could serve no purpose now, other than to provoke a massacre. I was only just in time. I felt the twin barrels of a shotgun pressed between my shoulder blades, forcing me back into the main body.

★   ★   ★

The mood of our new captors was very different from the friendly and generally cheerful attitude of the 'peasants' who first found us. These others were hostile and abrupt in manner, calling us *Psarakia* (little fishes), the name always given to escapees caught near the coast or on the beaches. For me it brought back memories of my first contact with Kodros and the mess I made of my 'fish pond' rendezvous with Jack. Then I thought of Maria and wondered whether I'd ever see her again. There was no doubt that we were in the tightest corner that any of us had yet faced. The Communists, having terrorized large sections of the population into submission – on the surface anyway – could rely on widespread, if not entirely whole-hearted, cooperation.

We were kicked and shoved around, but not bound immediately. Instead we were crammed into a nearby shepherd's hut, where we were made to take off all our clothes. These were then searched in the background. The old lady was allowed to keep her clothes on, but was roughly searched by a girl Communist wearing a bandolier and carrying a gun like the others.

Luckily I no longer had anything incriminating on me; my identity card was sewn into one of the sleeve linings of my jacket, and they never found it, then or later. Some of the others were less fortunate. Papers with addresses of contacts in Cairo, notes of introduction to prominent officials, even gold coins for use as bribes (which always branded you a traitor in Communist eyes) were found on several of them. A few youngsters from humbler origins carried no such aids to preferential treatment, which undoubtedly saved their lives.

We spent the rest of the night crowded into the hut. It was bitterly cold. Icy draughts whistled through cracks in the timber walls. We huddled together to protect each other from the worst of it. Three of the lads completely enveloped the young school teacher – two with their arms round her from beneath, making a human couch for her to lie on, and one from above. It must have been God's blessing upon her, poor girl. She hadn't long to live.

At daybreak we were marched off on a 20 kilometre trek, over mountain paths and goat tracks to the village of Episkopi. The sun rose behind us and shone on a ragged little band of dejected humanity, stooping and stumbling through the scrub and up dry watercourses choked with boulders. A pair of eagles circled high above us, watching and waiting for we knew not what.

In the early afternoon we picked our way down the rocky bed of a creek to the village of Pirgi, about half-way to our destination. We were allowed to squat in the village street, and were given a handful of olives and some water each. Many of our guards were little more than children, in their early teens – bombastic and shrill, brandishing their weapons with terrifying gusto and calling each other by grand nicknames, like 'quartermaster', 'navigator', sergeant-major'.

It became clear in Pirgi that the two older women were at the limit of their endurance, and would never make it to Episkopi. So rather than have them collapse and arouse genuine pity among the villagers who saw them, which might lead to murmurings of dissent, they were set free and told to find their way home. The rest of us (we were now thirty all told) were kicked and dragged to our feet and forced to struggle on, with frequent thumps and clouts from shotgun butts to keep us moving.

In the main street of Episkopi, when we reached it about an hour after sunset, there were German soldiers standing about in groups or lounging against the walls of the houses. None of them took any notice of us. We were herded into a large church which was freezing cold, night and day. We were held there for three days, awaiting interrogation by two senior EAM officials.

One of these officials, their Political Commissar, was a truly bestial individual – short but stocky, with a black beard and yellow eyes (like a panther's, I remember thinking). He was a brutal and exceptionally violent fellow, who beat people mercilessly during interrogation. We were (I think deliberately) moved to an upper floor in the church, from which we could hear him in the room beneath us, yelling and swearing at his victims; they screaming or moaning as they were fiercely attacked, or their voices cracked and quavering with fear, as they tried vainly to counter his accusations.

When the other interrogator (and official prosecutor) turned up next day, we recognized each other at once. Formerly an Army major, now a Communist *kapetanio*, he had attended the Military Academy with my two young officer friends. He had also been secretary of a sports club to which I belonged. 'You, George Bisbas!' he exclaimed when he saw me. In his eyes I was, of course, a traitor, as indeed was he in mine. His slightly hunched shoulders and mean little glittering eyes reminded me forcibly of a hyena.

But for some reason, my friends and I were not seriously interrogated at this time. The intention, I believe, was to leave us till last, when the other interrogations had given a lead to the kind of information they must endeavour to extract from us 'by any means in their power'.

In due course we were moved on again, up into the mountains, bound for the village of Steni, near the top of 5,700 ft Mount Dhirfis, where EAM had their Divisional HQ. It was a long hard climb, lasting three full days, over rough and stony tracks. And at every village we came to, a People's Court was set up by the *kapetanio*, carrying his official briefcase more or less as a badge of office. He was very proud of that briefcase.

The courts were held in the open air just outside the village. They always consisted of five 'judges', three of them *andartes* and two local villagers chosen by the *kapetanio*, who also selected, more or less at random, the unfortunates from among us who were to be tried. There might be just one or two or a small group of four or five, all charged with the same offence. The judges were seated on chairs, the prisoner or prisoners and their guards standing before them, with villagers of all ages – men, women and always a number of small boys, come 'to see the fun' – sitting on the ground or standing around them. When all were assembled, the *kapetanio* stood on another chair (still carrying his briefcase) and read out the charge, which never varied: 'Traitor to the cause of the People', or words to that effect.

This was always received in silence – a shocked and deathly silence, accentuated on one occasion by a sudden clamour of crows from a nearby hillside. The *kapetanio* then made a short speech, which also varied little. The prisoner or prisoners might attempt to reply, but were always cut short, and the 'judges' asked straightaway for their verdicts. They wrote these on little slips of paper, rolled up carefully and dropped into a box brought round by another *andarte*.

With great ceremony and a final flourish, the *kapetanio* undid each slip and read out what was written on it. This was always 'Guilty' – except in one case, where one of the villagers chosen to be a judge happened to be the village priest. (He had been wearing old clothes and digging his garden when he was selected.) With apologies, but firmly, he refused to condemn a fellow human to death. For that was what it was. As soon as judgement was passed by the senior *andarte* on the panel of judges, the prisoner was taken away and shot, and left for the villagers to bury, while the rest of us were marched straight off on the next stage of our journey.

The first court of our march was held in the village of Manikia, at the foot of the Mavrovouni mountains, whose grey cliffs and crags, rising abruptly out of greener hillsides, formed a grim setting for the proceedings. And the first, indeed the only prisoner to be tried, was none other than the young school teacher. What they could possibly have against her was hard to understand, but the *kapetanio* was quite definite in his indictment. 'A betrayer to the Gestapo of our heroic Resistance fighters,' he declared in ringing tones.

The poor girl was dumbfounded, white and trembling. Betrayal to the Gestapo was the vilest crime known to any Greek at that time, whether a member of the Resistance or not. It was also the crime of which EAM always accused those whom they particularly disliked. And among these, of course, were school teachers, unless they had become Communists or joined the Resistance themselves. If they had not, they were looked on as 'lackeys' to the establishment, who paid them to poison the minds of the young with their 'filthy capitalist doctrines'.

The poor girl protested. She wept. She appealed to the villagers themselves, who averted their eyes, though some wept with her. But it was no good. She was dragged away screaming. A little later shots rang out and the screaming ceased. It was the most sickening display that any of us had ever witnessed of the horrors – the senseless horrors – which men with a raging thirst for power can inflict upon others. But it was not the only one. There were more to follow.

★ ★ ★

The track to the next village, Ano Mistros, followed the tortuous and boulder-strewn bed of a stream as far as Kato Seta, and then climbed up into mountainous country; in all, a distance of some 12 kilometres, which nevertheless took us all day. We spent the night under guard at various houses, and next morning another court was held, at which two more of our number were 'tried' and duly executed. The day after that we finally reached Steni, where we remained for the next ten days.

Here my two friends and I were billeted in a house where, to our surprise, we were joined by a young artillery officer, who had recently been recruited by the Communists and had been sent to guard us. It was, in fact, his own house. He and my two young officer friends knew each other quite well, and seemed pleased to have met up again. After the occupation of Greece by the Germans and Italians it was fairly common for people without any real Marxist tendencies, including some Army officers, to support ELAS, the military wing of EAM who, together with EDES, the right wing guerrilla formation, were the most effective forces to continue the fight against the invaders. This young fellow had been made local commander of ELAS artillery, and seemed quite content to do his job as he'd been taught to do it, leaving policy matters and suchlike to others.

At Steni, People's Courts were held every day in the village school, a comparatively large building with several rooms, one of them the main assembly hall. Here, the farce of a so-called public trial was re-enacted day after day with undiminished ceremony, and the convicted prisoners taken to the village cemetery for execution.

On the tenth day of our detention, it came at last to our turn – those that were left of us – to undergo interrogation followed by trial. And looking back now on the next few hours I am struck by the lasting effect the sheer brutishness of the ensuing events had upon me. The pain and shock of the physical violence itself is difficult to recall, but the cold hatred and almost animal ferocity on the faces of our young executioners – some of them no more than sixteen or seventeen years old – is something I shall never forget.

After several hours, or so it seemed, of alternative beatings and quite friendly interludes with coffee and cigarettes (a fairly standard interrogator's trick) the proceedings were cut short and we were marched away without further ado to the cemetery to be shot. I remember feeling almost relieved that our ordeal was over and could not be repeated. I shook myself and faced up smiling to the young men with Schmeissers at the ready. It would be a quick release, I thought, and almost painless . . . when a loud shout from the direction of the village, followed by the sound of running feet and the arrival of a breathless messenger, brought matters to a standstill. The *kapetanio* took the message held out to him by the runner and read it carefully twice. Then he turned to the *andarte* in charge. 'Take them back to the village,' he said curtly.

A higher authority, we heard later, had decided that we must be interrogated professionally by the EAM Intelligence Officer, who would shortly be visiting Steni. But when this official would arrive was uncertain, so we were transferred in the meantime (there were only nine of us now) to a small school in the nearby village of Ayios Nikolaos, where we found three other prisoners – Andrew Effter, an American lieutenant and two SOE W/T operators, both sergeants. One of the sergeants had had his legs deliberately broken during interrogation the day before.

We remained at Ayios Nikolaos for three and a half weeks, during which time it was the responsibility of the president of the village council to provide us with food, as well as men to guard us. The food we were offered was in fact rather better than we had been accustomed to, and I suppose it was inevitable that as the weeks went by we should become quite friendly with our guards. Then came 5 December, the eve of the feast of St Nikolaos, when all hands, young and old, in his namesake village were needed to prepare for their customary celebrations.

But what was to be done about the prisoners' guards? There were eight of them working in shifts. They were badly needed for the heavier work in getting things ready, and it didn't take the president long to decide that the best way of also keeping an eye on the prisoners would be to invite them to take part as well.

We accepted with alacrity, and were soon busy with tables and chairs, lights, jugs, bottles and glasses, and the making of a mammoth bonfire on an open space just outside the village. And those of us who still had a little money secreted about their persons – including one of the Americans who had managed to hide a gold sovereign in the heel of one boot – contributed towards the cost of *tsipouro* and *retsina*, which were to be the principal drinks at the party.

It was a good party; one of the best I can remember from those difficult times. It went on until the early hours with dancing, singing and bazouki music, shouting and stamping, getting fiercer and fiercer and louder and louder as the night wore on. We plied our guards most assiduously with *tsipouro* and soon they were all dead drunk or snoring. But we managed to dispose of our own drinks in other ways without arousing suspicion.

At one o'clock in the morning we lay down, pretending to sleep, but were actually in a state of barely suppressed excitement. At 2.00 a.m., one of the young officers crept round and gave each of us a shake. We slipped away in three pairs plus myself and my two school-friends, each group taking a different direction. My friends and I walked till dawn, when we found a deserted (and still stinking) goat shed, in which we were able to get a few hours' sleep. I had had the foresight, during the evening, to slip some of the party food into the blouse of my tunic, and noticed that some of the others, including my two friends, did the same. We now had to husband these supplies most rigorously, not knowing how long it would take us to reach safety.

Soon after daybreak we moved out into the scrub, and remained hidden there till nightfall. We were in a terrible state to look at, with bruised faces and torn clothing, which might have aroused suspicion in any Communist sympathizers we chanced to meet. And we had no papers except my hidden identity card, which I was determined not to show to anybody, since there was no way of telling, on sight, who were Communists and who weren't.

Eventually, after two most arduous night marches, we reached Chalkis and skulked in the undergrowth a little way from the town until the small hours, when we made our way down to the waterfront. There we were lucky to find a small boat with oars in her, and twenty minutes later reached the mainland.

★   ★   ★

There is little more to tell. It took us the best part of another week to get to Athens. For now there were German checkpoints and patrols to look out for as well as Communists. During the day we hid under culverts, in woodland caves and reed beds, whatever we could find in a countryside becoming increasingly formal and cultivated as we approached the city. We took appalling risks at times when we called (singly) at cottages – and once spoke to a truck driver – to beg for water or a little to eat. But in the end we reached the suburb of Kifissia and the house of another old school-friend, who gave us food and shelter until we felt strong enough to face our families and the emotional scenes which must (and did) follow.

The Insurance Company Director's Tales

CHAPTER TWENTY-FIVE

Triumph and Disaster

If you can dream and not make dreams your master,
If you can think and not make thoughts your aim,
If you can meet with Triumph and Disaster,
And treat those two impostors just the same . . .

Rudyard Kipling

As a young lieutenant in the South Wales Borderers I had had an interesting war so far: the campaign to put down the Rashid Ali revolt, followed by the occupation of Iraq; the push northwards into the Caucasus to block any German advance through Southern Russia to the Mosul and Kirkuk oilfields; then eastwards with a British mission to Pahlevi[1] on the Caspian. Here, where the brilliant blue sea was bordered by snow-capped mountains in the lands of the ancient Seljuks and Assassins, we linked up with a Russian team organizing lines of communication for released Polish soldiers (captured by the Russians earlier) to form the Polish 1st Corps assembling in Cairo – cheerful young fellows in khaki drill, who came down by sea from the north and were passed on via a chain of transit camps to Baghdad and eventually Egypt.

But now – stagnation as duty officer in Camp LG5, surrounded by limitless wastes of sand and rock in the Syrian desert. I pulled every string I could (there weren't many in that desolate outpost) to get back to my regiment, which was by then in Tobruk, and at last my posting came through. But I never reached them. While I was on my way, Tobruk was over-run and most of the Division defending it killed or captured. The remnants re-formed in Cyprus, where the survivors of three British regiments were amalgamated, but the new unit would clearly not become fully operational for some time.

However, a new turn of events – the formation of MI9, an organization for helping captured or stranded soldiers, airmen and others to escape from enemy territory – provided me with a position of great interest; I was appointed G3(I) and MI9 representative on Divisional HQ staff, based in Cyprus, and for many months became immersed in Aegean military as well as political affairs. It was a fascinating field; and since at that stage the whole of the Aegean was German-held, all our activities had to be clandestine, with movement mostly by caique at night under conditions of the utmost secrecy. I was immediately on my guard, therefore, when one day a friendly, but somewhat impetuous, US Army captain came to see me, to ask whether he could help in any way. His offer was clearly genuine, but I couldn't at first see how a lone American would fit into our organization; so I asked him how he saw himself being of use to us. 'Waal,' he replied, 'could you use a Liberator bomber for anything?'

Then came the day, in the summer of 1944, when some Greek caiques flying white ensigns entered Kyrenia harbour en route for their training area on the west coast of the island. It was an inspiring sight, for me in particular. Before the war, at the age of fourteen, I had learned to sail my father's day sailer, and later cruised with friends in larger sea-going craft; so when I was offered, by its Senior Officer, the post of Intelligence Officer to the Levant Schooner Flotilla, I accepted at once. And three weeks later I joined the lads in Beirut.

★ ★ ★

The advanced base for Aegean operations was at Port Deremen, in the Gulf of Kos, where John Campbell was at that time COMARO I. I took passage up there in a Fairmile ML, and remember especially, at dawn on the day after leaving Famagusta, raising the Taurus Mountains, with snow-capped Tahtali Dağ brooding over the Bay of Antalya. Then Castelorizo and on past the Seven Capes, but at night. My nearer acquaintance with them, in daylight and at close quarters, was in the future.

Next morning we rounded Cape Krio and in the afternoon entered a land-locked sound enclosed by steep-sided hills covered with pine forest. The bay was inhabited – infested one might almost say – by an extraordinary assembly of craft, from small caiques, larger caiques and portly schooners; HDMLs, Fairmiles, a motor fishing vessel, motor boats, waterboats, workshop boats and suchlike, to say nothing of dinghies, dories and sail boats, threading their way among the bobbing heads of naked bathers, splashing and yelling to each other across the water.

I reported to the elegant Lieutenant-Commander (E) John Campbell, whose intelligence officer I was to become, and also met the plump and jovial Gordon Hogg, Signals Officer to the LSF – a friend to all and confidant of many, whose unfailing good humour was an important cementing factor among the motley crowd of sailors, soldiers and two airmen, who at different times formed the crews of raiding caiques.

My main task, at first, was to debrief the caique and ML skippers on their return from operations, and add the information they gave me to the daily reports coming in from Alexandria and Cairo. It was not exciting work, but often tantalizing, as I listened to tales of interesting and frequently colourful exploits in enemy waters, and sometimes to lyrical accounts of long and leisurely sails through the islands. But suddenly one day – in the autumn of 1944, I think it was – the whole concourse took off, like a flock of starlings, to settle again further north on the island and harbour of Khios, opposite Izmir.

Now the naval war in the Aegean took on a new complexion altogether. The Germans were clearly pulling back, and our job was to harass them. Then Turkey came in on the side of the Allies, and life became positively cosmopolitan for all of us. That is to say, we were now able to land in Turkey itself (forbidden to us before) and, when the occasion warranted, enjoy some of the luxuries offered by a thriving modern city. Even one or two splendid yachts belonging to Levantine families were offered to our senior officers as Headquarters ships: *Eliki* and *Lillias* were two of them. And later on Dougie Russell, during his tour of duty as COMARO I, brought Rosalie, his Hungarian wife, up from Beirut to live on board.

★　★　★

By the spring of 1945 the war in Europe was nearly over. The Germans had withdrawn all their forces from Greece to reinforce their hard-pressed northern armies. In the islands they had left only Crete, Rhodes and Leros with substantial garrisons, which were hemmed in and closely watched by the Navy and the RAF, to prevent them from joining their comrades in the north. Otherwise there was little to worry about in the Aegean – except for the terrible plight of the island populations, tyrannized and pillaged by the retreating Germans and the growing power of the Communist organization EAM, with its military wing, ELAS.

It was this that gave my life a new and interesting slant. The operational caiques of the LSF were to be handed over to the Royal Hellenic Navy and their crews dispersed; but three large vessels, commanded by Army officers (we had four in the flotilla at the time), were to be fitted out in Famagusta for certain specialized tasks. And since I was the only one not seriously occupied just then, I was sent down to Cyprus to select the vessels from a number laid up there, and start fitting them out.

The most immediate of the 'specialized tasks' was to monitor the German withdrawal from the Aegean islands, and report back to FOLEM on the rapidly changing military and political scene. In particular, attempts by EAM and ELAS to take over from the retreating Germans, which threatened the whole structure of political life and the future of democracy in Greece, had to be closely watched. And to enable us to keep in constant touch, day and night, with Alexandria, we were to be provided with two W/T operators.

This sounded like an exceptionally interesting assignment, and I set about it with a will, assisted by 'Snow White² (no less) and his staff, who happily by this time had grown less critical of Army officers in command of ships. My brief was to find three sturdy caiques with powerful engines (their own or new ones)³ to be named LS43, LS45 and LS46. I was to command the first to be ready for sea; Bill Turnbull and Jack 'Gaffer' Charrington the other two. My naval crew, when they arrived, must have been hand-picked by an experienced caique officer – no doubt the skipper of one of the LSF boats handed over to the Greeks. All were 'caiqui' lads with excellent records, and as keen on the new job we were going to do as I was.

★   ★   ★

We sailed one morning early in May, round the south coast of Cyprus, past Paphos, then up to Turkey at Cape Khelidonia. A south-westerly wind headed us for most of the first 75 miles of the way; but after passing the Akrotiri promontory our course was more northerly and we were able to make sail on the port tack.

The sun went down, and it grew quickly dark. Off Paphos we altered course again. Now we had the wind abeam and freshening. The sea was getting up too as the sky clouded over. We reefed the mainsail, but were still doing 8 knots and a little more. Our dinghy, towing astern, began to take water; we luffed up, eased sheets and slowed the engine to get it aboard. The crew worked like clockwork.

By the time we raised the Turkish mountains, at dawn next day, the wind had veered and the glass was rising. We tacked and steered west-north-west. Then the sun came up, and with it the enticing smell of coffee competing with bacon and tomatoes (young Reg, our seaman/gunner was cook-of-the-day). Ahead of us the pink island of Hipsili stood out bright and welcoming against darker headlands beyond.

Straight-armed, steadying myself against the cabin-top, legs braced to the roll and lurch of the ship, I stood with a feeling almost of triumph (after all the problems of fitting out and storing) at being at last on our way. And now, looking back close on fifty years, I can recall that feeling still. In the forenoon we passed between Castelorizo and the Turkish shore, hugging the coast as we approached Patara and the Seven Capes. They looked forbidding in the early evening light, parallel ranges ending abruptly in cliffs which fell sheer into the sea from many hundreds of feet. And west of the Xanthus River there was no sign of any sheltering inlet; nor any gully, or even a goat track by which a shipwrecked seaman, cast up on the rocks below, might climb to the coast road crossing the cliff-tops high above (or, for that matter, a coastguard scramble his way down). Had I appreciated the significance of this last fact, and its bearing upon what happened later, I might have been more watchful.

We motored happily on from headland to headland, with sails furled, against a moderate breeze which had now turned westerly. Then all at once the coxswain sitting on the main hatch amidships called out, pointing over our starboard quarter. I looked round and was surprised to see a small vessel standing out to sea from the cliffs. She looked like a patrol boat and had either been lying unnoticed against the land, or there must be a creek of sorts over there, screened by rocks and so invisible to us a mile offshore.

The patrol boat stood straight out to sea; and when she reached our wake she turned to follow us. She was faster than we were, doing, I suppose, 9 or 10 knots to our 8. I assumed that she was a Turkish coastguard. Nevertheless, for form's sake, I called the crew to action stations, and told the senior 'Sparker' to challenge her with the Aldis lamp.

As was to be expected, she made the correct reply; the Turks, having recently come into the war on our side, were passed our daily recognition signals. However, as she came closer, we could see that she was, in fact, a British HDML. She flew no ensign, but as she turned into our wake, a red and white flag was hoisted to her starboard signal yardarm. Since we were both heading directly into wind, I could only see it edge on, but took it to be the white ensign. The crew stood down, and Sparks returned the Aldis lamp to its stowage just inside the cabin hatchway.

The ML continued to close, overhauling us quite fast now. Soon she would be within hailing distance, and I expected at any moment to hear her loud-hailer blaring out. I was a bit puzzled not to see anyone on her bridge, but assumed that they were all in the wheelhouse – and quite suddenly she pulled out to port and, to our horror, we saw that what we had taken for a white ensign was, in fact, the red and white flag of the German Transport Command. She surged past, about a boat's length off, then suddenly went hard a'starboard and rammed us amidships, smashing through our port bulwarks and riding right up on to our main hatch, where she hung like a stranded whale.

My first instinct had been to cut the engine; and for the moment I could think of nothing else to do. Then all at once, while the fore part of the ML still hung there, a dozen soldiers emerged from her armoured wheelhouse and leaped down on to our deck brandishing sub-machine-guns. On a hook in our own wheelhouse we had a slip of paper on which were written the recognition signals for that day and the next. I made a grab for it, but the butt of a sub-machine-gun cracked down on the back of my neck and the paper was snatched from me. The ML, with her screws now turning astern, slid back into the water, apparently undamaged. Her stem and forefoot must have been heavily sheathed and reinforced, or she would certainly have come off second best in collision with a solidly built Greek caique. In fact, plans for such an operation (and training for the boarding party) must have been made well in advance.

We were all herded below under guard in LS43, while German seamen at her wheel and in her engine-room turned her to follow the ML back inshore. In the darkness below, we sat or stood in silence, each occupied with his own thoughts. The weight of utter defeat, compared with the high hopes and expectations of so short a time before, was crippling. For my part, this sudden transformation of heady triumph into bleak disaster was almost more than I could bear. But I had to bear it. My ship might be gone, but her company were with me still. And it was my responsibility to advise and influence them in any way I could.

For a long time the silence continued, to the background music of engine beats, the swish and gurgle of water passing down the ship's side, the creak of blocks and rigging aloft. We might, indeed, have remained for hours a demoralized bunch of losers, if it hadn't been for the overriding claims of healthy young constitutions. . . .

'Bout time we had a bit of grub, ain't it?'

The basic good sense of the remark, delivered in young Reg's bright Londoner's twang, dropped into the brooding silence like a frog into lake waters, sending rings of consciousness outwards to us all and bringing us back at last to reality. We wouldn't be together and alone for very much longer; perhaps only twenty minutes or so. Therefore the first and most important matter to be settled, as we grabbed a scratch meal, was what we were all going to say under interrogation. Above all, we must convince our captors that we were on our maiden voyage as a relief and rehabilitation vessel for the islands, and that none of our crew had been up to the Aegean before, or knew anything about hostilities up there; otherwise we would undoubtedly be pressed (a euphemism for tortured) to disclose whatever military information they thought (or hoped) we might possess.

Our actual interrogations a day or two later were, in fact, very different – in some ways amusingly different – from anything we had prepared ourselves to meet. But we couldn't know that, and in the meantime our deliberations were brought to an end by the sudden slowing of the engine and the slamming back of the cabin hatch cover above us.

'*Heraus*! und bind ze ship!' shouted a rasping voice, which we all recognized as belonging to the leader of the boarding party.

★ ★ ★

Night was coming on as we entered what looked like a miniature Lulworth Cove[4] tucked away behind a large outcrop of rock at the base of the cliffs. The ML was already moored to a rough jetty of boulders. Timber fendering – the trunk of a medium-sized pine tree, by the look of it – was floating in the water across the jetty's face, secured by chains.

We tied up alongside the ML, and while the boys were busy at this, I sat myself down on the main hatch and took the chance to look about me. In the afterglow of sunset I could make out a pathway leading up to a small leaf-shelter on top of the outcrop – the sort of shelter you can see in summer-time all over southern Turkey and Cyprus, used by farmers to watch day and night over their melon and pumpkin crops. Here it fulfilled a similar role as the Germans' lookout post.

The boulders of the jetty had obviously been recently piled there: the pine-log fender still had its bark on. I wondered who had put all this in place – a working party from Rhodes or (one couldn't avoid the suspicion) local labour? There had always been close contact between Rhodes and Marmarice, the Turkish port opposite; and Turkey had only recently come into the war. So friendships would doubtless have continued, with advice if not assistance; for example, the choice of this cove, completely inaccessible from above and invisible from seaward.

Even so, it came as a shock to find what amounted to an enemy base on Turkish soil. Our own agreements with Turkey for the use of her territorial waters stopped well short of this. And yet . . . had we for all these years been thinking of ourselves as a sort of chosen race, beloved of the Turks, who gave us the freedom of their coasts and denied it to our enemies? When all along, down here on the south coast anyway, the opposite had been the case?

There had probably been quite close collaboration between friends in Marmarice and the Italians, if not the Germans. But how had these particular Germans got hold of our daily recognition signals? . . . Of course! When Turkey entered the war the signals had necessarily been passed to coastal authorities everywhere – including Marmarice!

These reflections were interrupted by a quiet and cultured voice saying, in good English, 'Good evening. I hope we have not made you too uncomfortable here on board.'

I turned my head to see a tall, imposing figure standing beside me. There was just enough afterglow on the side of a somewhat gaunt and leathery face with deep-sunk eyes to show a straight high-bridged nose above a thin-lipped yet sensitive mouth and firm chin.

'We'll manage,' I said, perhaps a little defiantly. From his uniform cap and jacket and general air of quiet authority I took him to be the captain of the ML.

'I've come', he said, 'to apologize for a most unseamanlike assault upon your ship.' I said nothing, and he went on: 'It was also unsporting to delay hoisting our colours until we were both head-to-wind, so that you couldn't see them properly. Unfortunately, here in Turkish waters, I had no option.'

'You could have left us alone.'

'Regrettably not. My orders were to capture you without any gunfire from either ship which could be heard ashore.'

'Would your friends there object?' The mild sarcasm in my voice seemed to pass him by.

'Probably not, but yours would, and make a fuss which could be embarrassing. . . . As you'll discover tomorrow, we are completely cut off on Rhodes – not only from the rest of our forces, but from any news or information we can trust – I mean free from propaganda doctoring (yours as well as ours).'

'Well, what's your plan then? We can't help you much over here.'

'No. So as soon as the British destroyer patrol has passed through the straits – about midnight usually – we'll head for Rhodes harbour. It wouldn't do, after all the trouble we've taken, to have you shot up by your own people . . .' (This with a quick smile that lit up his whole face) '. . . and us as well.'

'You've got our recognition signals.'

'Yes, but one of the destroyers might be curious and start asking awkward questions. I must beg you to be patient; my orders are to get you to Rhodes unharmed, and I shall do my best to obey them.'

I couldn't help admiring this soft-spoken, gentlemanly fellow, and wondered where he'd come from. He looked about thirty-five, maybe forty; a reservist of course, who was trying not to allow the everyday brutalities of service life to impinge too far upon his natural instincts as . . . a writer? . . . a teacher? . . . perhaps even a scientist?

'We'd like some supper,' I said, to clear the air.

He stiffened. 'My apologies again. Please make full use of your amenities. I will see to it that you are not disturbed.' He clicked his heels, saluted and was gone.

⋆   ⋆   ⋆

We sat around in the starlight while Reg rustled up an enormous meal; we started with two kinds of soup, followed by tinned cold roast turkey, sausages, cranberry jelly, baked beans and mashed potatoes; peaches, pineapple chunks and cream; two cans of beer per man; and in the end, double tots of rum to have with our coffee. I would have turned the whole jar over to the boys, but for the risk that one or two of them might get roaring drunk and start a fight with our guards, which could only lead to shooting and probably one or two deaths.

The moon, in its last quarter, had set earlier on; but there was enough light from Venus that evening to cast faint shadows, as we lolled on the hatches and bulwarks feeling full, and at last reasonably relaxed. We no longer had control of our own or anyone else's destinies, so why worry – except for the nagging regret that we hadn't been able to pile in any more of the magnificent food we'd brought with us before catering staff on Rhodes grabbed the lot, which they would certainly do as soon as we arrived. However, we did manage to pass a fair amount to the German troops and sailors on board, who hadn't treated us too badly, though I took the precaution of handing the rum jar personally to their captain (whose name, by the way, was Hergesheimer) for safe keeping.[5]

It was quite an evening – a commissioning and decommissioning party rolled into one. In particular it gave us all a chance to get to know each other in a new and different atmosphere from the normal run of naval occasions. Discipline was still there, but it was a relaxed discipline, deriving from the realization that there were difficult times ahead which we'd have to face together or founder one by one.

The coxswain, a cockney type in his late twenties, was the focal point of our small community: a first-class seaman, serious and introspective at times, but cheerful with the crew, and he always got the best out of them. He was able to fall in with the spirit of our present situation and keep the atmosphere generally friendly. 'OK, Shorty,' I heard him say to a long and lugubrious German corporal sitting on the cabin top, sub-machine-gun cocked and ready across his knees, 'OK then, let's see you shoot the top off this can for us, and you can have half what's in it.' The German didn't understand, but he smiled wanly and leaned back against the ventilator cowling making himself more comfortable.

Soon after midnight we were all bundled below again, and heard the engine start up. We knew there was a good five and a half hours' run ahead of us, so most of us slept or dozed, till after what felt like twelve hours at least on passage, old Rasping Rupert's 'Heraus!' brought us up on deck to find the ship edging alongside in the fishing harbour of the port of Rhodes. The ML had berthed elsewhere; and although she was our enemy, we felt ourselves in a strange way abandoned.

However, 'We still have each other, darlings', as Stoker Wall, our engineer, put it, making us all laugh. And there was just time for a hearty breakfast of bread, corned beef and tea (none of us had much of an appetite after the 'fancy gorge' of the evening before). Then a couple of trucks drew up on the quayside. We were herded into them and trundled up to the castle where we were put into three separate cells and locked up.

[1]   Now Anzali.

[2]   The Naval Officer in Charge, Cyprus; *see* Chapter 16 'Learning the Ropes'.

[3]   In fact they were all fitted with 120 hp Caterpillar diesels, and each armed with two 0.5 in Colt-Browning machine-guns.

[4]   A beauty spot on the Dorset coast.

[5]   Editor's Note: In an article in the 1978 edition of *The Cruising Association Bulletin*, Robert Ballantine (see Chapter 3) wrote: 'One of the few vestiges of naval routine aboard LS3 was the appearance of the coxswain daily at 11.00, with the rum jar tucked under his arm, emerging from the hold to dish out generous tots. We took some gallons of the stuff with us from Beirut and were probably the only ships in the Navy not expected to account for it in detail on our return to base. (My recollection is that Coxswain Hallybone kept it under his bunk! At all events I never had any trouble with rum!)

CHAPTER TWENTY-SIX

Feeling the Pinch

My only fear was that if our captors discovered that we were bound for the Aegean in a semi-political role, and that I was actually an intelligence officer, our interrogation would be an exceptionally harsh one. So I had been at pains to point out to the whole crew that they must describe our mission as purely humanitarian, that we were intending to load food and supplies at Izmir for the starving Aegean islanders. After several years without home leave (in my case five) we had all been transformed from eager youngsters into hardened citizens of the world, so although I could no longer exercise any real authority over them, I knew that they could hold their own against the wiles of all but the most cunning interrogators.

Stoker 'Tiddly' Wall, our engineer, for example – a lively lad, several years older than he looked, which was about twenty-three – would not be easy to bamboozle. He was game for anything and a leading light among the crew, largely due, I think, to a wild and colourful history (duly noted on his conduct sheet). Then there were the W/T operators. We had two, so that we could keep a continuous listening watch. And this in itself might have aroused suspicion. I considered asking the younger one (aged about twenty) to claim that he was an ordinary seaman, but decided that this would arouse greater suspicion and might get him into serious trouble if found out. The senior operator was a slow-spoken fellow who always meant what he said and was quite happy as long as he had a bit of radio to play with. He had been a dedicated radio ham from the age of sixteen and was never without the basics – a crystal and a cat's whisker – which he carried in his wallet. And finally there was Reg Osborn, our young seaman/gunner ('Guns' to everyone), a stockily built lad with dark curly hair, who would have made an excellent pirate of the old school, but was in fact a capable seaman, who could always be relied on for a job well done, afloat or ashore.[1]

We were all interrogated separately and, to my surprise, my own interrogation turned out to be very different from what I had expected. First, as a matter of form, I was asked about our voyage and what we had seen of their hide-out on the Turkish coast. But my interrogators were obviously not really interested in my replies, and quickly turned to a very different subject – namely what the future held for themselves personally, now that the war was nearly over; and, in particular, what was likely to be agreed at the San Francisco Conference.[2]

They were completely isolated on Rhodes, and didn't even read the newspapers, which would always be several weeks out of date when they received them. Apart, therefore, from radio broadcasts, which they all knew were heavily angled by their Ministry of Propaganda, they had no news at all from the outside world. My interrogation was, in fact, a purely personal enquiry by the interrogating officers themselves, to assess their own chances of a reasonably happy future. The same was the case with all the Germans we had to deal with. They were only concerned with what would happen to *them*; and would we, for example, intercede on their behalf if they treated us well in captivity.

But the interrogation of the rest of our crew was in some ways different from mine. Reg Osborn has given this graphic account:

> For interrogation we were taken one by one down a long corridor with rooms on either side and sentries at every door. I wondered what tortured creatures lay huddled behind those doors. Or was this Kafka-esque set-up intended to reduce us to a suitable state of terror before interrogation?
>
> The corridor opened into a large Italian-style room, lavishly furnished, with an enormous desk set against the long wall opposite the entrance. At this desk sat a most elegant individual, slim and very well turned out, in a light grey uniform and smoking a strong-smelling Turkish cigarette in a holder which must have been at least 9 in long. His manner was supercilious but friendly. After noting down my name, number and rank, he leaned back still smiling, and observed, 'Your comrades have told us everything they know about you and what you have all been doing.'
>
> This was such an obvious and clumsy device, that I felt at once reassured. 'Then you won't be wanting any more from me, will you?'
>
> 'Oh yes . . . we want confirmation; your friends may have been lying.'
>
> 'Well anyway, the war is all but over, so why are you going to ask me a lot of silly questions which can't possibly be of any value to you?'
>
> 'You are wrong,' he said sternly. 'The war is by no means over. And Germany is going to win it . . . we have already bombed your Parliament House. Our rockets are devastating London.'
>
> It was all very transparent and rather childish. Did he expect me, I wondered, to break down and exclaim, 'Oh, God! What have you done to my country, my home, my family?' (In fact, when I got home a few months later I did discover that part of my family – my uncle and aunt and all their children – had indeed been killed when their house was hit by a doodlebug. But at the time I simply laughed.)
>
> He got up, still smiling his supercilious smile, and strolled languidly to the window, his long cigarette holder protruding between thin and slightly twisted lips. The cigarette had gone out, but he continued to puff at it in silence. Evidently he was trying to put me at my ease by his relaxed and generally unthreatening manner.
>
> It was comic opera, no more. There was no ill-feeling, nor any immediacy about his attitude, though I was probably too young and

inexperienced to understand and fear Hitler's Commando Order of 18 October 1942, under which Alan Tuckey and his crew had been handed over to the Gestapo for 'special treatment' (a euphemism for execution).

When he returned to his desk, he observed that I was not in uniform (which I denied; I had my cap with me) and could therefore be treated as a spy. He also held up the 9 in knife which I used for rope-work. I had ground it down from an Italian bayonet.

However, I was dismissed. When I got outside the door, my escort had disappeared, and none of the sentries in that long and forbidding corridor was interested in me. I could have walked straight out of the building. Morale was obviously at a low ebb throughout the garrison.

When my guard eventually returned, he took me down to join the others, who had already been interrogated, in what looked like an armoury. The walls were lined with rifles and automatics, all with chains through their trigger guards which, with time and a little ingenuity, might well, we thought, be removed. Boxes of ammunition stood against one wall.

While we were there a small and squat, but very fierce-looking *Feldwebel* came in. He was horrified to find us there, and we heard him yelling at some unfortunate fellow outside. If we succeeded in freeing any of those weapons, he was saying, we could easily create a dangerous situation.

The upshot was that we were taken back to the prison in which we had first been held. Next day, however, they transferred us to Koskino village, some 2 miles south of Rhodes town. Late in the afternoon we stopped to pick up a scrawny-looking character standing at the roadside under guard. He was hauled protesting into the truck; there was quite a struggle and a bit of a punch-up to get him there. He seemed shocked and frightened and answered our questions in monosyllables. But when we finally reached the villa and had settled in, he loosened up. It appeared that he was a Ukrainian POW, who had escaped from a working party but was later recaptured. We questioned him for quite a while, and it wasn't long before we decided that his story didn't ring true – that he was in fact a 'stool pigeon' planted on us by the Germans. He must have realized that we suspected him, and that he'd be in for a rough time if he stayed with us, because at 'Colours' next morning he broke ranks and went over to the guard, who immediately let him out of the compound.

The incident pleased us, because it meant that our interrogators hadn't obtained any worthwhile information from the 'comrades who have told us all about you and what you have all been doing', so they'd sent in this Ukrainian to see if he could find out any more.

*   *   *

At Koskino we were housed in a villa consisting of two semi-detached houses surrounded by barbed wire and a minefield. We were given the freedom of the two houses, which we had to share with some twenty-five Greek Sacred Company prisoners. I was the only officer, so I had a room to myself. The Greeks had been there for nearly a month and had organized cooking and eating facilities.

After a while we began to receive weekly parcels of food and comforts from Red Cross headquarters in Izmir, whose representative, Rene Carretti, visited us from time to time. With these parcels to supplement our rations, we were now much better fed than the garrison troops themselves, who had to send regular working parties out into the countryside to dig for roots. The German commander of the battalion responsible for our district always attended the distribution of parcels. He was a regular soldier who had been wounded on the Russian front, and he looked with contempt upon the second-line troops – a rag-tag of Germans, Poles, Hungarians and even a few Ukrainians – who formed the garrison. He would pick out a tin of bully beef and fling it into a nearby meadow. The wretched soldiers, always desperately hungry, would rush to retrieve it; but just as the first man reached the tin, he would suddenly call them all to attention and order the man nearest the tin to bring it back to him.

The *Feldwebel* in charge of the unit guarding the villa was a very different character – friendly, easy-going and by no means a Nazi at heart. He came up to me quietly one day and, after looking round to make sure that there was no one within earshot, said in a conspiratorial whisper, 'If you plan escape, I like coming vid you. I have map of Rhodes.' Whether this was genuine or a trap I never found out.

But the question now was indeed whether or not we should try to escape. To decide about this we needed to know more about the state of the war. There would be no point in risking our lives on an extremely hazardous enterprise if, in a few days' time, we could be carried to Allied territory in a British ship. But, as I said, no one on the island really knew how things were going. At this point our 'Sparker' – the radio ham who always carried a crystal and cat's whisker in his pocket – said that he thought he could contrive a set which would pick up broadcasts from Cairo, if he could somehow get hold of enough wire to make an aerial. 'Tiddly' Wall, who was always full of ideas, volunteered at once to plunder the minefield for as much wire from remotely controlled mines as was needed.

The villa's defences consisted of a barbed wire fence behind which was a continuous concertina of barbed wire rolls lying on the ground. Mines were laid under both of these, and were also buried at random out to a distance of 15 or 20 yards from the wire. You could sometimes see where mines had been buried by the disturbed earth covering them. But you could never be sure that the disturbance hadn't been left deliberately visible so as to mislead you, while the mines themselves were hidden elsewhere.

None of this deterred Wall. He crept out under the fence one night, while Sparks lifted the bottom strand with a stick to let him through; then he carefully parted two of the concertina rolls, and after nearly an hour had collected several hundred yards of wire. With this, he and Sparks constructed an effective aerial by winding it round and round among the rafters in one of the attics. They finally connected it to the crystal and cat's whisker assembly, and the latter to a makeshift earphone, made from a cigarette tin covered with candle wax as an insulator, on to which had been wound a hundred turns of single-strand electric wire. Whether the whole contraption was connected in some way to the electric lighting system, I don't remember – if I ever knew.

Sparks and Wall worked in the loft in between roll-calls, which occurred five times a day; and for several days it was a matter of continuous trial and error. Then one day they came down with the exciting news that they'd picked up a snatch of conversation from Cairo containing the words 'successful advance' and later 'closing in on Berlin'.

★ ★ ★

The Germans were becoming more and more anxious. One could tell it from their worried looks and ever more ingratiating manner. One day Wall, who had become increasingly impatient since they picked up those words from Cairo Radio, crept under the wire and managed to thread his way through the minefield. He waved to his pals and set off boldly towards the sea. For some reason, the sentry on that side of the compound didn't see him go. But an hour or two later he was picked up by a coast watch patrol, who treated him kindly and brought him back to the compound. There were no repercussions, not even a lecture from the battalion commander.

Reg Osborn recalls that:

While at the villa we had to fetch water from a nearby village well, where we became friendly with some of the villagers. We sometimes gave them chocolates from our Red Cross parcels. It was from them that we first heard the rumour of an SAS or SBS raid to rescue us. And sure enough, soon after midnight on May 2nd we heard explosions and the rattle of machine-gun fire from down the coast.

It wasn't, in fact, a rescue attempt, we heard later, but a raid on Alimnia Island, off the south-west coast of Rhodes. However, it must have alerted the German staff to the possibility of a rescue bid, because the next day, without any warning, we were moved from the villa to a collection of log-cabins, known as a *Feldpost*, in the mountains. We were told at 9 a.m. that trucks would arrive to pick us up at noon. There was no time to dismantle our radio aerial from the loft, so we tore it down and took it with us, hoping to find some way of using or disposing of it later.

A few days after our arrival at the *Feldpost*, at one of our roll-calls, an Order of the Day from General Wagner was read out to us in harsh but ringing tones by the battalion commander. It told us that 'Whatever may happen on the mainland, the Third Reich will live for ever on the island of Rhodes.'

This was greeted with sniggers and, from the rear ranks, outright laughter. And it was after that that we began to think about making a serious attempt to escape. 'Tiddly' Wall it was who first put it into words: 'Can't 'ang about 'ere much longer. We'll get bloody sleepin' sickness.'

We had made friends earlier on with a couple of local Italians, who offered to help us. If we could escape, they said, they'd find us a safe hiding place. It so happened that a sheep had blundered into the barbed wire a day or two before, detonating some of the mines buried beneath it; and we could see that none of them had been replaced. So it was only the mines laid outside the wire that we would have to negotiate.

No one wanted to go first, of course. Then some enthusiast (I don't remember who it was) piped up with 'Why not measure everyone's feet, and the man with the biggest feet goes first. If he gets through, we can all follow in his footsteps.'

There were nine of us in the escaping party. In the end we divided into three groups and drew lots and, believe it or not, the group who drew the short straw and had to go first, got through! They rendezvoused with one of the Italians (the other didn't show up) who led them into the mountains, where they hid in a village.

When they failed to turn up at the next roll-call there was a fuss, of course. Our guards were doubled and a whole new pattern of mines was laid down, so no one else tried to escape. We must have been looked on, in a way, as hostages, and therefore bargaining counters, who mustn't be allowed to get away. Those who had were still up in the mountains, living rough on whatever scraps of food the villagers could spare them (mostly roots) when a few days later the Rhodes garrison surrendered and after that the rest of us were free to come and go as we pleased and eat whatever we liked.

We had been up at the *Feldpost* for no more than four or five days when one morning we were fallen in and addressed by an elderly, and very friendly colonel. 'The war is over,' he said, 'and General Wagner has ordered your immediate release and repatriation.' (Photo 38)

We were taken by truck down to Rhodes harbour, where Rene Carretti had arranged for a British landing craft to come alongside and transport us to Simi. Before we embarked he took photographs which showed us all to be in good condition and reasonably well fed. But before the landing craft berthed, while we stood there waiting for it, I was approached by two senior German officers, one after the other, who wanted to know whether we were satisfied with our treatment as POWs. They were very concerned that we should have nothing to complain of.

When the landing craft eventually reached Simi, instead of the enthusiastic welcome from old friends and a few days 'stand easy' which I'd

38 The surrender of Rhodes: a German general boards a British destroyer.

been looking forward to, I was transferred straightaway to the ML in which the new Naval Officer in Charge and the Army commander who would receive General Wagner's surrender were to take passage to Rhodes. I was required for certain formalities to do with the release of the prisoners and any enquiries about their treatment which might arise.

I was more interested, however, to find out, if I could, what had happened to my ship, LS43. I had heard that her bulwarks, stove in when rammed off the Seven Capes, had been repaired; and that she had been taken down to Alimnia Island, where a German observation post had been set up. They had anchored her in a small cove just inside the entrance to a deep bay. So John Hamer of MO4 took me down in his caique to look for her. When we found her at last, I almost wished we hadn't. She had been holed and was lying beached in 6 ft of water which just covered her engine. If she were pumped out and hauled further up the beach she might, I thought, be salvaged; but she was in a sorry state.

While John and I were examining the hole in her side from his dinghy, the Greek coxswain dived to check on a pile of what looked like junk on the sea floor beneath her. He found a quantity of arms and ammunition, and brought up with him a Mauser pistol which he was still holding in one hand as he put both hands on the dinghy's transom to haul himself aboard. In the struggle to lift himself out of the water, his grip must have tightened and pressed the Mauser's trigger. It fired a round, which hit John Hamer in the hip, passed through his bladder and came out of the opposite hip. He had to be rushed to hospital, where he was operated on and after two months had fully recovered.

But that was the last I ever saw of LS43, my first and last command in the Levant Schooner Flotilla. And for me the war in the Aegean was over. I was posted to 21st Army Group in Germany, while Jack Charrington and Bill Turnbull, in the other two caiques fitted out at Famagusta, now concerned themselves with the rehabilitation of all the Greek Islands of the Southern Cyclades.

[1] After the war he became a successful press photographer.
[2] 25 April–26 June 1945.